ADAPSO Reunion Transcript

May 2-4, 2002

ISBN: 1-4140-0267-X (e-book)
ISBN: 1-4140-0268-8 (Paperback)

This book is printed on acid free paper.

Published by iBusiness Press, Inc. in conjunction with 1stBooks Library ®

1stBooks – rev. 09/11/03

Table of Contents

Acknowledgments

Thanks to the many, many people who helped to make ADAPSO Reunion 2002 a great success. If this transcript provides insight into the challenges and opportunities faced by companies in the early computer software and services industry, and ADAPSO's role in guiding those young companies through turbulent times, it is because of the contributions made by everyone who helped to make the reunion happen.

Thanks to our cosponsors for their support in developing the concept for the meeting and providing the context—both historical and contemporary—that framed the workshop sessions: the Charles Babbage Institute, the Smithsonian Institution's National Museum of American History, the *IEEE Annals of the History of Computing*, and the Information Technology Association of America.

Thanks to our moderators and co-moderators who kept the discussions on target and insured that the key issues were covered, while making the process of remembering the "old days at ADAPSO" fun for everyone. And thanks to our volunteer rapporteurs who so ably assisted with logistics and coordination.

Thanks to everyone who participated in the workshop discussions for contributing their recollections and experience so that ADAPSO's legacy will be preserved.

Special thanks to Ed Bride, Jerry Dreyer, Olga Grkavac, Doug Jerger and Dave Sturtevant whose deep knowledge of the industry's history and of the people who played significant roles in its development was invaluable.

Special thanks as well to Carol Anne Ances whose creativity, resourcefulness, and unfailing good humor contributed enormously to the production of this book.

But, most of all, very special thanks to Burt Grad whose industry knowledge, organizational skills and unswerving commitment were vital to the success of the reunion and to helping to insure that the final result—this transcript—would be a source of pride to everyone who participated.

Luanne Johnson, Editor

About the Software History Center

The Software History Center is dedicated to preserving the history of the software industry, one of the largest and most influential industries in the world today. The industry originated with the entrepreneurial computer software and services companies of the 1950s and 1960s and grew dramatically through the 1970s and 1980s to become a market force rivaling that of the computer hardware companies. By the 1990s, it had become the supplier of technical know-how that transformed the way people worked, played and communicated every day of their lives. SHC is working to preserve for future generations information about the companies, people, products, and events that shaped the evolution of this vital industry.

In addition to sponsoring ADAPSO Reunion 2002, other projects undertaken by SHC in 2000-2002 were:

- Organizing a workshop of industry pioneers to discuss their experiences founding companies in the early years of the industry and publishing the transcript of the meeting ("One for the History Books" Workshop).

- Development of a database of computer software and services companies founded in the 1950s, 1960s and 1970s which is accessible on the SHC's website.

- Publication of a special issue of the *IEEE Annals of the History of Computing* (24:1) on the beginnings of the software products industry.

- Arranging for the archiving of historically significant materials from ADAPSO and ADAPSO's General Counsel Milton Wessel at the Charles Babbage Institute at the University of Minnesota.

- Organizing and editing oral histories of fifteen computer software and services pioneers conducted by seven computer historians with the transcripts now available through the website of the Charles Babbage Institute.

Further information is available at www.softwarehistory.org.

Software History Center Board of Directors

Introduction

On February 3, 1960, Bill Evans, a professional association manager from Willow Grove, Pennsylvania, met in New York City with Romuald Slimak, manager of the Univac Service Centers division of Sperry Rand Corporation, and C. W. Graf, Jr., manager of advertising and sales promotion for the Service Bureau Corporation, an IBM subsidiary. Evans, an executive with the National Office Management Association, was exploring the idea of organizing a trade association representing the nascent computer services industry.

This meeting led to others held throughout the year, each meeting attracting a greater number of participants with representatives from large and small companies. The organizing committee considered several names for the new organization including the Office Services Technical Institute, Inc. and the Data Activating Technical Association (DATA), but finally settled on the Association of Data Processing Service Organizations (ADAPSO). The first membership meeting of the new organization was held in January, 1961, and Slimak was elected president.

Minutes of these organizing meetings show that there was a continuous attempt to balance the membership between small computer services companies serving a single local market, larger services companies with branches in multiple cities, and the service centers of the computer hardware manufacturers. So, from the very beginning, ADAPSO established itself as a trade association committed to representing a broad spectrum of the industry from the smallest to the largest companies, with the inevitable give-and-take that would follow as the association endeavored to be responsive to the needs of companies at very different levels of operation and stages of growth. The industry grew and expanded through the next decades in parallel with ever-increasing computer power and ever-expanding customer demands for applications of that power to solve business and technical problems. And ADAPSO expanded its definition of the industry it represented to encompass timesharing companies, professional software services companies, software product companies, network-based information services companies, turnkey companies, and myriad variations on each of these. What all of these companies had in common was that their businesses were based on the know-how required to deliver useful applications of computer power into the hands of the people who needed it.

In 1991, the association changed its name to the Information Technology Association of America (ITAA) and it continues to provide leadership today to an industry of a size and complexity far beyond that envisioned by ADAPSO's founders.

On May 3-4, 2002, the Software History Center assembled a group of people who had been active in ADAPSO in its early decades to discuss their involvement in ADAPSO and analyze the benefits they and their companies had received as a result of ADAPSO's services to the industry. The meeting opened with a cocktail reception and dinner on Friday evening, May 3, highlighted by the personal recollections of Senator Frank Lautenberg, a founder of Automatic Data Processing, and ADAPSO President in1967-68.

The full day meeting on Saturday began with presentations by representatives from the Software History Center and the four cosponsoring organizations for the meeting: the Charles Babbage Institute, the Smithsonian Institution's National Museum of American History, the *IEEE Annals of the History of Computing*, and the Information Technology Association of America. The luncheon speaker was Dr. Martin Campbell-Kelly of the University of Warwick, author of *From Airline Reservations to Sonic the Hedge-Hog: A History of the Software Industry.*

The rest of the Saturday program consisted of a series of ten workshops, each of which explored one of the many and varied programs that ADAPSO pursued on behalf of its membership. Each workshop was co-moderated by an industry leader who had been active in ADAPSO during the time period being covered and by a professional historian.

This book is a transcript of the plenary sessions and those ten workshops and is intended to be a reference source for those who, now and in the future, seek to understand the impact of ADAPSO on the development of the computer software and services industry. It is also, for those of us who were part of it, a way to preserve our memories of a truly extraordinary organization that brought together a remarkably diverse group of people, many of whom were intense competitors, and turned them into friends, colleagues and allies in the cause of ensuring that this emerging industry would function in a fair and non-restrictive competitive environment.

Attendees

Albert, Sam
Allison, David K.
Ances, Carol Anne
Aspray, William
Bergin, Tim
Blankenship, Betty
Blankenship, Buck
Blumberg, Joe
Bride, Edward J.
Brizdle, Barbara
Campbell, David
Campbell-Kelly, Martin
Carlson, Bart
Carpenter, Richard
Ceruzzi, Paul
Coleman, Bruce
Crandall, Rick
Dent, T. Lowell
Dreyer, Jerry
Durbin, Gary
Ensmenger, Nathan
Esch, Arthur
Frana, Philip L.
Goetz, Martin
Goetz, Norma
Goldberg, Jay
Goldstein, Bernard
Gracza, John
Grad, Burt
Grier, David A.
Haigh, Thomas
Jerger, Doug
Johnson, Luanne

Johnston, Julia
Jones, Kim
Keane, John
Keet, Lee
Keet, Nancy
Krammer, Joan
Lautenberg, Sen. Frank
Maguire, John N.
Maples, Mike
Markoski, Joseph
Miller, Harris N.
Nugent, Mike
Palenski, Ronald J.
Piscopo, Joe
Rollins, John W.
Saunders, Mary Jane
Schachter, Oscar
Schachter, Amy
Schnell, Linda
Schoenberg, Larry
Sherman, David
Sinback, Warner
Sturtevant, David
Tasker, Joe
Thatcher, Dick
Treleavan, James
Virgo, Elizabeth M.
Weissman, Robert
Welke, Larry
Wessel, Joan
Wormser, David
Yeaton, Jack
Yost, Jeffrey

Plenary Sessions
Luanne Johnson, Software History Center
Saturday Morning Plenary Session

Welcome and good morning. Thank you all for coming to see your old friends and help us record some of the history of ADAPSO. I'd like to start off our Saturday session by telling you about the Software History Center.

Our mission is to preserve for future generations information about the companies, people, products and events that shaped the computer software and services industry. We have several goals toward fulfilling that mission.

- We want to figure out where there are materials that still exist that record what happened in the early days of the industry. Since so many of the companies are gone through acquisitions or dissolution, a lot of the materials that still exist about the early companies are in the personal files of the founders and the employees. That makes them hard to find and we're trying to figure out who might have those materials and, when we find them, encourage their preservation.

- We're trying to identify the people who have personal knowledge of the events that shaped the industry and support the preservation of their recollections. We're encouraging people to write memoirs and we're doing oral histories. We've got a very extensive oral history program going to get those recollections recorded and preserved.

- We want to disseminate this information about the industry's history. In your registration packets, you saw one of the examples of that with our special issue of the IEEE *Annals of the History of Computing* which focuses on the beginnings of the software product industry. We also have a web site where we're disseminating information about early companies in the industry and people who played important roles in the industry's formation.

- And, finally, we want to encourage and support research on the history of the industry. There are a number of historians who have

1

come to this meeting who are interested in the history of this industry as a potential field of study. So we are encouraging research and historical analysis of the industry's beginnings.

Our scope is all sectors of what was traditionally called the computer software and services industry. Although we call ourselves the Software History Center, our focus is broader than the software products sector because the history of all those sectors is really intertwined. Many of the most important companies overlap sectors so one really can't separate out any one sector and understand its history. What all of these companies have in common is that their businesses were based on know-how that is manifested in software.

Our focus is on business history. We believe that the vision and creativity required to develop and serve markets for technology is as crucial as the ability to develop the technology in the first place. A substantial amount of work has been done in computer history by a number of different organizations. There's been a lot of focus on the development of hardware technology and, more recently, on the evolution of software technology. That's a very, very important field of study and we're pleased to see that happening. But our focus is on how companies identified markets for the technology and then created business models to serve them. Those were inventions as well. We're interested in the experiments that people did on how to create a model for a successful company. I think everybody in this room has probably been involved in a few experiments that didn't work so well. That creative process is what we're trying to document and record.

Our current emphasis is on companies from the pre-PC era—companies that were founded before 1980 and wrote software for or provided services on mainframes, minicomputers, small business systems. It's not that we don't think that the other companies are important but because we feel that the records of these companies are the ones that are most vulnerable to loss. So many of the companies are gone. The people who might have records in their personal files are getting older. They're retiring and moving to their retirement homes. And they're going to throw those records out when they move. So we're focusing on that era right now because that's where we feel there's an urgency to prevent records from being lost.

I'll give you a little bit of background on how the Software History Center got started. Burt Grad and I have both been interested in the history of the industry for quite some time. After I left ITAA, I wanted to pursue the industry's history in more depth. In 1997, Burt suggested that we start a website to promote the idea that people ought to be preserving this history. So we set that up, but didn't really get much serious interest.

But then in November of 1999, *Fortune* magazine did an end-of-millennium article in which they named the top four businessmen of the 20th Century including Bill Gates. And they made this statement: Before Gates and Allen started Microsoft, pure software companies did not exist. [*Laughter*]

That got our attention. [*Laughter*]

I was actually very angry. I wrote a letter to the editor, which they published. I said that a magazine that purports to be about business should be able to do the research to get their facts right, and so on and so forth. But as I thought about it, I realized that if you were a journalist working under a tight deadline, where would you go to get those facts? Where was the source of information? There were scattered bits of information, some of it at the Charles Babbage Institute and here and there, but where would you go to find out about software companies that existed before Microsoft?

So at that point, we realized that this information gap was an even more serious problem than we had thought. Up to that point, we'd had a vague idea that if we drew attention to the problem, somebody somewhere would do something about it.

That was the turning point at which we said: Somebody somewhere isn't going to do something. We're going to have to do something. So we went to some key people in the industry for help. Specifically, we went to Rick Crandall to identify somebody who might give us some help and as a result of that we got some seed money from Computer Associates which allowed us to form a non-profit corporation. Ron Palenski got involved with us at that point to help get the corporation set up. So the Software History Center was incorporated in February of 2000.

Our funding plan was to go out and get pledges from a few individuals to get enough money to cover the first two years of operation. We wanted to have a track record of having accomplished some specific things before we tried to launch an annual fund drive and go out to the industry generally to ask for money. We wanted to show the kind of things that we felt needed to be done and that we were an organization that could do them.

So we went after the funding to get going and some very, very generous people helped us with funding to cover the first two years of operations.

And now we are launching a broader fund-raising campaign to ask people throughout the industry to help us preserve its history. There's a brochure in your registration packet, so please take a look at it.

I want to explain that we have no intention of being a bricks and mortar organization. We're not a museum or an archive. We're an education and outreach organization. We want to serve as an information resource about the industry's history and as a focal point for efforts by other organizations and volunteers.

We're working through partnerships with other organizations. We work very closely with the Charles Babbage Institute at the University of Minnesota. They have wonderful archive facilities. We're encouraging people to look to them as an archive where their files can be preserved. We're working closely with the IEEE *Annals of the History of Computing*. You've seen the results of that with the issue that we distributed to everyone here. We'll be doing more of that. We're working with the Smithsonian National Museum of American History on special projects such as the oral history program that we did yesterday where we brought in 13 people to be interviewed by professional historians. David Allison from the National Museum of American History coordinated that effort. Those oral history transcripts will go to the Babbage Institute and be part of the archival record of the industry there.

Other accomplishments are this reunion which will result in a transcript of the information collected in our workshops today about ADAPSO activities. And in September of 2000, we held a "One for the History Books" workshop in conjunction with a conference that the Babbage Institute did in Palo Alto. In that case we had 30 people who sat around for part of a day talking about their experiences starting companies in the '60s and '70s. Again, we created a transcript. That information is now preserved.

And we have our website. It contains an overview of industry history and the goal is to have a pretty comprehensive database of companies that were founded in the '50s, '60s and '70s, and a list of people who played important roles in the industry's development. So now there is a place for journalists to go to find out that there were a lot of companies out there before Microsoft.

We're working with ITAA to preserve what is left of the ADAPSO files. Many of the ADAPSO records have been lost over the years but what is left will be archived at the Babbage Institute.

As a result of our efforts, Larry Welke has given all of his files with the ICP Directories to the Babbage Institute. That's a wonderful record of the software products that were out there in the late '60s through the '70s. Now that's all been preserved.

Marty Goetz has donated his very extensive records on ADR and ADAPSO to CBI and he's also written a marvelous memoir of his career, the first part of which was published in our special issue of the *Annals*.

Among the things that have happened is that CBI has now created a finding aid to assist researchers in locating ADAPSO materials in their archive. They had a number of ADAPSO materials that had been contributed by various individuals and companies as part of larger collections. That's now been structured that so you can find materials related to ADAPSO that are already there at their archive.

Last night you heard from Joan Wessel that all of Milt Wessel's files are going to that archive and, of course, that's a wonderful contribution in terms of ADAPSO history.

And Tom O'Rourke is working on creating a website for Tymshare history. I had invited him to come to this meeting but he wasn't able to. So, instead I went to visit him and spent several hours interviewing him and recording his recollections. He got very interested in preserving Tymshare history. So he's created a website where former Tymshare employees can contribute their recollections of Tymshare history. And he's also going to donate his files to the Babbage Institute.

Those are the kinds of things we've done so far. In the future, we want to do more special issues of the *Annals* covering other sectors of the industry and other eras.

We want to do more oral histories. There are so many people whose ideas and recollections we need to capture.

We want to expand our company database on the website. That takes a lot of research to develop a good list of companies and then find someone who knows enough about each one to be able to put together a pretty complete set of facts on it.

We want to expand the list of people that we have on the web site and we want to add more biographical detail. Arthur Norberg, the Executive Director of the Babbage Institute, and I have discussed creating a biographical database modeled on the one created by the Center for the History of Physics which would provide researchers of all kinds with readily available biographical information on people who were influential in the development of software.

We're going to continue doing our outreach to individuals regarding the importance of preserving any records they have. If you've got materials in your files relating to the companies you founded or have been involved with, please make sure they don't get thrown out. I can't tell you how many people I've talked to over the last couple of years who have said, "Oh, I just threw that stuff away last year." Please don't throw it away. Give us a chance to find out whether it is something that needs to be saved. Don't assume it has no value.

And we want to do ongoing outreach to companies and to associations that are still in existence to establish a plan to make sure their records get preserved. We want to encourage them to take advantage of resources like the archivists at the Babbage Institute who will give free consultation in records management that will help them set up a system to make sure their records get preserved.

Those are the kinds of things we want to do as we move forward.

Here's how you can help us. Make a commitment to save any records you have. Put together an inventory of what you've got in those boxes in the basement or the garage or wherever. Correlate it to your personal resume or timeline so that you can relate the files to various phases of your life. Contact CBI for an evaluation. The archivists up there will talk to you about what should be saved, what should not be saved, what has historical value. And although we work very closely with CBI, if you prefer to work with a different organization, that's fine, too. Some people feel like they'd like to donate their personal records to their alma mater. That's fine. The important thing is to make sure that your records get evaluated by someone who knows how to determine what their historical value is. And then donate them or put a codicil in your will to make sure that in the long run those records end up somewhere where they will be preserved and made accessible to researchers studying the history of the industry.

There are other things you can do. Write or dictate a memoir. Volunteer to work with us to collect information about a specific company as the employees from Tymshare are doing. Go find the people who were involved and get their information and add that to the record. Or pick an ADAPSO section or program and volunteer to reconstruct the list of companies that were involved in it. Just getting the data together and writing it down and getting it preserved is important. Talk to us about what you'd like to do, the part that you feel is important, and we'll figure out a way to make that happen.

And, of course, you can help by providing us with some financial support. Because of the kind of organization we are—we're new, we're small, we're not affiliated with an academic organization—we don't have the right profile to be able to get significant grants of any kind. So, how much of this we're going to be able to do is really going to depend on how much support we can generate from the industry itself. We'll go as far as we can based on the level of support that we get from the industry.

So thank you. Thank you for coming. Thank you for helping with the workshops today where we're going to put you all to work talking about your ADAPSO experiences. Let us know what you think about our efforts. And have fun!

[*Applause*]

David Allison, Smithsonian National Museum of American History
Saturday Morning Plenary Session

Luanne Johnson: There are four organizations that helped to make this event happen: the Smithsonian National Museum of American History, the IEEE *Annals of the History of Computing*, the Charles Babbage Institute and the Information Technology Association of America. I've asked representatives from each to spend a few minutes telling us about their organizations.

We'll hear first from Dr. David Allison of the National Museum of American History. Some of you probably attended the 1990 combined ADAPSO Conference and World Congress. We had about 1200 people, 900 from ADAPSO and 300 from around the world. It was in Washington, DC, and our opening cocktail event the first evening was held at the Information Age Exhibit at the Smithsonian which had just recently opened. We had a wonderful time.

The man I'm going to introduce to you now is the curator of that exhibit. Dr. David Allison, Director of the Information Technology and Society Division at the Smithsonian National Museum of American History.

[Applause]

David Allison: Thanks, Luanne. As Luanne said, I head a division called Information Technology and Society at the National Museum of American History. And in some ways we converged at the Museum even before the industry did because that division contains the history of computing, history of communications—telegraph, telephone, radio, television, etc.—history of photography, history of printing, history of graphic arts, and even numismatics, the history of money.

We saw six years ago that all those fields had a natural relationship to each other because they were all about different forms of information. As we looked to the future of collecting in those fields, it was going to be necessary to see how digitizing and information technology spread across all of them and to look for linkages in our collecting plans. And that has now happened.

Luanne mentioned the Information Age Exhibit. We are in the early stages now of doing a complete renovation of it. Ten years for an exhibit like Information Age is like fifty or sixty years for another exhibit. So it is more than overdue. I brought some brochures that you can pick up out in front to tell you a little bit about what we are planning.

The working title for the new exhibit is "Global Connections." That exhibit will include not just computing and communications, the subjects of Information Age, but all the other disciplines I mentioned as well. We also will have more of a social focus, because the audiences that come to the Smithsonian are much more interested in the impact that information technology has had on their lives and the lives of other Americans than they are in just the technology.

So our theme in the new exhibition will be "communications and community," how information technology has affected us at home, at school, at work and in our nation. We will also look at the relationship of our nation to countries around the world. It is an interesting time, because we're working with designers, our own team and outside consultants, struggling to figure out how we're going to present a 21st century exhibit to the American people and to the huge audiences that come to the Smithsonian from around the world.

That is all I'm going to say about what we are doing at the Smithsonian because I want to spend a few minutes echoing and maybe expanding on what Luanne said about the importance of what the Software History Center is doing.

I have heard some people at this conference say, "Why is this important? Nobody really cares about what we did ten years ago. It's not significant."

Well, I think we should try to put ourselves in the position of somebody looking back fifty, or a hundred, years from now at the post-war era in the United States. We need to ask ourselves, "If somebody looks back at that time, what are they going to think is the significant contribution that this society at the pinnacle of its world power and influence made to civilization?"

What is their vote going to be? It is not going to be our system of democracy. We can't claim credit for that. We built on what the Greeks did. It is not going to be our free market system. That is not an American innovation. It is also something from an earlier time.

But in this post-war era, the field of information technology, particularly software, is new. It is something that has clearly shaped our economy, has shaped economies around the world, and has brought people around the world into different kinds of relationships with each other. It is a truly revolutionary force.

If this is not the most significant contribution of this period in history, it will certainly be near the top. Think about it. Software has truly been a fundamental intellectual contribution to the history of mankind.

What other society, what other period in history can say that it created a new means of communication, a way that people can talk to and control machines. It transformed the world.

A hundred years from now people are going to want to know: How did this happen? Who were those people? Why did they do this? What were the issues that brought this about? It is an important question now, but the further we get from it, the more significant it will become.

Now I want to say a word about history. Many people think history is the study of the past. It's not the study of the past. It's the study of what we *save* from the past. There can be no history if there is nothing to study. If we don't save the records, if we don't save recollections, images, sounds, thoughts, if we don't save this material, there will be no understanding of what happened because there will be nothing to interpret.

We really need to think about that. I'll tell you one story from my own experience. It's not a software story, it's a story about electronics. I did my doctoral dissertation at Princeton on the development of radar, particularly the invention of radar at the Naval Research Laboratory in the 1920s and 1930s. Many people think that the British invented radar but, in fact radar was invented in many different places, including the United States.

One of the critical documents that I wanted to find was the document that identified when the word "radar" was coined. Now you would think that would be an easy document to find. "Radar", the word, must be documented in a lot of places. So I went to the source of the document in the records of the Naval Research Laboratory. It wasn't there. I found the file. I found, actually, the card that said, "This is where the document is," but the document wasn't in the file.

Since there wasn't a carbon copy in the file, I decided to go look where the original was sent. So I went to the office of the Chief of Naval Operations where the document was sent. It wasn't there.

So, where was I going to look? Was it completely lost? There was a man named Stanford Hooper who was the program manager in the Bureau of Engineering . He had the document, or a copy of it, and saved it in his personal papers, which were later deposited in the Library of Congress. And that's where this document was preserved—the only copy as far as I know.

So, don't underestimate what Luanne is saying about the importance of saving your personal records. Don't assume that somebody else must have saved it somewhere. Because in fast-moving, innovative companies, that is probably not true.

I want to leave you with one final thought. People say that history never changes. It is done. The only thing that can change is the future. But that is not true either.

History is constantly in flux. We continually reinterpret and rethink our past. Consider Harry Truman. If you look back on the 1950s, Harry Truman was usually considered a failed President. People thought he had not been up to the task of running the country. They believed that Eisenhower had to come in and take charge. Yet, today, people have reinterpreted the importance of Harry Truman to the history of the United States. Now many think of Truman as one of our best Presidents.

Think about a subject like slavery. If you look at history textbooks in the United States a few generations ago, slavery is almost a footnote. Studying it did not seem very important. Today, most scholars will say the experience of this country with black slavery was among the most important episodes of our national history. It fundamentally changed who we are. They argue that we must study it carefully if we are going to become a successful multicultural country in the future.

So do not believe that there will be just one interpretation of the history of software and information technology. We need to save documentation so that, as our society changes, people will have an opportunity to go back and reinterpret the significance of this important development in our history, and how it informs our future.

We don't know yet what kind of questions those historians of the future will be most interested in. Just as people twenty years ago didn't know what historians of slavery would be interested in, or historians of the Truman Presidency. What we do know is that we must give them the opportunity to understand. That is why we at the Smithsonian are delighted to partner with Luanne and Burt and the Software History Center. We have very important work to do, and we are delighted that they have taken the personal initiative to move forward. We thank all of you for being here, and for giving us your recollections. Most importantly, we thank you for helping us preserve this important piece of American history.

[*Applause*]

Jeffrey Yost, Charles Babbage Institute
Saturday Morning Plenary Session

Luanne Johnson: The Charles Babbage Institute was established twenty-five years ago. It's affiliated with the University of Minnesota and its extensive collection of information about the history of information processing is heavily used by all kinds of researchers, academic and otherwise. Its initial focus was primarily on hardware but more recently they've begun extensive work on the history of software. I'd like to introduce Dr. Jeffrey Yost, Associate Director of the Charles Babbage Institute.

[*Applause*]

Jeffrey Yost: It's my pleasure to be here today and to be part of this Software History Center event. I'd especially like to thank Luanne and Burt for all they've done. It's been great working with them on this and other projects.

Though some strong scholarship has been done on the history of software, much of it by historians taking part in this event, it's still greatly understudied, as is the study of the role of trade organizations in the development of industries. Noted historian Louis Galambos did a wonderful study of textile trade organizations, but trade associations in most industries have been ignored and that certainly has been true of ADAPSO.

For these reasons, it's especially exciting to be here with software industry pioneers, ADAPSO leaders, and fellow historians to celebrate, recount and interpret the history of ADAPSO and its role in the software industry.

Many of you know CBI very well. The Institute is proud to be celebrating its 25th anniversary this year. For those of you less familiar with CBI, we are a research center and archives dedicated to the history of information technology. We are located at the Andersen Library at the University of Minnesota and we're supported by the school's engineering college as well as the university library, the Charles Babbage Foundation and friends of CBI. Our staff includes our director, Arthur Norberg, I am the associate director, our archivist is Elisabeth Kaplan, and Philip Frana is the Software History Project Manager. Phil is also here with us today. Our assistant archivist is Carrie Seib and our secretary is Lisa Deutz. We also get a great deal of help from undergraduate and graduate assistants.

As an historian of business and technology, I feel the best way to understand an organization is to look at its history. I'm going to attempt the daunting task of trying to provide you with a sense of CBI's 25-year history, as well as current projects and future prospectives, all within about five minutes.

I'm going to talk about five senses of CBI: our purpose, our programs, our products and services, our sense of community, and future possibilities. First, our sense of purpose. Former ERA engineer and Dataproducts founder, Erwin Tomash, formed CBI in 1977 to provide leadership in the preservation and interpretation of the history of computing. We've had many different types of projects since then and worked with many different people and groups, but we've never deviated from this basic mission.

We advance our mission through the synergy of our two fundamental programs: historical research and archives. We conduct and publish research to advance the history of information technology as well as to build connections and knowledge important to our collection development efforts. We collect, preserve and make accessible a world-class set of primary resources to study the history of information technology.

CBI has many products and services. In our history, CBI staff has more than 85 publications. Most books by current and former staff extended from major research projects funded by competitive grants from the National Science Foundation, DARPA, the National Endowment for the Humanities, the National Historical Publications and Records Commission, and others. CBI also publishes articles on history, historiography, archival theory and biography.

From shortly after the Institute's founding, CBI historians have conducted research-grade oral histories on computing, software and networking. We now hold more than 330 oral histories and are currently targeting the history of software development and the software industry as part of our Software History Project.

We also provide access to many other types of resources. We have more than 6,000 cubic feet of archival records on companies, individuals, trade organizations, and many other areas. The CBI archives also hold more than 10,000 photographs and extensive film and video footage. Our dedicated staff of historians and archivists are always willing to help out researchers.

CBI staff, however, is just part of a much larger CBI international community. Through the CBI/Tomash fellowship, the Institute has supported 21 doctoral scholars researching the technical, business, social and cultural history of information technology. Our first two fellows, both here today, William Aspray and Paul Ceruzzi, are representative of the continuing contributions and leadership to the field made by CBI/Tomash fellows. Also here today are two of our most recent fellows, Tom Haigh and Nathan Ensmenger. Both have published some terrific articles over the past year on the history of software and are establishing themselves as new leaders in this field.

Our sponsored and cosponsored conferences such as recent software history conferences held at Xerox PARC and in Paderborn, Germany, have brought together leading historians, scientists, technologists, and industrialists to advance a number of topics and methodological approaches.

Looking to the future, CBI continues to acquire important new collections in software, networking and computing. I'd like to reiterate Luanne's words to please contact us and our archivist, Elisabeth Kaplan, regarding any records you may have of potential significance.

On the research end, CBI is currently completing studies of the early computer industry, continuing work on our half million dollar NSF-sponsored project entitled "Building a Future for Software History," and exploring the possibilities of new projects in areas such as the history of medical informatics and management in the software industry.

CBI is also building new infrastructure for scholarship. The tools and content of our website are continuously being expanded. For example, we recently added a database of all our oral histories and put those online as PDF files. And they're being downloaded at a rate of over 400 a month. They've always been very popular but that's greatly exceeded our expectations.

And we've also placed on the website, as part of the Software History Project, a large bibliography of resources useful to the study of the history of software that contains over 2,000 citations.

I am running out of time, but I would like to reiterate my thanks to Luanne and Burt and to express the enthusiasm and dedication of the CBI staff as we continue to conduct important new research, and extend and strengthen our collections in an effort to facilitate and advance the study of the history of information technology.

Thank you very much.

[*Applause*]

Plenary Session Photos

Luanne Johnson opening the Plenary Session

Senator Frank Lautenberg

Rick Crandall

David K. Allison, Smithsonian Institution National Museum of American History

Jeffrey Yost, Charles Babbage Institute

Tim Bergin, IEEE Annals

Harris Miller, ITAA

Martin Campbell-Kelly, Keynote Speaker, Warwick University, UK

Joan Wessel contributing Milt Wessel's papers to CBI

Rick Crandall and control panel from an SDS940

ADAPSO photo displays

Luanne Johnson and Burt Grad, Software History Center Founders

Tim Bergin, *IEEE Annals of the History of Computing*
Saturday Morning Plenary Session

Luanne Johnson: The next person up is Dr. Tim Bergin, who is the Editor-in-Chief of the IEEE *Annals of the History of Computing*, a distinguished publication that's been around for a long time and is now beginning to have a focus on software history. The *Annals* is also a cosponsor of this Conference, and has donated copies of previous articles which you will find in your packet.

[Applause]

Tim Bergin: When you are the fourth speaker, there is the risk that everybody in front of you said everything you thought about saying. So let me just say that, in a sense, Luanne gave us a mission statement. When you look at business history, you see organizations that succeeded because they had a mission statement, because they had leaders, because they had enthusiasm. And if Burt and Luanne don't have all of the above, I don't know who does.

David Allison gave you a broad view of history and why it's important. I don't think that I need to tell you much more about that. Your presence here indicates that you recognize how important it is that we preserve the history of our industry.

Jeff Yost talked about archiving the records. I guess for most of my adult life I've enjoyed reading *National Geographic*, especially archeology and paleontology, and the big thing that jumps out at you is that there are gaps in the fossil record. I'd be the last person to put you in the fossil category *[laughter]* but, on the other hand, if your records aren't at the Charles Babbage Institute or some other archive, then future researchers and historians will never get a chance to look at them.

Last weekend, I was at CBI for a different kind of conference, The Second Workshop on Using History to Improve Undergraduate Computer Science Teaching. When they took us down into the catacombs, I got to see Marty Goetz's records, Bob Head's records, some of Jean Sammet's records, so I have first hand knowledge of the excellent job they do.

So why am I here?

Well, if we go out twenty years I hope that someone will want to know something about the history of the software industry. They might think that the statement in *Fortune* in November 1999 that Luanne referred to sounds a little suspicious. Wasn't there something before Bill Gates?

You have two ways to get that kind of knowledge. You can get on an aircraft, fly to Minneapolis, take the risk of snow—it snowed Saturday and Sunday last weekend [*laughter*]—and dig through miles of records.

But that's not a very efficient way to do anything. This is where the historian comes in. What historians do is that they study the record and distill from it the essence of what happened. Historians provide a short cut, if you will. And I would give you the argument that no student, no professor and very, very few other people, will go out to CBI and do all the work necessary to understand why *you* made a difference; why what *you* did was important.

And I'd ask you not to judge the importance of what you did. Let history be that judge through the eyes of the people who will work on those records.

So, how does the *IEEE Annals of the History of Computing* play a role in this? Well, *Annals* is *the* archival journal. If you're writing something on the history of information technology, then *Annals* is the place to publish that information. As an archival journal, we have papers written by historians and practitioners. The special issue that you received in your registration packet has a couple of articles by historians. It also contains memoirs written by practitioners, based on their experiences. I've had the pleasure of working with Marty Goetz on his memoirs. At dinner last night, someone said how much they enjoyed the first part of Marty's memoir. Well, let me say that if you enjoyed the first part, wait until you see the second part; it's really insightful. He gets to the bone, and lets us see what he did, what his colleagues did, why they were successful, and why the future needs to understand that.

Annals also has articles on the industry's heritage. We'd like to see the history of ADAPSO written. Going home on the Metro last night, Paul Ceruzzi asked, "Why ADAPSO? Why not some other trade organization?" Well, the answer is because Luanne and Burt saw a need, contacted people and put forth a couple of years effort to make this day possible. We'll have to hope that someone does the same for the other professional organizations in our industry.

So *Annals* has scholarly papers and practitioners' memoirs, but we also have departments which contain short biographies, book reviews, and anecdotes. Anecdotes are short pieces, maybe just a few pages, in which practitioners share interesting stories about episodes in their careers.

In your registration packets, there is a letter on *Annals* stationery from Anne Fitzpatrick, the editor of the Anecdotes department. We hope that each of you will sit down and write some interesting little tidbit about your career, and send it to Anne.

And, finally, there is our Events and Sightings department. Nathan Ensmenger, who is here today, is one of the editors of that department. A report on this conference will appear in Events and Sightings in the next issue and thereby document that it happened!

Let me finish with a short story. I grew up in New York City and a number of years ago the Tip Top Bread Company had an advertisement in the days of black-and-white television. An elderly lady gets on an elevator wearing a hat with a little flower on top. A workman gets on the elevator wearing blue overalls and carrying a tool box. He says, "Good morning, madam," and tips his hat. When he tips his hat, the lady notices that he has a light bulb tattooed on the top of his head. After a few moments, the lady finally says, "I don't mean to be disrespectful but why do you have a light bulb tattooed on your head?" The workman answers, "Well, madam, it was New Year's Eve and I thought it was good idea at the time." [*Laughter*]

When I first talked to Burt and Luanne about the special issue on the software products industry, I thought it was a good idea. Given the feedback I've gotten from people across the country and around the world, it was an *excellent* idea. And I'm grateful to Burt and Luanne and the people who wrote the articles.

I hope it's only the beginning. I hope we will have more special issues, more papers, more anecdotes, and more memoirs from people in this audience.

Finally, there's also a yellow subscription blank in your registration packet. I hope those of you that are not presently subscribing to *Annals* will do so. If you email me, and my address is on the masthead, I'll be happy to send you some back issues.

I look forward to our sessions this morning and this afternoon.

[*Applause*]

Harris Miller, Information Technology Association of America
Saturday Morning Plenary Session

Luanne Johnson: Our fourth cosponsor is ITAA, as ADAPSO is now known, represented by ITAA President Harris Miller.

[Applause]

Harris Miller: Thank you, Luanne. I want to add my congratulations to you and Burt and the others who put this together. I also want to say how pleased I am after having traveled around the country the last two years spending a lot of time with CEOs of ITAA member companies to be with people in the IT industry who actually have some money.

[Laughter]

It's tough out there, folks. We're hoping the industry will get better soon, but times have been tough.

I'm a little intimidated by being here to talk about the IT industry because of the collective knowledge represented here. But what I want to do is give you an update on what ITAA is today and to make the point that understanding the history of this organization, understanding the history of all of you who helped to found it and sustain it and grow it as part of the industry, is very important. Because as David said, IT is the contribution of the American society in this post-war era and the challenges that you faced as you started this industry and moved it forward are still being felt today.

In terms of ITAA, we have about 500 companies. We've moved beyond the initial services and software industry to a broad range of companies. We now have an Interactive TV council comprised of companies involved in that new segment of the industry. But, of course, the more traditional software and service companies are also involved within the association.

Our core mission has changed quite a bit. Obviously, ADAPSO pursued public policy issues from its earliest days, but my background is in public policy. So, to a large extent, we are a lobbying organization disguised as a trade association. Over a third of the staff have direct public policy experience working on the House or the Senate or the Administration or all three, as I did earlier in my career. Joe Tasker, whom some of you may have met last night, our General Counsel and Senior VP for Public Policy, ran Compaq's Washington office for ten years. Allen Miller, who heads our global public policy, ran EDS's international public policy program for ten years. So we're very much involved in this agenda setting.

And why is that important? Well, again, to refer to David Allison's comments, if you look through the history of most of the industrial age sectors that have developed, soon thereafter you see government regulation. So whether it's the railroads, airlines, pharmaceuticals, electricity, you name it, it's regulated by the government. There's one sector, though, that is not regulated by the government. And that is the information technology sector, except for telecommunications.

Some could say that that is by pure accident. But some would say that that is because of an effort to keep ourselves unregulated and I think, in fact, the challenges are even stronger today than they have been. There are more bills in the Congress today and in the state legislatures today and in Brussels in the European Commission than there have ever been.

In areas like taxation and privacy and security, those issues are out there right now presenting major challenges. So we are very involved across a range of issues. Just earlier this week, the Undersecretary of Commerce and the Special Assistant to the Secretary of Commerce, Phil Bond, who used to work as an industry lobbyist for Hewlett Packard, in a speech in Utah said the IT industry is still not putting enough energy into its public policy agenda. There is still much more to be done.

So the public policy issues are important and that's a lot of what we do. Obviously, we continue to focus on business development, particularly for our smaller and mid-size companies, but the kind of networking that you did in the earlier days of ADAPSO is not nearly as popular today as it was then. There are so many other venues, conferences, events, local associations, other national associations, which provide that sort of opportunity.

Many of the events we do now are very specialized and very focused. For example, on Monday and Tuesday, we're holding our fifth annual convocation focusing on the IT workforce shortage. This event actually sold out two weeks ago, we had such intense interest. But only about a third of the attendees are industry people. About two-thirds are from education and government. So it's a different kind of event than you were used to.

We also hold a lot of very visible public policy events. Thursday of this week we hosted an event at the Hay Adams Hotel with over 200 attendees to work with the new Critical Infrastructure Protection Board that President Bush has appointed headed by his cybersecurity czar, Dick Clark. About a third of the attendees were from government and two-thirds from industry, focusing on the cybersecurity issue.

And we still do some studies and reports. One of them is called "Digital Planet" which we do in conjunction with IDC which is a biennial survey of the global IT market. We do an annual survey of the IT workforce shortage. We'll be releasing that on Monday. The new one is called "Bouncing Back." We get tremendous press visibility out of that.

And we do a monthly online-based survey of the health and condition of the IT services industry which gets a lot of play and coverage, too.

How are we set up currently? We have a fifteen-member Board of Directors. Gary Greenfield, former CEO of Merant, who is our current Board Chairman wanted to be here with you all today, but he had to be in Europe and couldn't be back in time. We have a very active and engaged board, primarily CEOs of software and services companies. We currently have four divisions:

- Enterprise Solutions, which some of you know as Systems Integration. And, yes, Olga Grkavac is still the head of that division. Olga also wanted to be with you today, but unfortunately, her father is ill and she had to be in Wisconsin with him. Olga just celebrated her 21st anniversary at ITAA so I know that many of you have worked with her.

- IC&C is the Internet Commerce and Communications Division. We still work with Joe Markoski's firm on telecom issues at the FCC and on Capitol Hill. But there are also a lot of Internet issues, such as privacy and other issues related to that.

- The IT Services Division is primarily the commercial companies in the IT Services business.

- And the Software Division is primarily the enterprise software companies. Rich Carpenter, who is here today, sits on the Board of Directors of that Division.

I also want to mention our international organization, WITSA. Luanne mentioned the World Congress back in 1990. WITSA, the World Information Technology and Services Alliance, does go on. ADAPSO was one of the founders in 1978. We just added our 46th country. We're probably going to add another half dozen at our meeting this fall in Geneva. We just held the 13th World Congress on IT in Adelaide, Australia. We had 1800 people from 55 countries there.

Positively Broadband is an initiative we launched last October. There's a lot of debate about broadband but most of the debate, at least inside of the Beltway here, is focused on the supply side, who should control the last mile. It's the fight between the Bell Operating Companies and the competitors. But we went out and did the hard data analysis and about 80% of the country does have access to broadband but only about 10% of the people use it. We did some surveys and asked people why and they said, "I don't want to pay that much money for faster email. It just isn't worth it. You have to give me an additional value proposition."

So we've been focusing on various applications and trying to shift the debate. And I'm very pleased to say that in just six months, the whole tenor of the debate has shifted. The President, the Secretary of Commerce, and the CEO of Telstra during our World Congress have given speeches focusing on the fact that we need to create content, to convince people that broadband is worth their time and effort to sign up for.

We have a Defense Transformation program. A lot of people who were not interested in the government marketplace a couple of years ago, particularly during the height of the dotcom boom, have suddenly decided Uncle Sam is, in fact, a *great* customer. Maybe the margins aren't so great but he does tend to pay and pay regularly.

We're also trying to get the government marketplace changed and we've had a lot of success over the last six years. We're still far from nirvana but at least it's beginning to look more like the commercial marketplace.

When Olga Grkavac does training seminars for program managers in the federal government, they always ask the question, "In the commercial marketplace, when someone loses an attempt to get a contract, how does the bid protest system work?" So she has to explain to them that the commercial marketplace doesn't *have* a bid protest system. [*Laughter*]

30

That's something that's unique to the government. So we're trying to get them to understand that's not necessarily the way to do business.

ITAA was the first organization to call for the appointment of an e-government czar and we were very pleased that President Bush appointed Mark Forman to that position last summer. Mark, as many of you know, comes out of our industry. We were also the first organization to call for the appointment of a cybersecurity czar and Dick Clark was appointed to that position by President Bush in October.

Our Information Security program is one of our most visible and active. As many of you know, ITAA was a leader in the Y2K program and we morphed that into our information security program. Many of our first information security meetings were held in very small phone booths. We couldn't get anybody interested. It wasn't a priority, it wasn't an issue. It began to grow considerably the last couple of years with some of the very visible denial-of-service attacks, for example, in February of 2000. President Clinton asked me at the time to organize a meeting at the White House and I brought 25 of our companies in to meet with him and his cabinet officials to discuss cybersecurity. Obviously, 9/11 and the appointment of Dick Clark as the federal cybersecurity czar has raised this issue even higher in visibility.

Our international program is very important. Many of our companies, big and small, earn 50%, 60%, 70% of their revenue overseas so making sure that those markets stay open or become even more open is important. Also, harmonization so that our companies don't have to deal with different rules and regulations in areas like cyber crime and tax and privacy when they operate in the US versus Europe versus Asia. It's a big challenge. The Europeans, in particular, for all kinds of historical reasons, are very much more inclined to regulate than we are here in the US.

We're also involved in ICANN, which is the Internet naming organization, it's the phone book for the Internet. In some ways, it's a very technical and boring issue but it has a lot to do with Internet governance and whether the industry really can govern itself or whether we're going to have to turn it back over to government to do so.

Our work force program is an area in which we've been a leader. We've been working very closely with the education community and the government community. At our conference starting Monday, our speakers will be people like Secretary of Labor Elaine Chao and Jim Goodnight of SAS along with a number of leading academics. We're bringing together leaders in education, government and industry to talk about having a work force which is large enough, is well-trained and available to make sure that the US IT industry can remain not only competitive but be a leader globally.

There are also some community-related programs that we're involved with such as Stay Safe Online. ITAA is a founding member of that, working with other business organizations like the Chamber of Congress and the National Association of Manufacturers and the US Government, trying to educate average consumers and small businesses about cybersecurity because the Internet is such an open technology, everybody has to be part of good cyber hygiene.

The Cyber Citizen Partnership is a partnership between ITAA and the Department of Justice to try to educate young people. It's hugely problematic for people in industry, for people in government, that there are so many so-called "script kiddies" out there who think it's cute to figure out if they can hack. In fact, it's even worse that their parents think, "Isn't Johnny smart? Isn't Susie smart? They just brought down the Pentagon website." We have to begin to educate them that they have to be good cyber citizens.

You know, the pre-Socratic philosopher Heraclitus said, "You never stand in the same river twice." Which basically means change is constant. And certainly that is true at ITAA. One of the fun things about this job in the now seven years I've been in it, every day is a different day, everything is new. But at the same time, we also know that without understanding our history and the tradition of our industry, people cannot really fully appreciate how significant our industry is.

ITAA is very pleased and honored to be turning over the ADAPSO files to CBI and hope that they will contribute to the work of current and future historians. We're very, very pleased and honored to have an affiliation with the work that Luanne and Burt and others are doing with the Software History Center and we look forward to at least 41 more years of ITAA.

Thank you very much.

[*Applause*]

Martin Campbell-Kelly, University of Warwick
Saturday Luncheon Speech

Martin Campbell-Kelly is a reader in computer science, specializing in the history of computing, at the University of Warwick, England. His latest book, From Airline Reservations to Sonic the Hedgehog: A History of the Software Industry, *was published by MIT Press in early 2003. His previous books include the official history of Britain's leading computer company,* ICL: A Business and Technical History, *which won the UK Wadsworth Prize for Business History, and an accessible history of the computer co-authored with William Aspray,* Computer: A History of the Information Machine. *He is editor of the* Collected Works of Charles Babbage.

Dr. Campbell-Kelly has held research fellowships with the Smithsonian Institution, the National Archive for the History of Computing, and the Dibner Institute. He is an editor of Computer Journal, *and the* Encyclopedia of Computer Science and Engineering *and is on the editorial board of the* IEEE Annals of the History of Computing. *He is a council member of the British Society for the History of Mathematics and the Computer Conservation Society, and serves on the experts panel of Nominet UK.*

History and the History of Software

I want to start by congratulating Luanne and Burt on the wonderful job they have done establishing the Software History Center. There are many specialist historical societies, but often they become collecting or preservation organizations and their labors do not contribute much to the creation of real history. I am so pleased that the Software History Center has involved professional organizations like the Smithsonian Institution and the Charles Babbage Institute, as well as individual historians like myself. I think the results of this weekend will be a real addition to the store of knowledge about the software industry.

When they were planning this meeting, Luanne and Burt asked if I would give a short talk from the perspective of someone actively engaged in writing about the history of the software industry. Luanne suggested I might like talk about some of my opinions and conclusions. Unfortunately, I think there may be fifty industry experts in this room with fifty different opinions. Instead I'd like to talk about my view of the history of software within the general field of history. Of course there are ten historians here with ten different opinions about this subject too—I'll have to deal with those off line!

A few years from now our grandchildren—or as I look about me, perhaps great-grandchildren—will begin to study the history of the late twentieth century. It will be history of wars, of sexual liberation and its consequences, of feminism and post-feminism. But above all I think it will be a history of technology—especially information technology. How will historians write these histories of the late twentieth century? Principally by mining information from specialist histories—like the one I have just written on the software industry. These historians call "secondary sources."

People often use the metaphor of the "river of history," and the kind of history I write is one of the tributaries that feed this river. I never like this analogy because it suggests that if my particular tributary—that is, the history of the software industry—is cut off, then it will be scarcely noticed in the general flood of events. Instead, I prefer to think of my kind of history as being a piece of a jigsaw puzzle. If there is a piece missing the picture is simply incomplete. How many pieces in a jigsaw puzzle? Five hundred, a thousand? It is a good analogy, because I believe that software is one of the most important five hundred things that happened in the late twentieth century.

My book is a secondary source. To write it I used primary sources. Without sources there can be no history. What one has is myths, speculation, or invention. For example, in Europe we call the centuries between the fall of the Roman Empire and the medieval period the "Dark Age." It is so called because no written records exist that can shine light on the period. Very little real history has been written on the Dark Age because historians have no materials to work with. What we have instead are myths and legends, of which *The Tales of King Arthur and the Knights of the Round Table* are perhaps the best known.

In England, history starts to get true and detailed for the sixteenth century—the Elizabethan period and the Age of Shakespeare. We have very rich accounts of the wars with Spain for example, that we all learned in history at school. These histories are based on political and royal records. They are relatively few in number and could probably be accommodated in the present room.

You might think that after 400 or so years the history of the sixteenth century would have been "done" and we could move on to the next thing. But this is not so. New generations ask new questions of the primary sources which are therefore forever indispensable. For example I have a colleague who is working on a history of glove-making, which was once based in Worcester in the English midlands. Sixteenth-century glove-making sounds inconsequential, but consider the questions my friend is asking: How were gloves actually made? Where did the leather and cotton thread (though perhaps not *cotton* thread) come from? How did the goods get from Worcester to London, the primary market? How did the maker get paid—and the workers? How were glove factories organized—indeed, *were* there glove factories as such? So, while glove-making may sound less than earth-shattering its history has the potential to tell us as much about life in the Elizabethan era as the chronicles of Kings and Queens and Wars. Glove-making is part of the fabric of life and its history tells us much about how the different parts of society cooperated.

So how does one find out about Elizabethan glove-making? It sounds impossible at such a distance in time. But this is exactly what historians are trained to do, and the source materials they use are Artifacts and Records. We have artifacts in the form of actual gloves preserved in museums and private collections. We have records such as parish registers—in which are recorded the lives of glove-makers, and even glove-making dynasties. We also have the account books kept by manufacturers, merchants, and the private houses that bought gloves.

Let me fast forward through the centuries to consider the software industry. Writing its history is not very different. We have artifacts (for example, computer programs) and we have business records of different kinds. And we have oral histories—a vital source not available to scholars of the Elizabethan period.

I'd like to say a few words about each:

Artifacts present a problem for the software historian. More effort by well meaning amateurs is going into the preservation of programs than any other historical activity in software. Of course it is very useful to have some software artifacts preserved, but they do not provide historical insight in proportion to their number. Think of my friend the historian of glove-making—he gained important insights into early glove-making by examining the physical construction of a glove. But even he—and this is a man who has come to love gloves—accepts that a few examples are sufficient to his purpose.

Business records, perhaps not surprisingly, have been my most important source in writing about the software industry. The most useful is the single-volume company history. Unfortunately histories of Microsoft outnumber all the histories of the remaining companies by a ratio of about 2:1! I will come back to the contemporary obsession with Microsoft later. The most useful company histories were written by professional historians, it is true. But they do not have to be, and often the primary records are insufficient to justify the employment of a professional historian anyway. Some excellent histories have been written by company founders and Chief Executive Officers. For example, John Imlay's *Jungle Rules* (1994) is not a book any historian would have written, but it is nonetheless full of insights about Imlay's stewardship of MSA. My personal favorite is Richard MacNeal's *History of the MacNeal-Schwendler Corporation* (now the MSC Software Corp.) written in 1988, when the company had just a couple of hundred employees and sales were around ten million dollars—it is a very rare example of a history of a medium-sized software company before it became large. Where no company history has been commissioned by a firm it is very useful to historians if records are preserved. Access is often sensitive for commercial reasons, but historians understand this. And we urge business people not to preserve just high-level documents such as Annual Report and Board Minutes. That random sales pamphlet or other piece of ephemera may be truly interesting to the historian—and forever interesting.

Industry-analyst reports. The conventional business history is often described as being written from the "inside looking out." The reports of industry analysts give us another view—from the outside looking in. The phenomenon of the industry analyst arose almost in parallel with the rise of the software industry, and you know their names: ICP, IDC, INPUT, Gartner, Frost & Sullivan, etc. The Library of Congress has about fifty reports covering the period 1970-1990. This is but a very small fraction of what was actually produced. For example, a surviving catalogue of INPUT shows it alone produced 1500 reports in the period 1976-1993. I asked my research assistant to contact all the industry analysts we could locate to see if they had any historical material, but none admitted to any records going back further than ten years. So thousands—perhaps as many as ten thousand—reports are simply lost forever. But let me stress: historians do not ask you to save *everything*. After all, it would be difficult to actually digest ten thousand reports. But unquestionably a lot of valuable data has been lost, and preserving a selected one or two percent of the reports would have prevented this loss.

Trade Magazines were exceptionally useful. The best was *Datamation*, published 1956-1997 in hardcopy form, covered almost the entire span of my book. *Datamation* has since become web-based and one therefore cannot be certain what will survive for historians twenty years from now. *Software News* (edited by Ed Bride) and *Business Software Review* (produced by Larry Welke) were also valuable. *Software News* has a wonderful set of company profiles of significant firms (often before they became industrial giants). *Business Software Review* reported, especially, the annual Million Dollar Award ceremonies for leading software products. These magazines convey a sense of community largely absent from more formal reporting. Incidentally, I know of no complete holdings of these software magazines. For example, when we contacted *Software Magazine* they had nothing older than three years, and did not even realize they had once been called *Software News*!

Oral History is what we are here for this weekend. Oral history is the recollections and testimony of the people who made history for the people who will write it. It is the kind of material historians of the sixteenth century would die for! For me, oral history has two purposes. First, it adds a human dimension to what would otherwise be primarily a technical or economic story. Second, it records data that is not captured by conventional sources. Let me illustrate.

In September 2000 the Software History Center organized a workshop at which several industry participants described the early years of their businesses. These histories were rich in human incident. A particularly evocative example concerned Joe Piscopo's decision to found Pansophic in 1969. Joe was then a recent graduate in computer science, had just completed a graduate course in business studies, and was wondering what to do next. He described an encounter at a social gathering. The story Joe told was reminiscent of the scene in the movie *The Graduate* where a family friend whispers the word "plastics" to Dustin Hoffmann. Except for Joe it was "software." Joe got funds from family sources and during the next few months built a product called PanValet. To avoid the problem of marketing he tried to sell PanValet to IBM for half a million dollars. IBM declined— which says as much for IBM's judgment as it does for Joe's exuberance of youth, because PanValet went on to do hundreds of millions dollars of business. It is stories like these that bring to life the rather dry statistic that "about 3000 software companies were started in the 1960s."

Oral history helps to fill in some of the gaps in the historical record. In researching my book there were several aspects I never resolved to my satisfaction. (Books are like software in this respect—there comes a point where you have to go with what you have got, and ship.) For example, I never fully understood the granting of patents and intellectual property protection generally; likewise the accounting for software assets, the role of the "Big Five" in the software industry, the relations of software entrepreneurs with IBM and the banks, and the social networks that existed between leaders of firms. In theory a historian could get to grips with these topics, but the effort needed would be disproportionate for a single-volume history. I'm delighted that these are exactly the kind of topics Luanne and Burt have slated for discussion this weekend. The transcripts will make life much easier for the historian of the future.

When people come to write the popular history of the information technology industry of the twentieth century—unless we set the record straight—it will be seen as a history dominated by two companies: IBM and Microsoft. Each will be seen as a Colossus bestriding the third and fourth quarters of the twentieth century respectively.

In the case of IBM I think this is a fair characterization—it was there at the beginning of the computer revolution, and during the third quarter of the twentieth century it owned three-quarters of the world market and profoundly shaped the mainframe industry. In the case of Microsoft this characterization—that it shaped the industrial scene of the last 25 years of the twentieth century—is simply untrue. Even today Microsoft accounts for only 10% of software sales, and in 1995 when Microsoft-mania and the first antitrust suits were filed, it was a lot less than that. It was not even the biggest *software* company in the world. That was IBM, but no one outside the industry seemed to be aware of this—certainly no one in the Department of Justice.

So, why the consuming interest in Microsoft? I believe there are two reasons. First, Bill Gates is the richest man in the world, and that is of universal fascination. It was exactly the kind of attention and notoriety that John D. Rockefeller gained in the early years of the twentieth century. Second, I think that Microsoft is the only software company the general public knows about. If you like, it is because consumer lobbyists such as Ralph Nader can see on their desktop PCs the nature and extent of Microsoft's monopoly in operating systems, office software, and Internet Explorer. They rightly see this as an abuse of monopoly power. But the desktop PC is but one sector of the computer world, and arguably not the most important.

If the consumer lobby and the Department of Justice knew more about software and more about the IT industry, they would realize that Microsoft does not present the most serious monopolistic threat. In my book, I studied two software products that seem at least as worthy of investigation as Internet Explorer—IBM's CICS and SAP's R/3. The statistics of CICS are impressive: it is used by 99 of the *Fortune 100* companies; it accounts for 16 percent of cycles executed on IBM mainframes; 20 billion transactions per day are performed using CICS; and it constitutes some 95 percent of the market for teleprocessing software. SAP R/3 is not yet so pervasive as CICS, but it is used by many business corporations and they are utterly dependent on it. If CICS or R/3 become intolerably expensive, U.S. industry would either have to put up with it or suffer enormous disruption. There are no easy substitutes. If Microsoft's Internet Explorer became intolerably expensive tomorrow? We would switch to Netscape Navigator.

Another factor overlooked by most writers is that the software industry did not start with Microsoft in 1975. The first software company, CUC, began twenty years earlier in 1954. And most of the practices of the industry were shaped by pioneer firms such as CSC, Informatics, and ADR. Compared with these firms, the likes of Pansophic or AGS are Johnny-come-latelys, but even they had been in business several years before Microsoft got started.

Let me close with a few remarks about what we can and cannot achieve this weekend.

First, we cannot have much immediate impact on the history of the software industry, simply because it is such a recent phenomenon. Let me explain. We now all accept that the creation of the railroads in the nineteenth century made the twentieth century what it became—an era of unparalleled economic prosperity. But it was not until the 1950s that this became widely understood. If one reads the histories of railroads in the 1920s (say), they are largely technical histories about system building or histories of dominant industrial barons such as Carnegie, Vanderbilt, and Pullman. In fact, very much the kind of history that is being written about the software industry today, including mine.

It was not until 1977 that the Harvard historian Alfred Chandler brought to light in *The Visible Hand* the true significance of the railroad in shaping the modern economy, and he set the agenda for much of the business history of the last 25 years. It seems that almost nothing was untouched by the railroad. My favorite example is the breakfast cereal. Kellogg's Cornflakes exists because the railroad made it possible to ship pre-prepared food long distances in short times at a very low cost. It killed the porridge "industry" and shaped our breakfast eating habits to the present day.

I think by the year 2050, that is the kind of change that software will have brought to society. It is commonplace to think of computers and software as creating in the twentieth century an information infrastructure, in the same way the railroads established a transport infrastructure in the nineteenth century. I feel certain this is right, but even so I think it will be a long time before we can grasp its full implications.

However, what we *can* do this weekend is to create primary sources so that future historians will have materials to work with. The records we create this weekend really are that important. They will inform not only my generation of historians but the generations to come. Historians will be using these materials a hundred years from now. I guarantee it!

General ADAPSO Reunion Photos

Peg Jerger and Oscar Schachter

Martin Goetz, John Maguire and Lee Keet

Phillip Frana and Jeffrey Yost

David Campbell and Larry Welke

David Allison and Tim Bergin

John Rollins and John Gracza

Lee Keet, Marty Goetz and Dick Thatcher

Larry Schoenberg, Joan Krammer, Mary Jane Saunders, Julie Johnston, Ron Palenski, Ed Bride, Peg Jerger, Barbara Brizdle and Doug Jerger

John Maguire and Bernie Goldstein

T. Lowell Dent, Larry Schoenberg and Larry Welke

Barbara Brizdle and Elizabeth Virgo

Sam Albert and Ron Palenski

Bob Weissman, Rick Crandall and David Campbell

Buck and Betty Blankenship, Larry Schoenberg and Barbara Brizdle

Tom Haigh, Joe Piscopo, Martin Campbell-Kelly and Gary Durbin

Sam Albert, Bob Weissman and Ron Palenski

T. Lowell Dent, Sen. Frank Lautenberg, Bernie Goldstein and Larry
Schoenberg

Burt Grad and Rich Carpenter

Larry Welke and Rick Crandall

Joe Blumberg and Dick Thatcher

Jack Yeaton

Ed Bride, Joe Tasker, Joan Krammer, Betty Blankenship and Luanne Johnson

Arthur Esch

Marty Goetz, Jack Yeaton, Bruce Coleman and Nancy and Lee Keet

Jerry Dreyer and Mary Jane Saunders

Rich Carpenter, Buck and Betty Blankenship, Kim Jones and Mark Leonardi

Joe Markoski, David Sherman, David Allison, Jerry Dreyer and Jay Goldberg

Tom Haigh, Paul Ceruzzi, David Grier, Martin Campbell-Kelly, Tim Bergin (back to camera), Jeffrey Yost. and Nathan Ensmenger

Jack Yeaton and Burt Grad

Sam Albert and Mike Maples

Larry Schoenberg, Bart Carlson and Barbara Brizdle

In Memoriam: Sam Albert, deceased February, 2003

Workshop Sessions
Banking Litigation and Issues of the 1960s

Moderators: Bernie Goldstein and Tim Bergin

Rapporteur: Julie Johnston

Participants: David Allison   Frank Lautenberg

Lowell Dent   Joe Markoski

Luanne Johnson   Mike Nugent

Goldstein: I think I'm the only person here who attended the first ADAPSO meeting. There were 12 people sitting around a table like this. A fellow by the name of Bill Evans, who was a professional manager of trade associations and handled a number of small trade associations, had the foresight to believe that here was perhaps a new industry that was small enough that it could not afford full-time permanent leadership. He brought us together with the idea that we would be one of the associations that shared his services.

Nugent: Everyone should identify themselves and the company they were with at the time.

Goldstein: I was with a company called Computech. I was one of the founders of Computech and, like most companies in this industry, it disappeared into another company which then disappeared into yet another company. That is the history of this industry.

Let's go around the room with introductions.

Dent: My name is T. Lowell Dent, Jacksonville, Florida. I founded Computer Power, Inc. When I first joined ADAPSO, my company's name was Computing and Statistical Service Corporation. I joined ADAPSO in 1963, I believe.

Markoski: Joe Markoski, Squire, Sanders & Dempsey. I first went to an ADAPSO meeting in 1976.

Nugent: I'm Mike Nugent and I was an ADAPSO staff attorney from 1978 to 1983. I did much of the banking/regulatory litigation work during that time period.

Allison: I'm David Allison. I'm a curator at the Smithsonian Institution.

Johnston: Julie Johnston. I was a staff member at ADAPSO.

Johnson: Luanne Johnson, former President of ADAPSO and now President of the Software History Center.

Bergin: I'm Tim Bergin and I am on the computer science faculty at American University. I am also the Editor-in-Chief of the *IEEE Annals of the History of Computing.*

Goldstein: One of the speakers this morning said that the first issue that coalesced the association was IBM and its position in the market place. That isn't quite true, by my memory, and, as we were reminded this morning, those of us who remember history will write it our way. [*Laughter*]

And that, indeed, is what we'll do. IBM was very much present on the scene. They were the first monopolist we had to deal with. Their sales force helped create a very early period of this industry by selling excess capacity in the form of hardware, the EAM equipment and, later, the computing equipment. IBM then encouraged tabulating room managers to take this excess capacity and start small companies to begin offering services in the marketplace. As a result, in each city of reasonable size there began developing two, three or four of what we then called service bureaus or tabulating organizations that began providing services—usually financially-oriented—in the market place. There was no sense that an industry was being born.

So there would be three, four, five companies in a city. The first recognition that this constituted an industry was that the telephone Yellow Pages were willing to set up a section under which we could advertise. And you know their standards for setting up a section were not very high. [*Laughter*]

So, under the guidance of Bill Evans, ADAPSO was formed. The first program that ADAPSO pursued was to educate us as to how to run a company. There were no schools providing courses, there were no books published on how to run a company in this industry, so we had to teach ourselves. We'd come to meetings, which would be in modest motels outside the city center because that's all we could afford, and we would have how-to sessions. Perhaps, Lowell, you remember some of those.

Dent: If it was not too far to go, I would be there.

Goldstein: However, new members were slow to join. Bill Evans was getting on in years and not really a marketing man, so ADAPSO decided to look for a young man who would travel the United States and pitch membership in ADAPSO. But we could not get anybody to take that job. If you think about what that job was: staying in cheap motels, driving from city to city, and getting people together at lunch or dinner to encourage them to think that a trade association made sense, it wasn't a very desirable job. But I was at a crossroads in my career and had left my job as New York District Director for Control Data. So, in part selfishly, and in part for ADAPSO, I volunteered to do that job. Frank Lautenberg, I think, was the President of ADAPSO at that time.

By the way, it's interesting to note that this industry has given birth to a Senator, Frank Lautenberg; to a candidate for President of the United States, Ross Perot; and to a Dean of the Wharton School of the University of Pennsylvania, Tom Gerrity, who had been an executive at CSC. There are some men who have gone on later in their careers and done us great honor in terms of where we've been as an industry.

So I spent six to eight months traveling the United States, selling ADAPSO memberships, and that's a worse job than being an insurance salesman. [*Laughter*] Because it really was an intangible.

But as I went around the country, I found that a lot of these independents—who were, by definition, undercapitalized generalists offering these services—were very concerned about bank competition. Because the banks, stimulated by aggressive IBM salesmen or Boards of Directors were offering competing services. First of all, the banks had substantial access to capital. There was no capital flowing into this industry other than the capital that these founding members could take out of their pockets or borrow from family and friends. Secondly, the banks thought that there was a little magic in data processing and, therefore, many of them advertised that they were going to offer a free service. The game plan, obviously, was to attract demand deposits to the banks.

Nugent: Free payroll was one of the big services.

Goldstein: Yes, free payroll as well as other free services, and these independents that I spoke to were concerned about this and frightened, to be sure. Because there was no way that we were going to be able to survive that type of competition. So I came back to the ADAPSO Board and reported this. The Board felt that this was an opportunity to speak up for this brand-new industry and to take on the banks.

This was a very brave thing for ADAPSO to do. We fought the banks in the years that followed, both in the courts and through legislation. And it was really a David and Goliath battle. There was no way we could win, except that the banks were very weak enemies in this particular game. First of all, they were the beneficiaries of chartering by federal or state institutions and they were sensitive to that. They were a regulated industry by definition. Secondly, they weren't coalesced, because the banking industry was divided between the big banks and the small banks which didn't have the budgets to offer free services. For ADAPSO, it was not only an issue to win but an issue to energize the industry as to what it could do in this type of battle.

Johnson: You mentioned becoming aware of this in your trip around the country. Was it also an issue for you and for Computech at that time?

Goldstein: No, Computech didn't exist. Computech had been acquired by Control Data. It was during a hiatus in my life that I did this trip.

The banks made another mistake. Not only had they taken on this young industry, but they also simultaneously took on the travel agents and insurance agents. Now if there is anything that defined small American businesses in the United States at that particular time, it was the travel agents. They were really the backbone of middle-American business. So, girded for this experience, I went down to testify before Congressman Wright Patman and the House Banking Committee. Many of you who went to business school will recognize the name Wright Patman. He was sort of a Lyndon Johnson type of character from Texas and somebody the banks would have loved to push around but were frightened of.

Nugent: He *hated* the banks.

Goldstein: He hated the banks. And he gave us a reception at the House Banking Committee which was so welcoming that it infuriated the representatives of the American Banking Association who were present. We just hit his hot button. He hated the banks to begin with. He was a populist in terms of his political point-of-view and he opened the door for us. We gave him the story that had been prepared by Milt Wessel, who was ADAPSO's General Counsel. We came out of the House Banking

Committee with a laundry list of particular things that banks were not allowed to engage in, i.e., that were determined to be unfair competition.

Well, that was the House, which was very friendly, and then we went to the Senate. It was less friendly, more sophisticated, call it what you will, and we came out with a different....

[Ed. Note: At this point, Senator Frank Lautenberg entered the room.]

Come on in, Frank, I'm talking about you. Frank mentioned in his speech last evening that they embarrassed him, when he first became a Senator, with some of his testimony before the Senate Banking Committee.

We didn't do as well before the Senate committee and then, as is common in these situations, different legislation came out of the Senate. So there was a conference committee to resolve the differences.

Nugent: Who was the senator? Do you remember?

Lautenberg: Proxmire was the Chairman of the Banking Committee but McClelland, who may have been Chairman of a subcommittee, was the one that heard my testimony.

Johnston: I know who you are but please say it for the tape.

Lautenberg: I'm Frank Lautenberg.

Nugent: You were at ADP at that time?

Lautenberg: Oh, sure.

Goldstein: You were President of ADAPSO at the time.

Lautenberg: Right. '67-'68. Basically we were saying, "Hey, don't let those big, bad boys get all the business and we are here to plead the case of the entrepreneur." I wasn't really looking at the technology. I was looking at the banks' duplicitousness and how they were reaching out to grab everything and anything they could. But the Committee heard us and that was it. It didn't mean anything. I'll tell you where we beat the banks. It was on the pavement. That's where we beat them.

Allison: Well, from an historian's standpoint, the issue is: How fierce was this fight and what do you think were the turning points? Did the banks really contest this?

Lautenberg: There were several contenders on the banking side that we were concerned about. Citibank was aggressive as was Chemical Bank. ADP ultimately bought Chemical's payroll business. Bank of America was out there fairly aggressively.

Nugent: Also, Seattle First Bank.

Goldstein: Remember that the banking industry is a "monkey see, monkey do" industry. If Chemical offered a free service, Chase had to offer a free service. So there was an enormous amount of imitation.

Nugent: The banks were trying to use *their* excess computer capacity, too.

Goldstein: The banks, having been conned by their IBM salesmen, bought excess capacity and thought that they could turn out payroll for free, that it didn't cost anything. Well, they quickly learned that this was an industry where you can't produce results for free.

With different results coming out of the House and Senate, the conference committee produced what they called Regulation Y. Regulation Y was far more permissive than what had emerged from the Wright Patman committee because it restricted what applications banks could do but it used the word "financially-related". Well, what's "financially-related"? Practically everything: payroll, accounts payable, billing.

But, by then, a funny thing was happening. The banks realized that this was not an easy business, this was a tough business. Larger firms like Automatic Data Processing were beginning to develop and were growing by acquisition. The banks couldn't produce results for free and they weren't very innovative. Banking, in my mind, was not an innovative industry and they began losing the battle. They were slowed up by the years of process before Patman and the Senate Committee and they began to leave the business. As Frank has just said, he bought Chemical's data processing operation.

Lautenberg: We bought Citibank's Quotron not too long ago after they struggled and dumped $100 million into it.

Goldstein: So, this fight with the banks which we took on, in part to generate membership for ADAPSO, and in part to protect those members we already had, really was won, There was a remark made by one of the speakers this morning that this is one of the few industries that is not a regulated industry. In my mind, one of the reasons that we're not a regulated industry is we had early success—success that we didn't have the budget or the experience to undertake—and we won. We really won this battle against the banks and the banks never emerged as important players in this business.

Nugent: Just parenthetically, at that time Citibank had gotten around the Bank Holding Company Act, which limited what banks could do in non-banking businesses, by creating a one bank holding company.

Lautenberg: What was the year?

Nugent: I think it was '68 or '69. Congress said, "Wait a minute, since the law only applies to multibank holding companies, and this is a one bank holding company, we're going to hold hearings and try to revise the law to get Citibank." It created an opportunity for everyone who saw banks getting into new businesses to come in and say that they should be limited to that which is closely related to banking.   So the insurance agents, the data processing crowd, the travel agents, started suing. I think ADAPSO v. Camp was at that time.

Markoski: That case went all the way to the Supreme Court and established the principle that a competitor had a right to sue the government to enforce something. It was a landmark case.

Goldstein: You know, this story could not be told without talking about Milt Wessel. Milton was a litigation attorney with the law firm Kaye, Scholer, Fierman, Hays & Handler in New York City when he was retained by ADAPSO.

Nugent: He prosecuted the Mafia.

Goldstein: He was a Special Attorney General at the time that the FBI broke up the Mafia meeting in Apalachin, New York, and arrested a lot of the leaders.

I introduced Milton to ADAPSO. I had gone to his firm because one of our employees stole some software and I was outraged and I ended up with Milton Wessel. He became very intellectually interested in this industry.

And he played a *very* important part not just in the bank situation but in developing a philosophy and a legal framework for the tie-in concept: the implicit tie-in sale when an organization that controls one line of commerce uses that to have an unfair advantage in another line of commerce. The philosophic concept of the tie-in sale, honed and developed by Milton, became an important base for the other activities that ADAPSO took on as time went on, for example, the IBM antitrust issue. We forget that IBM was a monopolist, but the best illustration I can think of for their monopoly is that when you upgraded your computer with IBM, you paid them an additional 25% and an engineer would come and take a part *out* of the machine. [*Laughter*] I'm not making that up. That's the way it worked. The machine ran faster with that part removed and therefore they were entitled to charge you more.

Bergin: They took off the governor.

Goldstein: That's exactly right. And who but a monopolist could do that? Data processing managers were afraid to order a Burroughs or Univac computer.

So what followed the banking issue was the IBM issue. And then we were twenty years earlier than the rest of the nation when we got concerned about auditing firms going into consulting. I remember that about twenty years ago ADAPSO produced a brochure that said it was a conflict of interest for accounting firms to provide data processing services to their audit clients. How right we were given the Enron situation today.

And following that was Microsoft where we showed more aggressiveness than the current Department of Justice in terms of pursuing what was a new monopolist on the scene. What did all of this add up to? We became a feisty organization and we attracted membership. We became the place where our voices were put together and we were able to accomplish things that we hadn't the muscle economically to accomplish. Because we had tasted victory in this bank fight and that gave us the heart and the strength to go on and deal with the subsequent threats to this industry.

And we got stronger and stronger. Public markets opened up to us, venture capital money opened up. That, too, became an excess. You know, every good idea goes to excess in the financial community and we're currently paying the price for that. But we became an organization that was known as one that could not be pushed around, that had a right to its own identity, that had a right to its standards. That's what the banking fight did for us, in my judgment. Would you agree with that, Luanne?

Johnson: Oh, absolutely. I think that it was not only the sense of success that gave ADAPSO members the confidence to go into these other arenas, but also the intellectual infrastructure that came out of the work that Milt did, which provided a framework to go forward in all of these other areas.

Goldstein: It's still being used today. I notice in the states' litigation against Microsoft, they are using the tie-in strength as part of the argument in terms of trying to reverse some of the compromise that emerged from the settlement of that case. Frank, what did ADAPSO mean to ADP?

Lautenberg: I've been thinking about this during these last 24 hours, about the nature of our industry as a community of entrepreneurs and proprietors. When I think of the ADP acquisition record, we were buying companies that were doing $100,000 a year in sales. What we wanted was to find someone who would work hard. It was like hiring a good employee with a credential because they didn't really offer much except that they were willing to work like jackasses to get the thing done.

There was a very pioneering character to the industry. I think there's a picture that has to be drawn about the entrepreneur, the proprietor, the small business owner: not a visionary, necessarily, but dedicated, committed, with a kind of mission. We were going to accomplish something. And the rest that flowed out of that was creativity of a fairly significant dimension. You know, we were working with new tools, and these tools enabled us to expand our thinking, enabled us to provide more service. I really think that it was a point in time in American history when we learned how you could use specialization to get work done. We were scared silly of the banks but they never had the capacity to provide the kind of service that we could provide. That was our store and we were watching the store. They were the money stores and they didn't know a hell of a lot about how to get things done. So, there's something even deeper that attaches to ADAPSO, in my view, than the evolution of technology as a part of life in America. There was also a cultural impact.

Johnson: One thing that you said in your speech last night really struck me. This was such an entrepreneurial industry. All over the country, in every metropolitan area of any size, there was a little company springing up to provide this service. The hardware manufacturers saw the business opportunity in the technology. But this was an industry that saw the business opportunity in the applications.

Lautenberg: Right.

Johnson: The services companies understood that there was a business there in how people were going to use this technology, as opposed to the business of providing the technology itself. You said that you didn't even really care about technology. ADP was focused on how to deliver this service and whatever technology was there to do that was the technology you were going to use. To me that was really an insight. It was the business opportunity in the *use* of the computers that grew out of this industry.

Lautenberg: Our first technological development was the use of a Volkswagen. [*Laughter*] We were able to deliver our products faster as a result.

Goldstein: Frank was much too modest in his remarks last evening. I remember at an ADAPSO meeting when he stated that ADP was announcing a million dollars of earnings as a break-through number that year. He gave us the early success of ADP and its growth into national and, eventually, international markets through acquisitions, and the fact that it became an early public player. His early success said that we could do it, too. He headed up a company that was really magnificent in terms of what it was consistently able to achieve in the marketplace, and that allowed us to be very brave—that we had a piece of that future as well.

Lautenberg: Thank you.

Goldstein: And so we weren't frightened to take on IBM or Microsoft. We decided during the Justice Department antitrust action against Microsoft that we were going to have open hearings and invite all members of the industry to come to these hearings and tell about their experiences with Microsoft's dominance in the marketplace as a monopolist. Those hearings were eventually cancelled because ADAPSO was beginning to be co-opted by large members with deep budgets, and Microsoft, after an enormous amount of work, got ADAPSO to cancel those hearings. ADAPSO hearings about Microsoft's monopoly were hitting the papers and creating enormous pressure on them and this was the way we thought we could aid the Justice Department action.

Lautenberg: There were always things out there to frighten us. I know how we felt when the PC came along: oh, my gosh, the companies would be able to do it themselves and wouldn't need ADP. Today, ADP has hundreds of thousands of small computers in customer installations. They're ours and the customers use them. Once again, we emerged as the user of the technology rather than being devoured by the technology. The industry has such strength in terms of the services that I think there's a lot more credit due to the industry than it has gotten. And, Luanne, this history is a wonderful project. This is exciting, and Bernie, I congratulate you and the others who have contributed to getting it going.

Johnson: Thank you.

Goldstein: It's interesting that the hardware companies have come around to recognizing that service may be more important than hardware.

Lautenberg: Look at IBM.

Goldstein: IBM, Hewlett-Packard, and Compaq all announced that service was going to be their new area of growth. Because, of course, as Frank said last night, the consumers didn't want to buy computes. It was rare that someone wanted to buy a compute. They wanted to buy results. This is an industry that entered the results marketplace and what we sold we priced on results. And, God forbid, if we didn't produce results, we didn't get paid.

Lautenberg: I think the experience with the banks is what got us started on the high road.

Nugent: Yes, that first round of battles was over excess capacity. And that resulted in the ruling that said banks can only do certain things with excess capacity, one of which was data processing if it was financially-related. But the banks didn't go away. They came back offering free timesharing services. I remember Rick Crandall of Comshare being involved and Tymshare being involved. So after the data centers group, it was the timesharing companies whose ox was getting gored.

Goldstein: They became part of ADAPSO as a result.

Nugent: Then the banks gave away software and the software companies started coming into ADAPSO because the banks were giving away free software. They were engaging in a whole range of computer services and so there were battles throughout the '70s and, really, into the early '80s.

Johnson: The banking industry seems to be somewhat of a slow learner.

Goldstein: The only successful thing they gave away was toasters. [*Laughter*]

Allison: One of the things that historians will want to know in trying to assess this battle is not just what the issues were but what did the team look like. You said a couple of times that you were small, you really weren't equipped to fight this battle and yet you fought it. Were there two guys, were there three people, what was the team that came together to take on this initiative?

Goldstein: The team was the Board of Directors of ADAPSO. That's where the running orders came from. And then some of us became the messengers and delivered the message, but it was the ADAPSO Board that endorsed this fight. Remember, the Board had a selfish game, too, because this was beginning to attract new members to ADAPSO. It became the organization to be part of. Members were attracted not just to the educational programs of ADAPSO, but ADAPSO as the industry spokesman.

Allison: There was a team of lawyers, too...a couple of lawyers?

Goldstein: There was one lawyer, Milt Wessel.

Lautenberg: You asked what kind of people, and you make me think about some of the people we had at the beginning: some roughnecks and some seriously intellectual people.

Nugent: It was a mix.

Lautenberg: And the business mission was an interesting thing. There were very few people with technical backgrounds in the earliest days. They could have been tradesmen or business people in a retail business. Or anything. They were entrepreneurs, and they found a way to put their talent to work. They grabbed the tools of the trade. It was an interesting evolution. In ADP's case, the three of us—Henry and Joseph Taub and myself—came from poor, uneducated working class families. Their father and my father both worked in the same silk mills. Henry Taub was an accountant, a very bright guy. He was 19 when he graduated, having worked full-time besides going to school. And he was 21 when he really put the muscle into ADP, then named Automatic Payrolls. But we weren't visionaries. We weren't people who looked out and said, "Some day ADP will be all over the world." But when Art Weinbach, who is now the Chairman and CEO, gives a speech to the employees, it's immediately translated into ten languages. That really tells you something about what happened. The company went from the streets of Paterson, New Jersey, in what was a virtual ghetto, to that kind of business opportunity and the impact it had on clients. We did so much for so many people and got paid for it. But it was an entrepreneurial business enterprise. And once it became based on computer technology, then, boy, the business just took off.

Goldstein: When David Allison interviewed me yesterday for my oral history he said, "I notice you were never a technologist." And I said, "Thank God." [*Laughter*]

Because if I were a technologist, I would be rapidly obsoleted in an industry in which technology was moving at such a rapid speed. So the survivors and leaders of this industry were not technologists at all. I doubt even Bill Gates is a technologist today. These were entrepreneurs. What is an entrepreneur? Someone who is a little crazy, who doesn't want to work for somebody else, and is willing to take personal and financial risk to start a business.

It was very typical for the head of the data processing department—what was then called the tabulating department—to tell the company he was working for that he could save the company money by setting up the department as a service bureau and selling the services to other companies. It was those men who became the early players in the industry. They were eventually followed by the business school graduates who were attracted to the business, but men of that type were the founders of this industry.

Lautenberg: It was also a particular time in our country. Our start was literally after World War II. Business was expanding and there were excellent opportunities there. But when you think of mistakes you made along the along the way—we were going to do bowling scores. [*Laughter*]

I started with ADP in 1952. We charged 25 cents per pay check. And we did everything. At one point, we even used to sit there and check their timecard calculations. And then we got bolder. We decided to charge for changes, and charge for the input not being ready on time. We found out that, as people began to understand how important we were to them, they were amenable. I won't say that price was no object but that wasn't the principal concern because the value-added was so good.

I remember a brokerage firm named Reynolds and Company, that was an offshoot of Reynolds Tobacco. The senior partner, the managing partner, of Reynolds and Company used to sit down on weekends and do the bloody payroll for 200 people because he didn't want anybody to know what other people were making. So when we came along, it was a godsend. And you found so many cases where this essentially clerical function had become a major event every week in the company because the one thing you couldn't stall was the payroll. So we just kept adding things and technology helped us enormously along the way. Now the customer does the input right from his office and when we print paychecks, we start up with blank paper. The printing of the checks are done at very high speeds including the company's logo and the color of the check and the numbering and the magnetics and everything else that goes on them.

I'm sorry that I have to leave. I have to catch a ride back to New Jersey and the airplane will not wait. But it's been great. I congratulate you, Luanne, and all of the people who have shown such interest. And, Bernie, you're a stalwart. I really respect you. So, I'd like to be of help if I can and see if I can whip up some interest at ADP.

Johnson: We'd love to see ADP do a corporate history.

Lautenberg: So would I, but we've always been too busy running the business.

Nugent: What other company names do you remember from those early days?

Goldstein: The problem with company names is that companies merged. It was a sign of success, not failure, to sell your business to another company. So these widely dispersed small-scale businesses in multiple cities that were offering local services became part of a larger organization. What did winning the bank battle do for us? It created the spirit of feistiness, it provided borders to this industry that were eventually respected by others. It allowed us resist pleas for government intervention and regulation, and we prospered. Horatio Alger stories abound in this industry and we've been very lucky.

Johnson: I went back and read through all the minutes of the ADAPSO Board meetings starting with the organizational meetings in 1960 through about 1985. I was looking for the first things that ADAPSO did. And one of the first things that it did was come up with a standard chart of accounts for the industry. Right there, you know you are talking about small companies in an emerging industry where they need help figuring out how to account properly for their income and expenses. At the same time, they're saying, "We're going to take on the banks." I think it's just fascinating that these small companies decided to take on a venerable, well-funded industry. I think that established the ADAPSO culture from then on. That commitment to serving the small companies, helping the entrepreneurs be better managers, and at the same time being willing to take on these really tough fights and challenges.

Nugent: I remember Milt telling the story about Computer Power but I never got a chance to meet you until today, Lowell.

Dent: In 1965, I called Bill Evans because a bank was going to put me out of business.

Goldstein: You were with Computer Power.

Dent: Right. Computing and Statistical Services at the time, later called Computer Power, in Jacksonville, FL. The Atlantic National Bank was literally trying to put me out of business.

When I started thinking about starting a computer service bureau, one of the first applications I planned to sell was medical billing. Doctors in our area were doing their own billing and accounting in-house. To service that market we developed a pretty good multiclient patient accounting/billing system.

I had discussed my plans for a computer service bureau with a number of people, including Mel Kahler, DP manager of Atlantic National Bank of Jacksonville, now part of First Union. Mel decided that he would like to have a part in any company that I started.

In an attempt to thwart my attempts to start a company, a friend with whom I had discussed my plans told the Chairman of the Board of the Atlantic National Bank that Mel planned to join me in a computer venture. The Chairman summoned Mel to his office and told Mel that he had to decide right then whether he was going to stay with the bank or join my venture.

Mel chose to join me, whereupon he was fired on the spot. My medical billing plans were mentioned during this meeting.

Mel joined my yet-to-be-incorporated company the next day and became my valuable and trusted partner from that day forward.

I was able to sell the Riverside Clinic, a medical partnership with about a dozen doctors, on using our service pretty quickly. In our excitement to land one of the most prestigious medical groups in the area, we cut prices to the bone and kept adding additional functionality with little or no remuneration. But we were looking forward to also converting their small private hospital after they saw what a good job we could do for them.

We successfully converted the group from a manual NCR bookkeeping machine system. In the process, we saved them money while improving cash flow, and we reported patient revenue by procedure and doctor, which was not possible in a timely manner on the old system.

After less than one year, the Atlantic National Bank took the account away from me with free but vastly inferior technology. It cost the clinic nothing to get their billing done by the bank. I had done a good job, the bank did a lousy job. In a few months, the medical group pulled their billing back in-house, but, by then, a new office manager was on board who preferred to continue with his in-house operation and never again go outside for accounting services after the experience with the bank.

This left us with nothing but unrecoverable development costs due to the early termination of our services because of the bank's "free" offering.

The bank also lost, rather than gained, deposits because some doctors moved to other banks. I lost a valuable client. Our client lost us as a trustworthy provider. Everybody lost.

Nugent: How did you know ADAPSO was around?

Dent: We got a questionnaire from ADAPSO in 1965. Do you remember that?

Goldstein: I do. We were collecting data to present to Congressman Patman.

Nugent: How many members were there at the time?

Goldstein: I don't really know.

Johnson: That information is available. Somebody would have to do a little research, but you'll recall that there was a time when every member that joined ADAPSO was approved by the Board. Therefore, the Board minutes recorded every new member that was approved to join at each meeting and also noted which members dropped out. By going through the minutes and seeing who came in and who dropped out, you could construct a list of who the members were at any point in time during the early years.

Markoski: How do you explain the fact that everyone was so active? Because, looking at ADAPSO from the outside, it seems as it got bigger, not all the members were involved the way they all were during this early period.

Goldstein: Well, the industry began segmenting into specialties and then there were the influences of various geographies. There were things that began to fracture the sense of unity that developed from the bank battle at the beginning of ADAPSO. You can see from Harris Miller's presentation this morning that what has survived is a different sort of association, but a valuable one with a very substantial budget of $6,000,000 doing things that we couldn't have dreamed of doing or that were not even necessary to do at that point in time. We could probably find similar stories in other industries. The reason this is of interest to us is because this was ours and it was new. We invented an industry.

Johnson: One of the things that I'm curious about is what you think was the beginning of the computer services industry. We can pinpoint a time when the software sector of the industry began. That began with CUC in 1955. That was the first software company.

Goldstein: Computer Usage Corporation.

Johnson: Right. But the services side is different. ADP came out of a services business that wasn't originally computer-based. It's a little harder to figure out the point at which the computer services industry begins. Obviously, there were enough companies in 1960 that it made sense to begin talking about creating an association. Bernie, what's your sense of how many companies were out there in the 1950s?

Goldstein: In any city of at least 200,000 population, you would find a firm. Some of them, as Frank said, used billing machines. They didn't use electro-mechanical machines at all. But they were there—a few of them in each city.

The reason the software industry came later is because IBM established an industry standard that software had no value. They gave it away. It becomes laughable in today's economics that they could have taken that position. But how can you have an industry when the principal firm in the industry is giving it away?

Allison: It seems like billing and payroll were the lead applications rather than inventory or something else like that. Is that a pretty clear pattern?

Goldstein: Well, they were repetitive. You could sell the same service to more than one client. Payroll was initially a very standard opening application.

Johnson: Payroll is one that you could generalize because there were regulatory influences as to how you did your payroll, unlike other types of applications like inventory.

Goldstein: And remember, many business organizations liked to contract out payroll because it kept sensitive information private.

Dent: I think most jobs had some kind of cycle, such as weekly or monthly. You would pick up the source documents, get the input prepared, take a couple of days to turn it around, and deliver it back to them. You didn't have electronic communications back then. I would use our Volkswagen Bus to pick up the source documents and deliver the reports. I would call ahead to the client to tell them that I was on the way and ask them to please have the check ready. I would hand over the reports and pick up the check, I hoped. I would then return via the bank with the check and a previously prepared deposit slip, often just in time to cover the payroll checks handed out that very morning.

Goldstein: Well, I think that maybe we have covered our topic. Is everyone satisfied that we have covered it? We haven't said everything but we've covered a lot.

Bergin: I have one question that might cause us to rethink the issue. Most of what I heard sounded like it was coming from the high moral ground that these small companies, because they were small, had a right to this business and the banks with their money and their connections didn't. But, really, you're talking about a political battle and you're the victors and the victors write the history.

What could banks have done to compete fairly? Why were they excluded?

Allison: Why wasn't it fair competition?

Goldstein: Because they were an industry that didn't allow competition. There were just so many banks that could be chartered.

Nugent: That's the key—the exclusive franchise given by the government. If you look at all the fair competition issues ADAPSO took on, it was banks, CPA's, telephone carriers, and others who had a government-conferred right to do certain things who were using that right to pay for business in unrelated fields. Banks were not just doing payroll, they were saying, "Give us your deposits and we'll give you the payroll for free." So they were using that deposit-gathering power to restrain competition in the payroll processing business.

Markoski: That principle has gone through every battle that ADAPSO has been involved with. Anybody can enter the industry, we don't care who you compete with, but if you've got a government franchise or something that I can't get, you can't use that to compete against me.

Allison: Doesn't that make the accounting situation a little different then?

Nugent: No, because they've got a franchise.

Allison: I see what you're saying. In that case, it's from the audit even though that's regulated in a different way.

Johnson: There's another example, too, where ADAPSO protested unfair competition from non-profit organizations who were offering, with their excess capacity, computer services. The non-profit organizations had a special tax-exempt situation that allowed them to do this at lesser cost. It wasn't fair that they used that tax-exempt franchise to compete against people who didn't have that opportunity.

Goldstein: So the image here is a young growing business that is putting its fingers in the dike as it becomes stronger and richer and able to survive.

Bergin: Let's see if I can summarize this. Legally, you had the law on your side, but the effort was to raise the dialogue up to where everybody saw that, and then the banks or others would have to back off—as opposed to getting new legal rights through ADAPSO's lobbying.

Nugent: It was illegal to explicitly tie something in but Milt's real contribution was to extend it to the implicit tie-in.

Bergin: So there was, in a sense, new law made because of the efforts of ADAPSO. It wasn't merely a matter of raising a dialogue.

Nugent: All of the rules for how AT&T, the banks, and IBM, engage in unrelated businesses were really influenced by ADAPSO. For example, in the telephone company case, AT&T couldn't use rate payer funding to fund R&D in computer services. That was the ADAPSO contribution. The same with the banks. They couldn't use bank personnel funded by the depositor to compete in other services. With the CPAs, there had to be a separation between one business and the other. ADAPSO really contributed to those rules of separation. How do you separate a competitive business from a non-competitive business? How does the money flow back and forth? How does promotion occur? That's where ADAPSO really contributed using existing law as the basis for the argument.

Bergin: I don't know whether those of you who are not academics know this, but the big topic in business schools in the early to mid-80s was *outsourcing* and the argument that organizations shouldn't waste their intellectual and other resources doing things that other people can do better because they do it full time. And so companies began outsourcing their personnel departments, payroll processing, and other functions not related to their core business.

It's a nice point to end on to realize that this industry began practices that had a major impact on the way that business operates today!

Goldstein: Well, it probably did start with us. Thank you, everybody.

ADAPSO Conferences Workshop

Moderators: Larry Welke and Nathan Ensmenger

Rapporteur: Linda Schnell

Participants:

Sam Albert	Jerry Dreyer
Betty Blankenship	Arthur Esch
Buck Blankenship	Kim Jones
Joe Blumberg	Mike Maples
Ed Bride	John Rollins
Barbara Brizdle	Dave Sturtevant
Bart Carlson	Jim Treleaven
Rich Carpenter	Bob Weissman
Bruce Coleman	Jack Yeaton

Welke: OK, we're running late so we only have whatever time is left. We're going to run it by the numbers. You'll notice that I'm the leader and you aren't. [*Laughter*] And Nathan is going to be the referee and Linda's going to keep score. OK?

We'll run this the way we used to run the planning committees for the conferences. And I would encourage everybody to tell it the way it really was, rather than how you would like people to think it was. Let's start by going around the room so that we get a record of everybody's name and company affiliation during the time period that we're talking about.

Betty Blankenship: I'm Betty Blankenship and I'm affiliated with Buck. [*Laughter*]

Blankenship: I'm Buck Blankenship and, in addition to being affiliated with Betty, back in those days I was with a company called Data Processing of the South from Charlotte, NC.

Welke: I'm Larry Welke. At that particular time, I was with International Computer Programs and I was involved with the conferences because of a fluke more than anything else. I had participated in bringing the software group into ADAPSO and, as a consequence, I was involved in planning the program content for the software group. And, then, I just sort of kept my hand in it because I've always looked upon the conferences as being a power point within the organization. Because whoever ran the program decided who was going to be in front of the audience and it was a real pivotal position in many, many ways. And I enjoyed exercising that pivot point.

Coleman: You enjoyed that power. Admit it. [*Laughter*]

Esch: Arthur Esch. When I joined ADAPSO in the '70s, I was with a company called Decision Strategy. We were interested in helping other software companies go from having batch products to having online products with CICS and IMS and things that I don't understand any more. And then in the '80s, I was with a company called Nabu Networks that was delivering software over broadband to the first of the PC marketplaces.

Coleman: Bruce Coleman. I was with Boole & Babbage in the '70s and with Informatics in the '80s. And I first joined ADAPSO because I didn't have a clue what I was doing and I hoped somebody else would. [*Laughter*]

Unidentified voice: Sorry to disappoint you. [*Laughter*]

Bride: Ed Bride. *Computerworld* in the early '70s and *Software News* and then *Software Magazine* in the '80s. I was a paid professional observer as opposed to a creator of the content for the conferences. But I thought of them as going to school so I went to a lot of planning meetings for the Software Industry Section which is what we were calling it at the time.

Carpenter: Rich Carpenter. I got active in ADAPSO in '83 when I formed Index Technology. Like Bruce, it was my first time in the software products business and I didn't really have much of a clue as to what I was doing. I wanted to get to know people who did, and ADAPSO was the place to go. The conferences were a key part of that for me, just linking up with people from our industry from all over the country. It was very beneficial.

Welke: Rather than continue, we'll go back and pick up the strays, the late arrivals, who nonetheless are relatively significant. Or were at one point. Could you please state your name and your affiliation? [*Laughter*]

Weissman: I used to be Bob Weissman. [*Laughter*] And my company was National CSS, one of the major timesharing players in the '60s and '70s.

Dreyer: I'm Jerry Dreyer. I joined ADAPSO as assistant to incoming president Frank Lautenberg in December of 1966. I became its executive vice president in July of 1967, the executive director two years later, and spent 19 years helping to run the organization.

Rollins: I'm John Rollins, founder of AZTECH Corporation in 1968. I sold the business in 2000 and I was CEO from 1970 until 2000. I got involved with ADAPSO, primarily the management conferences, because I needed to figure out what was going on in this industry, like Bruce and others here. It was a very dynamic industry, with a lot of tumult, lots of changes, things moving fast. I was trying to find the right business plan. Revenue models were of interest to me and I could meet people at these conferences that knew a lot more than I did about how to make money in software.

Welke: And often times it wasn't that you met people who knew more. You just *thought* they knew more. [*Laughter*]

Rollins: That's the important thing. I thought they knew more.

Ensmenger: My name is Nathan Ensmenger. I'm the token historian in the group. I teach at the University of Pennsylvania. I'm currently working on a book on software development and software workers in the 1950s, '60s, and early '70s. So this is of great interest to me.

Blumberg: Joe Blumberg. I originally got affiliated with ADAPSO through my work at Comshare in 1978. I never helped plan any of the conferences, but I was often a participant providing research information about what was going on in the industry. And in 1983, I formed a firm to do research on the industry and then acquired another research firm called Specifics in '91. I guess I have participated in every ADAPSO conference since 1978. For what that's worth, I can address it as a participant.

Yeaton: Jack Yeaton. I formed Merit Systems, a professional services firm, in '76. After we managed to get through the first couple of years and looked like we might live awhile, I looked for ways to learn more about the industry. We were starting to grow and move outside of our local office and that was kind of scary. So I started coming to the conferences in the late '70s or early '80s. About the third year or so that I attended, I met with a couple of the people that were on the board of the Professional Services Section with some suggestions about the conference program, and managed immediately to get elected to chair the next two planning committee meetings. And also immediately became a member of the section board.

Unidentified voice: What year was that, Jack?

79

Yeaton: That would have been in the early '80s, '83 or '84. What I discovered was that the more you got involved, the more you learned, and the more you realized what there was to learn. It was interesting because the first two or three times, just packing up and going to a conference and attending some sessions and packing up and going home, you wondered if it was a good idea. But when you started to get involved, it became a very important, useful part of trying to grow a business.

Treleaven: Jim Treleaven. I was with Univac in the late '60s and early '70s, then with the Service Bureau Corporation, which was part of IBM when I joined them, and part of Control Data when I left. And then with Interactive Data Corporation, which was a sister company of National CSS for quite awhile, into the '80s. I'm currently on the board of ITAA and of the Software Division. My attendance at the conferences has spanned the same period as Joe, but my attendance has not been as regular.

Welke: And we'll pick up one more stray.

Albert: My name is Sam Albert. I started in IBM in 1959 and—I don't use the R word—graduated in 1989. For 18 of the 30 years, I was responsible at IBM for all consultants in the world, all the CPAs in the world, as an industry. In 1981, they told me that nobody else wanted the software and services industry, so I was put in charge of it. So I took that on. I remember one of the other industry directors, one of the ones responsible for the manufacturing industry, saying that he had a real industry but I had the cats and dogs. It turns out that he was wrong in the final analysis.

I introduced Bob Berland from IBM to this organization and it was the start of a positive outlook on what IBM could bring to the table. Before that, although there were very good people representing IBM at ADAPSO, there was a lot of animosity and antipathy between IBM and ADAPSO members. In 1981, we ran an application software developers' conference at IBM attended by many people who were in charge of software firms and, from then on, Bob Berland and I tried to make IBM be seen as a friend rather than a foe of the software developers. I think it was a turning point and Bob became a very valued and respected member of ADAPSO.

Carlson: My name is Bart Carlson. I can't remember the exact year I first joined, but it was around 1980, representing the company I had at that time, National Systems Laboratories. I sold that in '84, and started another one called Group 1 Software. I was there until '86 and then I started Napersoft. I got involved with the program committee and did a lot as chairman of the

80

Software Program Committee for a couple of years in the late '80s and early' 90s. I was also president of the Software Division for a couple of years in the mid- to late '90s. And now I'm still working on new companies and chairman of all of them.

Welke: For other people they make rules like "three times and you're out". [*Laughter*]

Sturtevant: My name is Dave Sturtevant. I had the privilege of being vice president of public communications for ADAPSO from 1979 to 1987. My primary responsibilities were public relations, financial analyst relations, and bringing new members into the organization.

Maples: My name is Mike Maples. I was introduced to ADAPSO by Bob Berland. I worked for IBM and my area of interest at the time was intellectual property and protection of intellectual property assets. I attended some conferences, then changed jobs and went to Microsoft and was with Microsoft for eight years. I thought that ADAPSO was getting too broadly focused and worked with the software group for a number of years trying to get more of a software focus. Now I raise exotic deer and antelope. [*Laughter*]

Jones: My name is Kim Jones. I wish I had known about ADAPSO in the '70s when I founded my first software and services company called Genesys. I joined ADAPSO in the early '80s with the second company I founded called Forecross Corporation, where I still reside professionally. I, too, found that participating actively in the programs of ADAPSO had a huge payback to me and my company, and being active was a way to take advantage of the opportunities that were provided both within the conference sessions and also outside of the conferences.

I was very active with Mike, Bob Berland and others in the Software Division in the initial stages of dealing with what we called "openness" of software code. And it's been interesting personally and professionally to see that the people in the industry are really just people like me, however big their companies are in relation to my small one. In the end, we can talk shop and learn from each other in ways that one might not otherwise think about. I found the conferences to be hugely beneficial and attended them regularly for 10 or 12 years.

Welke: Of the people in this group, I have probably attended more ADAPSO meetings than anybody else. My first one was the fall of 1967, down in Houston. Twenty-three people—and that was the total ADAPSO membership at the time—got together. I don't know that you could call it a conference as much as it was just a bunch of guys who got together.

We had one speaker, Ross Perot. This was shortly after he started his company, EDS, and I will always remember that when he got up to speak, he stood on an orange crate in order to peer over the podium. And he was, well, an interesting speaker.

I don't know how we got to the point of planning a program where we had group meetings with a leader or a presenter. I don't know when we formalized the procedure. Jerry, maybe you can fill us in on this. I do know that as we brought the software group into the association, I got involved in planning a program for them. But I don't know what the rest of ADAPSO—the computer service sections—were doing.

Dreyer: We started having committees to plan the programs in 1967. But the problem was that we were trying to define an industry. We had all these less-than-synergistic companies involved and everybody had issues that they wanted to address. So we came up with the idea of having different sections for different types of businesses. Each section would get representation on a committee to formulate the program for the conferences. And seminars. Each group would select a representative to participate in developing the program so that everybody had a piece of the action at a conference.

Weissman: I don't know if others remember it, but my recollection is that, in the early '70s, the sections had become cohesive enough that there were growing pressures between the sections in terms of the allocation of resources. I particularly remember an ADAPSO meeting in Mexico City where the software group was seriously considering breaking away from ADAPSO because it was looking for, I think, $100,000 in funding for a PR media program and...

Coleman: Yeah.

Weissman: And since the demographics of the membership were highly skewed, with the biggest dues being paid by the remote processing services companies, it created some real tensions. The remote processing companies were asking why the hell they should pay, in effect, $98,000 of the $100,000 so these little software companies could go off and do their PR thing. Part of the process of governance of ADAPSO in the '70s was transcending those tensions and creating coalitions that allowed us to operate as an association.

Welke: Yeah, I can remember that conference planning started with just a group of people who were interested in working on conferences, and whoever showed up contributed to the meeting and decided what was going to be put on the program. And then it became a political issue of: How many members of ADAPSO are software companies as opposed to timesharing companies as opposed to processing services? Well, if we have more members, then we need three people at the table and you only get one.

Unidentified voices: Oh, yeah. Yeah.

Welke: And, in retrospect, we spent too much time on that kind of political infighting. But you're right, Bob, it was a very serious issue at the time.

Carlson: It didn't go away. That actually carried into the '90s. In the '90s, the governance issue of participation and how many slots you got continued to be a major concern.

Yeaton: When I was on the board of the Professional Services Section, we had some very large services companies, but a survey we did showed that we had a very large number of members where the average size was about $3 - 4 million. This was back in the '80s. When you started to allocate resources, you had two or three companies paying 60-70% of the dues, but the real need in that section was to support the very small companies. And they had a whole set of issues that were different from the large professional services companies. So it was difficult, first, to get a program together and, secondly, to allocate resources. Because the guys who had all the needs and were the largest number of companies by far, didn't have the time or the resources to do a lot for the conferences.

Albert: That kind of competition continues today. I'm on the board of the Information Technology Services Division and that discussion occupies a good deal of time. They have accomplished a lot with recruiting smaller companies but it continues to fuel the kind of tension we're talking about.

Weissman: I think that one of the things that helped in the process was that as the association developed, it began to focus more on public policy issues. And when that happened, it became important to get raw numbers of members, to be able to go to the Hill and say we represent 1,000 companies instead of 23 companies. To say that there are this number of companies in your district or in your state, Mr. Representative, and you ought to pay attention to this issue. And so the small professional services, batch services, and software companies brought to the table, through their membership, the mere fact that they allowed the association to have a more important voice in public policy issues.

Yeaton: Larry, what was the largest number of member companies in ADAPSO?

Unidentified voices: 900. 700 or 800.

Dreyer: We were shooting at 1,000.

Sturtevant: The high water mark, I think, was 1987. We got just over 1,000 companies and very shortly thereafter, it started to slide.

Welke: For a number of different reasons, none of which are associated with conferences. [*Laughter*]

Dreyer: Some of the reduction in members occurred as a result of industry consolidation through mergers and acquisitions, many of which started at the conferences.

Maples: To go back to IBM, at one time there were a lot of executives of smaller companies trying to create a space in the IBM world who were brought together by an anti-IBM feeling. I sense that the meetings have changed so that, instead of having a few common enemies such as IBM, there's now more emphasis on policy, on influencing government for the good of the industry. I wonder how that has affected who attends the conferences and what goes on at the conferences.

Welke: I think you've got a good point, Mike. Several of you have commented on the fact that you went to the conferences because of the openness, and because of the fact that everybody was able to learn from each other. There was a culture of sharing that was established within ADAPSO by dint of, I think, the fact that the initial members were all small computer services companies and they were not competitive. There was a guy from San Diego and another guy from New York and somebody from Chicago and everybody had their local market. So the feeling was: I don't mind telling you what I'm doing because you're not my competitor because you're in a different city. But then as the companies grew and there was consolidation, the big company/small company differences came into play. The small companies still wanted to learn and they wanted to learn from the large companies. Well, the large companies were sometimes a little bit reluctant to share all of their knowledge with these little guys.

Unidentified voice: But I think *they* can learn from each other, too.

Carlson: We had the formal conference sessions and we had the board meetings. But the thing that facilitated that consolidation were the deals made in the hallways and coffee shops. People were putting deals together at ADAPSO meetings because they knew each other and it was a common place to meet, especially the late '70s and early '80s. I saw lots and lots of that happening.

In fact, a lot of the growth of the industry, I believe, came from that consolidation in all sectors, not just software. Look at ADP's growth. It happened where people had an IT services group in one section of the country and wanted to expand to Chicago or the West Coast. And it happened in software, also.

Rollins: Taking off from what Bart was just saying, my recollection of conferences is that they were a 48-hour period of time with so much packed into it. You'd come with a list of people you wanted to talk to and the conference sessions you wanted to attend. Then you'd buy tapes for the sessions that you hadn't had time to attend in person because you were doing a deal in the hallway. Or there were two sessions you wanted to attend in the same time slot and you could only go to one, so you bought the tapes for the other one.

Coleman: Until about five years ago, I still had the tapes of twenty or thirty sessions that I liked. You couldn't go to all of them because you had to attend board or committee meetings, so you'd buy the tapes and play them in your car when you were commuting. They were wonderful.

Rollins: I still have a few of the tapes.

Blankenship: John and others have spoken about the relationships that started out in the bar, at the cocktail party, at dinners and so forth. That kind of formalized itself into a series of roundtables. The first ones were called Presidents' Roundtables. There were, I don't know, maybe half a dozen of these subsets of ADAPSO that met apart from the ADAPSO meetings. I know some of the Presidents' Roundtable, for some reason, I'm not sure why, chose to meet in the most exotic places you can imagine.

85

Welke: Well, that was your experience. The one that I joined was a little bit different.

Dreyer: One of the things I worked with closely was the nominating committee. And seeing the people who participated in the conferences, I was able to go back to the committee and say that we've got some great, articulate, knowledgeable guys that should be considered for the section boards or the ADAPSO Board. The conferences were an opportunity to evaluate the people in the membership.

Rollins: Getting back to the planning sessions for the conferences. You described some of the early ones in the '60s as being small and informal. My recollection of the first one I was asked to chair—I don't remember the year, but I know the conference was held at the Shoreham Hotel in Washington DC sometime in the late '70s—was that things were really down to a system by then. I was sort of a young kid brought in to chair this planning committee, and Jerry taught me all the things I needed to know to run the meeting, to line up the sessions, and to do this and do that. ADAPSO had a good staff. We met in Jerry's office with half a dozen people, I think, for a planning meeting to organize that management conference. So there was actually very good discipline by the late '70s.

Sturtevant: The Washington conference at the Shoreham you are referring to was in September of '78.

Rollins: Thank you.

Weissman: I'd like to expand that discussion of association meetings to include the World Congresses, which evidently have continued over the years. I heard this morning that they'd had the 13th recently. The first one was held in 1976 in Barcelona. It was the first effort, and it was led by ADAPSO, to create a forum where participants in the computer services/software industry globally could get together and meet each other. And that was successful enough that we decided that we would run them every four years. Obviously, that cycle is shortened. The second one was held here in the United States at the St. Francis Hotel in San Francisco in 1980. We had about 1100 people at that conference from a number of countries. It was, in part, so that the learning experience could be more generalized, but it was also to make a statement that this was a real industry and a global industry and one of increasing power and importance.

Welke: It was also, Bob, a case of an increasing number of European firms who were coming into the United States market.

Sturtevant: The Barcelona conference was in 1978.

Weissman: There's a document floating around that says the Barcelona conference in 1978, but Jerry and I were there and we thought it was 1976.

Dreyer: Maybe we got there too early. [*Laughter*]

Weissman: Jerry and I remembered it as being '76 because in '78 we were involved in establishing the location and planning the program for the 1980 World Congress. We worked for more than two years putting together the '80 Congress. What is the document? Oh, it's the annual report and it says '78. Jerry?

Dreyer: I guess the first thing to go is your mind. [*Laughter*]

Weissman: I guess we've just proven the value of primary documents. [*Laughter*]

Maples: I have a question for the people who are active in ITAA now. I got the impression from Harris Miller's talk today that the organization has changed to focusing primarily on lobbying and less on conferences. And I suspect there are fewer members who run small companies and get together to network now than there were in the past. What is the character of the meetings they have now and how has that evolved?

Blumberg: When ADAPSO was really at its peak, attendance at the conferences was excellent. There was really a broad base of members attending. But attendance started to drop precipitously in the '90s. Last year, when they held a conference down in Florida, I counted 37 people in the room. At that point, ITAA made the decision to stay away from doing conferences. There were just too many conflicting organizations doing similar kinds of things. Now they're trying to focus on very targeted subject areas. I see where they're going to do a conference for IT services executives in June.

Albert: The IT Services Division Board, which I sit on, decided we needed a specialized conference since ITAA is no longer having general conferences. But there's been a change in the economics of conferences.

The events business has gone almost out of existence because of limited travel since 9/11.

Welke: Is the decline in conference attendance a consequence of the membership, the size or type of companies that are members now, or is it a function of the marketplace? Or is it a function of the fact that the industry has become more subject to political influence and that has changed the emphasis at ITAA?

Albert: I think there is a lot more competition for attendance at conferences. I'm not talking just about conferences of the type ITAA used to have, but about events in general. I'm a member of the New York New Media Association and they can't get people to come to the meetings because they can't get people to travel.

Carlson: I agree with what you're saying. I think what happened is the industry grew up and it went from hundreds of companies to tens of thousands of companies which changed the dynamic from the '60s to today. We also had periods when ADAPSO was not filling the need for that great expansion and so there were pockets where local associations began to fill the need of smaller startups and early stage companies for camaraderie and the opportunity to learn from each other. An example is Boston where the Mass Software Council has been around for a long time. There are now at least 26 local associations that I know of throughout the country in major urban areas, Chicago, Indianapolis, West Coast, all over the country.

In Chicago, we have the Chicago Software Association. I helped form that over ten years ago, and it has 600 or 700 member companies, just in the Chicago area. It serves some of the training, education, networking need that ADAPSO did when it was the only game in town in the '60s, '70s and early '80s. So now you have a way for people to go spend the day locally as opposed to flying to San Francisco or wherever.

Welke: And without spending two and a half thousand dollars in the process.

Albert: It's certainly true in New York. They have the New York Software Industry Association and they had an event where I'm sure the number of attendees approached 1,000. The speakers were Mayor Bloomberg and Senator Hillary Clinton.

Welke: Wow, what a combination. If you can turn out that kind of an audience with those speakers, imagine the potential. [*Laughter*]

Carlson: We have the same kind of thing in Chicago. Mayor Daley is very involved. He comes to the meetings. Many of the things he is trying to do are related to our industry such as: "How do we get gigabyte service to every single school and wire every house on the street?" And things of that nature.

Welke: Ed, you had a comment.

Bride: The idea of the local associations is one that ADAPSO embraced and helped spawn, so it became sort of logical when Harris Miller came in with his background in public policy to focus on that as what the ITAA constituency needed next. For networking, to talk about business problems, to talk about local legislation problems, you can now do that locally, instead of going to the national association.

Weissman: Is part of the reason for the decline in total membership also the lack of a set of overriding national level issues that can only be solved by a national association? Do you think that's part of the reason?

Bride: I'll bet that's a major part of it. I think that a lot of the reason the conferences drew a lot of people was because that was the only game in town. So when their primary value was subsumed by other organizations, absent the national issues, yeah, it was inevitable.

Yeaton: There were several initiatives by ADAPSO in the '80s to have regional participation and regional conferences. It would have been very specific, very directed, and a lot cheaper to attend. I know we tried on three occasions in the Midwest, and particularly in the Greater Detroit area, and it just didn't work. We'd get a few people together like Bob Jones of Computer Dynamics and Peter Karmanos from Compuware and several others, and it didn't work. I've never been quite sure why. Maybe we were too close as competitors, maybe the topics were wrong, but at least on three different occasions there were initiatives to have regional subsets, and then maybe go to one conference a year with a broader base. Why didn't that work? Bob Jones really put some effort into it. I helped him on two or three of them and it didn't go anywhere.

Welke: You just didn't try hard enough, Jack. [*Laughter*] In Indianapolis, I brought six guys together in 1985. It didn't work. We brought them together again in '86. It still didn't work. We did that until 1990 and, in the sixth year, we finally began expanding. At this point, we have 370 members.

Yeaton: What did you change that gained their interest so that it went from six to 370?

Welke: It was a matter of getting a couple of lead people to recognize that even they had something to learn in spite of the fact that they were allegedly the big fish in a small pond.

Albert: ITAA still has programs that are national in nature, as outlined by Harris in his talk this morning. One of them has to do with workforce. And another one has to do with taxation. These are national issues.

Welke: Richard, you had a comment way back when.

Carpenter: ADAPSO, in my experience and, more recently, ITAA, has always kind of ebbed and flowed based on the issues. At the first meeting I went to in '83, the issue was software piracy and "anti-duping" and I remember being impressed because there were CEOs of two or three microcomputer software companies who were actively participating and rolling up their sleeves and getting involved.

One phenomenon in the more recent history, that I think came at a low point in ITAA, was the emergence of the Web and the Internet. And I think that's had a profound impact by providing a number of issues, as Harris mentioned this morning. Everything from dealing with the global market place to Internet taxation, which has been a huge issue. But it's also been an enabler. I was very involved six or seven years ago in saying, "Gee, as an industry trade association shouldn't we be using this new Internet thing to inform our members of what's going on?" The good news now is that I almost get no real mail, paper mail, from ITAA any more but—I won't call it the bad news—I'm deluged with information that comes in via email. So that's had a very, very big impact, I think, on the way ITAA communicates with its members.

All of that, to the best of my knowledge, is made available to the local organizations. For example, the Software Division has been active on the stock options issue, and I started forwarding the information to the guy at the Mass Software Council who's working on stock options. I saw him at a meeting about a week ago and he said, "Oh, I get all that from ITAA." So I think ITAA can provide a lead role nationally, but then bring in Mass Software Council and try to influence Senators Kennedy and Kerry on issues. I think there's an important relationship between ITAA and the local organizations on policy issues. But Mass Software Council does almost all of what ADAPSO did for me when I was starting my company.

Sturtevant: I think there's another thing that has been left out as to the ebb and flow. In '85, '86, '87, the association got a real challenge from the Microcomputer Software Association which was a separate entity. It was the first time in the association's history that we didn't figure out how to incorporate a new group that was a logical extension of where the industry was headed. And, ultimately, we cut off a growth avenue as other companies were consolidating. We'd always managed previously to bring the next thing in. We failed there and I think that changed the dynamic at the same time that the regional associations were coming into play. So I think the two dynamics together really hurt us at that point.

Welke: Good point. You know, to be very blunt about it, I can remember the conversations we had relative to: "How do we react to this PC phenomenon that is under our feet?" And we did a crummy job of reacting to it. We did a very, very poor job.

Weissman: I remember, at the time, we sent an emissary to go talk to them to see if we could interest them in joining ADAPSO. And I remember the Board meeting where he came in to report. He said that it was going pretty well. They were interested in joining, but the biggest problem that they had expressed to him was their concern as to whether or not they could relate to a group of people as old as the people in ADAPSO. [*Laughter*] I looked around the table at the Board, and the average age of the ADAPSO Board at that point was late 30s. [*Laughter*]

Rollins: Right. Pretty old. Let me report on two other merger initiatives that I was involved with when I was on the ADAPSO Board, which was from 1984 to 1994. One was with the Information Industry Association where we attempted a merger of two non-profits. We had a lot in common, we all agreed it made a lot of sense. It never happened. And as I recall, the reason had to do with issues of who would be on the surviving board.

Unidentified voices: Yes. Yes. Yes.

Rollins: That's a common problem with non-profits, sorting out the governance. However, I was involved in another merger initiative when I was president of the VAR Division of ADAPSO which did work on a smaller scale. There was an independent group of IBM VARs called the Value Group. The Value Group had about thirty VARs across the United States, maybe more. Ultimately, about 30 of them joined ADAPSO, and we were successful in accomplishing that merger. And it was very simple. They all just dropped out of the Value Group. It dissolved, and they became members of the VAR Division and members of ADAPSO. So we grew.

Welke: As I recall, if we had done the merger with the Information Industry Association, the size of the Board would have exceeded the membership. [*Laughter*]

Rollins: You got it. Just an historical note. The Value Group merger occurred in 1987. I looked that up on my calendar.

Weissman: At the time of those IIA discussions, I was with Dun & Bradstreet Corporation, which was one of the major players in IIA. I actually hosted some of those meetings at the Dun & Bradstreet offices. And, as John points out, it was a failed effort. There was also an attempt to merge with CCIA. There was a common thread in both of those failures related to power-sharing and trust. You had two groups of people who did not know each other and did not have, therefore, enough trust to create an association. I think that that is one of the reasons why ADAPSO over a period of several decades was able to morph. Because there were distinct groups with separate interests, but quite apart from that, there were strong personal relationships which had developed as a result of attending ADAPSO meetings. And so there was a trust that came out of that which allowed people to make accommodations.

Welke: Good point.

Coleman: Following on that, I was thinking about what happened over time. Some of us software guys started showing up at ADAPSO meetings because there were little bits of the program that were of interest to us. We got to know the services people and the data center people and the personal relationships bridged the differences in interests. When it came to the PC folks, they were people that we didn't know. There was no strong sense of bond with "those guys." And I think as we grew larger, we lost the personal relationships that glued us together and inevitably the disparate groups were going to fly apart because we didn't have that glue.

Welke: Good point.

Esch: I think that back in the '70s and '80s, the thing that distinguished all of us was that we were the heads of companies. We weren't running divisions of larger organizations. When we came to the table, Bob Weissman sat down with Jim McCormack. They did a deal, shook hands and moved on to the next issue. I think that happened a lot. And it was the deals, it was the networking, it was the "do you want to go co-market together" discussions, that happened right there at the bar, at the cocktail party, at the coffee shop. To me, that was the real strength of ADAPSO and how it became, in fact, a sort of fraternity of people who, over ten or fifteen years, grew up together in this business. They were the people who actually made this business.

Rollins: They were entrepreneurs who had started their own businesses and were making deals. And were empowered to do so. And inclined to do so by their nature.

Unidentified voice: Yes, they were all entrepreneurs.

Coleman: I agree 100% with what you're saying Arthur, which is that the membership has changed from the entrepreneurs who were CEOs, to the senior management team. I wasn't here in the '60s, but from what I understand, there weren't too many companies that were over $100 million. [*Laughter*] There weren't too many of them that were over *$1 million*.

As they got bigger, they brought in professional management and the attendance at conferences changed from an entrepreneurial CEO/ founder kind of perspective to more of a mix of senior management. Now there are very large multinational worldwide companies. The CEO is off attending to business and working with ITAA is delegated to someone down the line. They are public companies, they have a whole different set of problems and we lost the mix.

Bride: You may remember that there was a National Computer Conference serving the computer industry for a couple of decades. As the industry matured, special interest conferences took little pieces of it, and the charter, the mission, was gone. NCC died. Taking some of the ADAPSO functions away were things like Comdex, which is where the micro guys go to do their networking. And then you have special interests such as the graphics groups, the new media groups. CASE is another example. Every technology grew up, had its special interest, and carved a little bit away from ADAPSO, and what we have left is not very much for conference value. And, therefore, not very many reasons to go to the conferences.

Jones: Larry, I certainly found all of the networking we did to be infinitely valuable. Like John, I made a list of people that I wanted to make sure to spend some time with in the hallways between sessions. But to some of the companies, those hallways were not just for discussing the sort of deals that Bart was alluding to, but opportunities to find the constituencies to whom they would sell. For companies like Joe Blumberg's that sell services to the industry, the conferences provided an opportunity for them to network with all of their potential prospects.

Welke: One comment that I want to make relative to the regional associations. They began to form back in the '80s. Massachusetts was one of the first, and then Washington got a very active group going, and the Software Entrepreneurs' Forum in Northern California was a very strong operation. That movement increased until we have, as Bart said, 26 or 30, or something like that.

Carlson: Twenty-six that I know of, but there probably are more.

Welke: There is an organization at this point called the Council of Regional Information Technology Associations. ADAPSO attempted for a time to support that organization but I'm not sure where that effort went.

Unidentified voice: They even held meetings at the ITAA conferences.

Rollins: Wasn't there a brief period when ADAPSO actually stated its membership as being 20,000 or 30,000 including all the members of the regional associations?

Unidentified voice: It still does.

[Ed. Note: In the early 1990s, ITAA actively supported the creation of the Council of Regional Information Technology Associations by providing staff support to organize and facilitate its meetings. A representative of CRITA was given a seat on the ITAA Board. ITAA provided information about government policy issues to the regional associations which were members of CRITA, and ITAA counted the thousands of members of those associations as affiliate members of ITAA. In March 2000, CRITA incorporated as a non-profit organization and subsequently spun off from

ITAA. Its website (www.crita.org) lists over 50 regional associations in the U.S. and Canada as CRITA members as of the date of this writing.]

Dreyer: In 1968, I presented to the Board of Directors of ADAPSO the idea of setting up local chapters. And I got Gordon Taubenheim, who was a member of the Board at that time, to use Cleveland to test the idea. We tried to get a chapter established and got five or six people who showed some significant interest. But when we went back to the Board again, they felt that having chapters would be divisive to the organization and its goals because of the dues issue. You would have to pay dues to the parent organization and you would have to pay dues to the local organization. So, ADAPSO did address the issue of chapters way back in '68 and thought it might fly, but then decided it was not in the association's best interest.

Welke: We've got roughly five, maybe 5-1/2 minutes, left. I'd like to go around the room and see who has a comment that they absolutely have to get on tape.

Blumberg: Those of us who were providing services to the industry often felt that the association was sort of closed and provincial because we wanted to attend the conferences as vendors and be able to have something like booth space, or a way to display what we could do for the conference attendees. And that was never an open issue, it was always closed for some reason.

Yeaton: The best you could do at that point was pick up someone's bar tab and put your name on it.

Bride: I'd like to address what Joe said because that's where getting involved in conference planning really helped. You'd show up and pound on the table a few times to get your topic on the program and then say, "By the way, I can provide a speaker, too, if you like." So you'd get a chance to get exposure to the attendees. You're right that there were only one or two conferences where they tried having exhibits to support the service organizations. But the conferences were a good way for the service companies to have a presence.

Welke: I was involved in conferences for almost all the twenty years that I was active with the Board and when I became Chairman of the association. There was an incredible amount of backroom dealing and wheeling in order to get a subject on or off a particular agenda. Anybody who denies that is lying.

Dreyer: Nobody denies it.

Welke: But that's a reality with any kind of an organization. And I think we even had gotten to the point where we were doing more than just conference planning in the back room. I mean, succession of leadership was very much an organized pattern.

Carpenter: One of the things that struck me at my first several meetings was the culture of the ADAPSO conferences, and the fact that someone like myself starting a company that had 20 people, had no concern whatsoever about approaching anyone, from any company of any size. I too had a list of all the people I wanted to make contact with. But how open people were—meeting, talking, sharing ideas—that's what kept me coming back.

Jones: One of the things that didn't get on the tape yet that I was heavily involved in was the Technology Information Service Committee which sponsored some reasonably successful spin-off conferences. We had three or four or five conferences on emerging technology that were very, very useful to the community of technologists that were members of ADAPSO. Or to people within their organizations that were focused on technology.

Rollins: Larry, I just thought of one other thing that attracted a certain number of members to ADAPSO, particularly small companies. There was a group insurance program. Many companies would join to get this medical insurance for their employees. There was a firm in New York called Leterman-Gortz that was the intermediary. I served on the ADAPSO Insurance Trust Board and was a trustee with two or three other people, over a period of many years, to help administer that trust and set rates. And they were very competitive rates. You join organizations for a lot of reasons, but that was a reason for many of the small companies.

Welke: Barbara, do you have any comment to make?

Brizdle: Perhaps you discussed it before I got here, but I was thinking how important camaraderie was throughout all the meetings. It was extremely easy to meet with people and, if you were new, it was very easy to be brought in and to be a part of everything which, I think, is a little unusual.

Sturtevant: Well, one of the things the staff did was try to make that easy. When we would get new members, we'd assign a current member to go and find that new member at their first conference, and bring them into the fold so that nobody was walking around lost. We literally paired them off. Your assignment at the first reception was to go and find this guy. And God love you guys, you went out and did it. But that got people involved much quicker than walking into a room and saying, "Oh god, I don't know anybody here."

Blumberg: One more thing that Kim triggered for me when he talked about spin-off conferences. There was a compelling need to share personnel information when I first started with Comshare. I kept asking what NCSS was paying for these people and what Tymshare was paying for these people. And none of that information was ever available. One of the things that happened as a result is that seven people got together in a room—it was NCSS and Cybernetics and Comshare and Informatics and GE Computer Services—and started something called the Computer Services Personnel Association which wound up sharing the information. And, in fact, conducted the first executive and management compensation studies that were done for ADAPSO. That was one of the successful spin-offs of groups getting together at conferences to say, "What do we need to share and how can we make that happen?"

Welke: OK, this could be the end of the meeting. Going once, going twice...

[*Laughter and applause*]

Accounting Issues Workshop

Moderators: Larry Schoenberg and Martin Campbell-Kelly

Rapporteur: Elizabeth Virgo

Participants: David Campbell   Doug Jerger
                                Gary Durbin   Harris Miller
                                David Grier   Jeff Yost
                                Thomas Haigh

Schoenberg: I'm Larry Schoenberg. My company was AGS Computers. I was the person who headed up the ADAPSO group when we first started working on accounting issues and spent, I think, seventeen years working with the AICPA and the FASB, failing to get most things satisfactorily resolved. However, we did publish some position papers. It was only after I left that AICPA and FASB reversed their positions.

This topic is called accounting issues but I think it should be redefined as financially-related issues. And I think it's important, at least in a historical perspective, to realize that, when these issues first came up in ADAPSO, ADAPSO was dominated by individuals who were the CEOs or COOs of companies. So, although this was a functional area of operations, it was approached from the perception of the CEO and COO, not that of senior financial people. Before we go further, it would be useful if every person here gave his name and background.

Miller: I'm Harris Miller. I'm the current president of ITAA. Accounting and finance issues are back big time, partly because of FASB getting involved in stock options which are very controversial. And partly because of some revenue recognition issues that have become very visible over the last few years involving some pretty visible companies like Computer Associates and MicroStrategy and others. And, of course, Enron has put everything back on the table, resuscitating the issue that you all fought through a couple decades ago.

But, beyond that, I think almost everything is on the table. When I got involved with ITAA in the mid-'90s, a lot of our companies said, we don't need ITAA to help us understand accounting issues, we understand it all. I actually had the CEO of a major company—that later made headlines because of their accounting practices—tell me that.

I think that egos got out of control and people were a little bit high-handed about these issues. And I think now people are coming together to say, OK, we better figure out what is the smartest thing to do as opposed to the cleverest thing to do. And this whole attitude of give us a loophole, we'll drive a horse through it, is now swinging back the other way. People are saying that their audits and financial reports are being watched a lot more carefully, and we better, as an industry, get our act together because it is affecting investor confidence.

Schoenberg: I love your comment about being clever because that really has been an overwhelming characteristic of how things have been done. One of the first statements I ever made to the accountants was, "Don't tell me about 'conservative' because 'conservative' is another way of saying biased." And if you're biased, sooner or later, someone will turn it on its head and we have had plenty of examples of that. I could never have dreamt up some of the ideas that people have come up with. So, once the connection between economic reality and accounting disappears, it's over. The game is over.

Grier: I'm David Grier. I'm the Associate Editor-in-Chief of the *Annals of the History of Computing*. So I am here more as an observer than a participant. I do have sort of an interesting connection though. My father ran the Burroughs Users Group for thirty-odd years and was affiliated with ADAPSO in the late '60s and early '70s. So I'm here to find out what the story is.

Haigh: I'm Thomas Haigh. I'm a historian of business and technology, specifically computing. I'm completing my Ph.D. at the University of Pennsylvania and currently teaching at Colby College.

Yost: I'm Jeff Yost. I'm Associate Director of the Charles Babbage Institute and have a strong interest in the business history of software.

Campbell: I'm David Campbell. I'm now Managing Director of a company called Innovation Advisors but, to make Larry Schoenberg feel young, I've had responsibility for running public companies in the software services business in five different decades. We did the IPO of Computer Task Group in '69 and I ran it all through the '70s, '80s, and '90s. And in 2000, I was CEO of another public company.

One of the things that's interesting is our industry's impact on financial statements and how they help investors. There was an era when balance sheets and tangible assets were how you reported the strength of a company and our industry changed things in a lot of ways. We changed it because we traded in intangible assets and people didn't understand much about that. We brought growth rates which were pretty extraordinary to the investment community. We were maybe the first industry that commonly thought in terms of double-digit growth rates. We created the first large market cap people-based companies—companies that had human assets that went down the elevator at the end of every day. A major battle that we had to fight was to get the investment community to realize that our companies really had value, even though at six o'clock at night everyone had gone home, and there was nobody there.

All of these issues dealing with accounting/financial reporting were related to needing to raise capital because we needed capital to fund the growth of the company. We needed capital and the accounting practices weren't designed for our kind of industry. And, frankly, it's a still-evolving art of how to represent the past and/or the future since all companies today are valued based on the forecasted future. And there is no financial representation that attests to a company's forecast of the future.

We still have significant disconnects in valuation models and in accounting models, so I think we are, frankly, still early in the evolving process of how investors get access to information to make decisions about the performance of companies. It's sort of an ever-evolving mystery and art.

Miller: We're involved with this whole value reporting initiative that companies are undertaking. We've put it on the back-burner for now because the ITAA Board is really uncomfortable with having new accounting rules. But we're continuing to have discussions about it with executives from NASDAQ as well as others. It's the same issue: how do you come up with a value of a company whose assets are intangible?

Durbin: I'm Gary Durbin. I was CEO of Tesseract Corporation. In the '70s and '80s, software accounting issues became critical for us, even though I didn't have any particular interest in accounting and considered that the responsibility of my CFO. But we were raising money. And if you're going to raise money, these become critical issues because there weren't any standards. There was any which way you wanted to do it. So you ended up explaining to investors how you were doing it and why what you were doing was rational, either from the software capitalization point of view or how to measure the assets if they weren't capitalized. Or why your revenue recognition policies made sense. We spent a tremendous amount of time doing that simply because there were no standards. So I became involved, as well as my CFO, Lyn Jensen, in the work to try to create some standards.

Schoenberg: I think Tesseract was actually the first company to testify.

Durbin: Yeah, we did testify at FASB. And preparing for that took a lot of work because we wanted to understand what was going on in the industry and try to present a good case. There were a number of companies who had strong positions and, in some cases, they wanted to change their position. I had a long talk with the CFO at MSA. They wanted the industry to tell them that the way they had had to do it in the past was wrong because, from their point of view, the accounting practices were limiting their ability to do R&D. And they were losing ground competitively because of it. So it was really significant for the industry, both for raising money in the early stages of a company, and for established companies in how they funded R&D.

Jerger: I'm Doug Jerger. During the '70s and '80s, I was CEO of a company called Fortex Data Corporation. It was a small software company but we had big customers. Our big interest in the accounting issue came from talking to Continental Bank. This was our banker who looked at our financials and said, "You don't have any assets here, nothing of value, right?" Eventually, we had a $150,000 loan from the bank, which for us was a *big* deal, and it was all secured by our accounts receivable. That was the only thing they would loan against.

Durbin: Same for us.

Jerger: So the work that ADAPSO did was wonderful for us. In the first half of the '90s, I was on the staff at ADAPSO/ITAA, and it was wonderful what Larry Schoenberg was doing with the accounting folks and the folks at FASB. He would disavow any knowledge of accounting and then kill them with his logic on the rationality or irrationality of the accounting principles. So, Larry, you really did do a wonderful thing for our industry in accounting.

Schoenberg: Thank you. Mentioning the issue of dealing with the bank, I remember many years ago going with Jay Goldberg, the founder of Software Design Associates, to a bank in New York City to attempt to get him a loan. They wouldn't lend him money on receivables because the receivables were based on services revenues. And I met Dave Campbell through a sales tax issue in New York State. What's sales tax have to do with accounting? Well, it was heavily connected to their perception of the business.

Jerger: We owe a great debt to a guy named Tony, our loan officer at Continental Bank, who worked with the construction industry. They didn't know which industry to put us in so they gave us to Tony. I called him one time, right after Christmas Day and said, "Tony, I'm in deep trouble and you've got to help. I've got to have some money because we've always covered payroll but with this one, we're in trouble." He said, "Are you sure?" I said, "Yeah." He said, "OK, you got it." That's when I went to the $150,000 level. He didn't really understand the business, but he liked us and decided it would be OK.

Campbell: To Larry's point, which is fascinating in terms of how accounting affects things, the sales tax issue came about because New York City got into deep trouble, and, therefore, New York State was in deep trouble, and they went looking for revenues that weren't subject to sales tax. They found some programming services companies and they said, "At the end of this process, what does the customer get?" Well, it's a stack of cards, so they decide that you're the manufacturer of tangible property, and that was the basis for applying sales tax. *Retroactively*, because nobody had previously filed sales tax returns and, therefore, there was no statute of limitations.

So, we got an invoice in 1976 for $586,000 and we had a $400,000 net worth. Sales tax, like payroll tax, is the personal responsibility of the officers of the company. So it was a bill to the four of us who were the officers for more than the net worth of the company. They were saying that what we did was manufacture a tangible property. None of the *banks* thought it was tangible property. [*Laughter*]

It was an example of how things can be interpreted to meet an objective.

Campbell-Kelly: I'm Martin Campbell-Kelly. I've been writing a history of the software industry, looking at the years 1955 to 1995, and accounting is one of the issues I've really not got to grips with in the book. Part of the background to the software industry is that one constantly reads about how difficult it was to finance a company where the assets could walk out the door. And yet, what we actually have is a thriving industry. And people got venture financing. When you look at the business press, you can't get a clear picture of the evolution of the accounting standards. But you pick up some little articles in the press that give you a sense that things are changing and that this must somehow be resolving the problem.

Schoenberg: Elizabeth, I'm not sure whether your title was provocateur, raconteur...*[Laughter]*

Virgo: I'm Elizabeth Virgo and I'm a consultant. The reason I'm here is because of a long link with Burt Grad. Burt and I did valuation studies. I don't know how many we did for you, Larry, but it was really at the start of this whole concept of accounting for intangibles. Burt and I started doing that, I think about 1978.

Schoenberg: Excellent choice in date, that's exactly the year.

Virgo: I can remember going to one of the FASB meetings and sitting there, really quite amazed that people did not understand this concept of intangibles. As I said, we evolved and developed processes for our clients, and some of the work was scrutinized by the IRS, which was equally interesting. *[Laughter]* This was my first choice of the workshops to attend.

Schoenberg: As I mentioned to some people who were here earlier, everyone who is here gets a stock option. Two people asked me, "What company?" Who cares? *[Laughter]*

Durbin: It's all lottery tickets, anyway.

Schoenberg: In preparing for this session, a list of subjects that ADAPSO addressed came up. I'll read them to you simply because it may trigger some thoughts in your mind. One of the first things on the list was creating a chart of accounts for service bureaus. Although I wasn't involved with that, one of the most important things that happened at one of the roundtables I was a member of—which was one of the earliest ones and still exists today, twenty-five years later—was a issue related to our participation in gathering industry data or financial numbers. Those of us who were in the business could not understand the survey. So we sat down together—the CEOs, not the financial guys—and actually worked out a common standard. You might say, "How could it be that you couldn't understand it?" I'll give you an example. You're in the labor business. Are social security taxes direct cost or indirect cost? This is not trivial in a labor business, it could amount to 10%. Where do technical support people fall? Are they direct labor or are they administrative cost?

It's not important how we resolved it, but the fact is sitting down allowed us to create something that benefited everyone. It doesn't matter if it was right or wrong. There is no right or wrong. It was a matter of creating a standard way of doing it. That kind of thing was really important and I believe the trade association provided the ability for people to get together and do it.

Financial ratios: this is the same kind of thing I just talked about but relates to things such as growth rate, employees, etc. One of the wildest ones I ever spent time with was, "What's the revenue per employee, and what is the turnover rate?" You know, in companies that are growing fast, the turnover rate varies tremendously whether you start with the number at the beginning of the year, the average number for the year, or whatever. And, I must say, Harris, one number you threw out in your talk this morning that amused many of us in the audience was the idea that the revenue per employee has gone down in the industry. Which, of course, is not true. We were looking at totally different data and statistics. But it's a good example. If the press or some analyst gets that data, they'll say the industry's less efficient that it used to be. So you've really got to be very careful how you use some of this stuff.

SIC codes: why are these relevant? SIC codes, the Standard Industrial Code, are the way the government categorizes companies for labor statistics. What we discovered was that companies which had evolved from different backgrounds did not identify themselves by the same SIC code, although anyone could see that they were in the same business. We still see it today. Not only are the SIC codes confusing but if you look at the people who do research on the industry and you look at the companies that they group together, it's a joke. I look at the *Business Week* and *Forbes* lists, and direct competitors are not listed in the same category! The most *direct* competitors. So, to someone running these companies, it's a pretty stupid set of discussions. But it turns out to be very important, and even more so in an historical sense. And those are the kinds of things that ADAPSO was involved in.

Jerger: We found that critical when we'd go on the Hill to talk about issues. They'd say, "Who are you guys?" And they'd pull out the SIC reports and couldn't see us anywhere. We'd say, "Wait, wait, we're really important, we're all over." They'd say, "Yeah, right."

Schoenberg: Roundtables and Workshops. The roundtables, I believe, were what kept many people in the association. A roundtable was a group of people who self-selected into an area of interest and met on a regular basis. The problem with roundtables was that they tended to get people who were pretty direct competitors in one place at one time. This raised some antitrust issues and, since Teddy Roosevelt, the U.S. has had relatively stringent antitrust laws.

So there were serious questions about whether the people in the roundtables were violating antitrust law. The presentations last night mentioned Milt Wessel, the former General Counsel of ADAPSO. He was a very seminal influence in ADAPSO, and lectured us constantly about antitrust. Well, I can say that over forty years, I've never heard anyone discuss pricing, which is considered the ultimate sin. But I must say I heard things discussed that one could reasonably conclude had the potential for being collusive. Even discussing financial ratios. Clearly, if you know someone's cost ratios, it doesn't take a genius to figure out that there is a connection between cost and price, although it's not a pure connection.

Campbell: Larry and I have been on a roundtable together for over twenty-five years, and one of the reasons they survived is because they are naturally adaptive, and so the issues today are totally different. Twenty-five years ago, it was how do you commission a paid salesman or whatever, and those things have changed dramatically. I never felt there was, frankly, even a hint of collusion relative to pricing but, one time, I found something that was on the edge of collusion. It was when you and I, Larry, were both looking at acquiring the same company and there was no reason to get into a bidding contest. The company of a third member of the roundtable was for sale. Either of us could have bought it and you ended up buying it. We never quite said, "Let's not get into a bidding contest." But I suppose you could say that it was a factor, and it's interesting whether competing on acquisition activities would come under the normal rules of price fixing.

Miller: We tried without success to get roundtables going when I started with ITAA in the mid-'90s. One of the reasons was that people said the information shared among the founders of the industry is now available from so many sources, they don't need to come together anymore. You can get industry analysts, you can get consultants, because the industry itself has matured. So the kind of basic things you guys were talking about in the '60s and '70s and early '80s, you can now pay somebody to give you that information.

Durbin: What the ADAPSO meetings were for me was educational. I came from the technical side of the business. There were all these management issues that I was blind to, and here were people who were just a little further along than I was. Sometimes I could contribute, but the learning experience was great because there were so many people groping for solutions. It was new stuff and I think it was the *new* character of it that was so important.

Campbell-Kelly: For people who are not familiar with ADAPSO, we're not getting a picture of what the roundtables were. How many people were there? What subset of those people were meeting? How often were they meeting and were you formulating policy that was being passed up into the organization or were you exchanging war stories and knowledge-sharing?

Schoenberg: First of all, the typical group was about twelve to fifteen people. People who wanted to be in a roundtable submitted their name and were invited to join or those that were already in a roundtable added names of potential new members. I was a part of the first two that were formed because I thought it was so valuable I wanted to see other roundtables get started.

The very first one was primarily people from service bureaus. I was the only person that wasn't. And the second one was essentially focused around professional services. The subjects that tended to be discussed were common business issues where smaller groups worked better and, as you would imagine, most of these evolved into social groups of a sort. I don't ever remember discussing ADAPSO issues.

Campbell: That second roundtable was actually a mix. We had software products people like John Maguire from Software AG, and Dick Thatcher from Atlantic Data Systems, and Bob Cook with VM Software. So it was a blend of services companies and software companies, and sometimes it was useful to have cross pollination. But the structure of the meetings, even today, is that one person has the group for an hour to say, "Here's my problem." And you just sort of talk about that problem so that it provides very personal support.

Everybody was young, frankly. The software and services industry was being created and the people running companies were in their 30's and 40's. They were sort of young to be running public companies or large companies and it was great to be able to share experiences. It's interesting that at the first meeting we actually had an outside moderator to make sure we didn't have any collusion. Right?

Schoenberg: In fact, Gil Mintz, one of the partners in Broadview Associates, moderated both of the first two groups.

Campbell: After the first meeting, we said we could do this without a moderator and we went off on our own. But we did worry about it. We had to make up the rules as we went along to some extent.

Jerger: I think in the late '80s, early '90s, there were probably thirty-five or forty titular roundtables. Maybe fifteen to twenty active ones. Does that sound right?

Campbell: Yeah.

Schoenberg: I certainly was aware of about fifteen.

Jerger: How often did they meet? I think it was quarterly.

Campbell: We meet every six months. We've been doing that for over twenty-five years.

Miller: The analogue that exists today, like the enterprise software roundtable which Rick Crandall runs, is not personal-based, it's criteria-based. You have to be a CEO of one of these large enterprise software companies. So, unlike the old roundtables that Larry and Dave were talking about, if you lose your CEO job, you don't get invited back. The new CEO gets invited.

Campbell: In the early years we maintained that rule. If you lost your job, you could come to one more meeting and then you were out. But after we had been meeting for about ten years, it happened the bonds had gotten strong enough that we started waiving the rules.

Schoenberg: There was no one with a job! [*Laughter*]

Campbell: It *did* evolve that way.

Schoenberg: I just realized that I misread the item in the list of topics that was given to me. It says in the note, "CFO Roundtables and Workshops." I didn't even notice "CFO" because, when we started, the organization was totally dominated by guys who ran companies. At some point in time, it became more functionally-driven and, actually, the first group to form a functional roundtable was not CFOs, but lawyers. Well, it didn't work because the lawyers wouldn't meet together.

At any rate, the next item that's listed is classification of software for sales and use tax and property tax. All of these things that sound trivial, like how to reduce your taxes, were highly interconnected. We were concerned with what you might call accounting issues, but they were actually issues related to the perception of value in the companies. We had this fantastic need to demonstrate that software companies had value. To whom? There's no simple answer to that question. To the world at large. Yes, people had trouble with banks Yes, they had trouble in the financial markets. But it was as much a matter of having created something that everyone said had no value. So it was a real emotional thing and only over time did it become something pursued by the accountants. The three original people assigned by the trade association to work on the accounting issues were myself, the CEO of AGS, Jim Porter, the VP of Marketing at Informatics, and Bill Graves, the COO of MSA. There was no accountant in the group. As people were replaced in the group, they tended to get replaced with accountants.

Durbin: There was a lead guy at Arthur Young who took a big position on the issues.

Schoenberg: Yes, Frank O'Brien. Frank worked for Arthur Young and he represented Informatics and a few other companies. He was a brilliant guy. But we got co-opted. The sequence of what happened was that we put out a white paper proposing changes to the accounting rules. I don't remember whether we sent it to the accounting groups but somehow the AICPA got hold of it. They called up and said, "You shouldn't be doing this, so we'll create a committee to work on it. You can assign three people to it and we'll assign three people to it and we'll work on the rules." And so that happened.

You know, any of us who have ever negotiated anything in our lives know that you should never negotiate with anyone but a decision-maker. Well, we made that mistake big time. We negotiated with the people on the committee, then the group as a whole negotiated with the FASB, then the FASB negotiated with the SEC and by the time it was done, we couldn't understand our own rules. They were absolutely incomprehensible to us. The political process did it.

From that activity developed the next subject which is revenue recognition.

Campbell-Kelly: One of the questions that I was unable to resolve in my book was that it's commonly stated that there was a problem with these intangible assets. And yet as I looked around, you have movie companies, you have firms who make encyclopedias, you have pharmaceutical companies, who also have intangible intellectual properties. If pharmaceutical companies are managing to account for intangible assets, then what was the problem in the software industry? Can you elaborate on that?

Durbin: We were trying to raise money in the late '70s. When we went to the venture capital community, they had already been badly burned by software companies claiming to have assets and then discovering that there was absolutely nothing there. This was because there were no standards for those valuations and for how costs were to be associated with the valuations and how those costs were to be tied into the revenues downstream. And if the revenue streams could not be evaluated, how could you deal with write-downs, and so forth? There were just absolutely no standards. So the rule that the VC's had was: take the intangibles off the valuation. We had this huge problem of trying to differentiate product companies from service companies. The product companies really did have assets. We had invested a lot of money. But the service companies' assets were just people and a lot of the investors couldn't make that differentiation. They wanted to put us in the service category. We were trying to make it clear that there was this other category which was a product business, and then determine how to value what we had.

What the VCs said was, "We'll take it off the balance sheet. We will not value at all the investments you've made. We're simply going to look your current revenue position." Well, if you've got an early stage company, that doesn't work. It was very difficult to get those valuations.

Miller: I think it also has to do with the physical manifestation of the intellectual property. In the pharmaceutical industry, the intellectual property is the formula for the pill, but yet you can show someone the pill—that's the physical manifestation. In the software industry the intellectual property is the code and, as Dave said, the physical manifestation of it used to be a deck of cards. And that's really different. So I think people had difficulty with it psychologically.

In movies, the intellectual property is a script, the physical manifestation is something you can sit in a movie theater and watch. But if you can't show people how that intellectual property exists in the physical world, they don't understand how to value it. Even today, when we lobby on the Hill, they say, "Where is the Internet?" Well, you know, it's not something you can point to. I can point to the Root A server that Verisign runs, but I can't point to that the way I can point to a pill factory, or a movie studio, or movie theaters where the movie studio's work is shown.

Durbin: The analogy of a computer being like a projector is very strong but we couldn't get there. Could not get there.

Schoenberg: First of all, you have to recognize that one of the motives of accountants in general is to report revenues at the end of the life of the company. [*Laughter*]

In fact, there was actually one standard which you would never use except when the company ended. And to give you a bizarre example like that, I'm involved with a company that is a spin-off of my original company. The company eventually sort of collapsed of its own weight and became a shell. Now here it is, many years later. You know how bad it is liquidating a company. How about if I told you the company has gone from zero to $80,000,000 and is reporting profits regularly? All because it's the end of the company. All these things from the tax reserves, or this or that reserve, are all starting to surface. You know there aren't any assets, but all the money is surfacing. With cash, I might add, in this case.

At any rate, what happened in those discussions was the movie analogy would come up and they would use several arguments against it. One argument would be the stability of the entity itself. So the longer it's been in business, the better the valuation. Many accounting rules, I find—even the ones they propose today—are tremendously favorable to the large companies at the expense of the small companies. Which also means stable companies versus growing companies.

The pharmaceutical analogy never came up. But as a general principle, the pharmaceutical companies expensed everything because they didn't care. They were so established that they didn't have to care. It's intriguing. If you listen to the companies who support more stringent financial standards, which usually means delaying revenue recognition and taking expenses early on, it's invariably the very profitable large companies. This is hardly a shock, because they gain from it *tremendously*. So the problem here was that we had small growing companies with very limited histories.

Campbell: There were some interesting debates within the industry relative to the accounting issues. For example, on the sales tax issue. Sales tax is defined state-by-state rather than by the federal government, and that creates the potential for mischief. The debate was: is there a difference between a professional services company doing a million dollar project for an insurance company and a software products company selling a million dollar product? Should they be treated differently for tax purposes? When sales tax was 7% and the average operating profit of the companies was about 7%, it was not a trivial issue. We simply didn't think we could afford the tax. And we were fighting against whether there should be any tax just about the time, in the late '70s, early '80s, when the PC came to the world with shrink-wrapped software sold over the retail store counter for $20. Now what's the difference between a $200,000 database system and a $20 VisiCalc? It was amazingly interesting and complex to try to get definitions. We ended up helping define the sales tax laws in New York and California. Then those became the patterns for lots of other states. But within the industry it was sometimes, "Yeah, we'll give up the software product guys." [*Laughter*] And they would say the same about the professional services guys. It was who got to the table first to sign the thing. And it was very interesting stuff because it was all pivoting around these definitions.

Durbin: But then we software products guys outfoxed you because we figured out that we could do electronic delivery so there was nothing tangible. We went to complete electronic delivery, so that we didn't even have to send a tape. We got tripped up a little bit, though, when we started doing some international sales because we couldn't make electronic transmissions, and Canada caught us taking a tape into Canada. And we had to try to say, "No, no, the tape is only worth twenty dollars." [*Laughter*]

Schoenberg: Actually there were other conflicts, too. I remember Marty Goetz trying to get some tax credit.

Campbell: The investment tax credit, right?

Schoenberg: It was more than investment tax, it was some sort of a local tax on products. I don't remember even what it was but to get these tax credits, he had to suddenly shift the definition to call it tangible even though for other purposes, he would call it intangible.

In my mind, all these issues always come back to what I started with: there is an economic reality. When laws and accounting rules move away from measuring economic reality to gimmickry, sooner or later you get into trouble. I mean, like with stock options. I know it's a very sore subject and I can understand why, but to argue that stock options have no economic value is ridiculous. It's just patently absurd. That doesn't answer the question of how they should be accounted for, right? But I suggested twenty years ago to several companies, including one represented here today, that we should have the stock strike price rise each year. And my thought was, not only was it economic reality, but, in fact, we would probably get around the problem of determining present value because it wouldn't have a present value. Or it would be really *de minimis*. I guess, by definition, it has to have some value, but it would go down humongously.

Durbin: Larry, could you talk a little bit about the conflict between the members of ADAPSO? You mentioned earlier about the difference between small companies like mine who were very early in the stage of things and had a strong interest in being able to show that the company had value and that we had real assets versus some of the more established companies. MSA had never capitalized a cent of software and they were ambivalent about it. On the one hand, they wanted to see it become the way to do things so that they could capitalize in the future, but they didn't want to have to go back and restate a whole bunch of stuff. And then you had IBM who had their own position.

What I found interesting when I went to the FASB was that their fundamental issue was: we're not going to do anything that makes IBM restate their balance sheet. So their inclination was to simply codify in the standard whatever IBM had been doing because that was the easy way to go.

Schoenberg: You know, Gary, I was involved in the ADAPSO effort from the beginning. I did not know until something like three years after the process started that IBM capitalized software.

Durbin: They had two billion dollars worth.

Schoenberg: It did not appear on their balance sheet, they never mentioned it. Only when they started to realize that the wording being developed for the standards could affect them, did they suddenly pop up. And they did something very clever. They tried to get the definition of who was covered by the standards to be only the software industry. The original draft didn't say software industry, it said software. But if you look at the original capitalization ruling, you will see that it excludes hardware

113

companies. It left open the question of what IBM is; it said for those companies in the computer services industry.

Another group that it excluded was users, for similar reasons, because they knew the users would capitalize it. *We* did not know the users would capitalize it. They knew it and they were getting all this back door input that we didn't really have.

It is definitely true that there were always conflicts between small and large in the trade association, but I can proudly say that, generally speaking, the larger companies—and certainly those that were involved in this decision—understood that they were representing a broader constituency. And a lot of the things we eventually fought through, including such things as how you had to adopt the standard, were focused around small companies.

I constantly raised the issue about the analysts. FASB said, "What do the analysts want?" Of course, this is a different time and we all know now what we think of analysts. [*Laughter*] But I thought that even back then, when FASB said, "We asked independent people, the analysts."

And I went off the wall. Independent??!! Now, their motive was not the same as it is now. Their motive was predictability. They didn't care about whether you had good results or bad results. They only wanted to be able to predict them. So, naturally, anything that spreads revenue, anything that does something along those lines, is clearly in their self-interest. But they were pure of heart. [*Laughter*]

At any rate, the small company versus large company issue was there. It's still there, Gary. It's a big part of the problem. The rules that they have adopted are horrendous for small companies. Much worse than the rules we would ever had made. They're terrible. And their justification is: can't measure them, no past history. Even in some of the most basic new rules they have a thing like "collectability." Well, how do you demonstrate collectability if you haven't been in the business very long?

Durbin: On the capitalization issue, you're absolutely right that the accountants wanted to look at it backwards. During the time we were building software at Tesseract, we couldn't capitalize. If we could have, we might have had maybe a million dollars on our books at any point in time, and that was writing down at a very fast clip. But then we went through an acquisition and the accountants came back in and said, "Oh, now we're going to take a look at this." Twenty-five million dollars was the asset they put on the books in the acquisition because now we were part of a public company. A twenty-five million dollar asset just appeared out of nowhere, and we had never been able to take advantage of the value up until that point.

Haigh: I have a related question. I'm interested in this issue of how purchasers would be able to account for software and I'm wondering, did ADAPSO have a position on that? Did you find the customer's ability or nonability to capitalize or depreciate a big ticket software purchase would actually make any difference to your company?

Durbin: We tried that pitch because we were selling big ticket software products—software licenses for a couple of million dollars—in the mid '80s and it didn't help.

Schoenberg: Well, the fact is, the buyer could capitalize it, period. What I don't know is how many did. I know it was common to capitalize software purchases, but common is not the same as prevalent. Many did it but maybe many didn't do it. I don't know. There was nothing to prevent you from capitalizing anything that was purchased.

Jerger: We had a smaller company, and our product cost about $300,000. It would get over a budget level and we'd get resistance. And we'd tell them to capitalize it. Usually it worked. [*Laughter*]

Durbin: Well, some of them would and some of them wouldn't. I don't think it ever made a difference in a deal that they could capitalize it. If we couldn't do the deal on the ROI, it didn't matter. Afterwards we'd get to the CFO and we'd tell him what games he could play and either he'd do it or not.

Haigh: So why was it much easier to handle the accounting on the customer side than it was for the suppliers?

Schoenberg: Because of the accounting rules. The accounting rules simply said, if you purchase something, you purchase something. Think about it as inventory that the customer has, OK? But the software company doesn't have inventory, it has a work in process.

Jerger: But if you paid cash for it, all of a sudden it became inventory.

Schoenberg: That's right. In fact, there's been all this talk lately about off balance sheet items. Well, a lot of the early off balance sheet accounting wasn't to make it look like you didn't have assets, it was to make it look like you *did* have assets—another perfect example of how dumb rules get turned on their head. The idea was that if you created a separate entity that you could buy the software from, then you could capitalize it. So we had the opposite of what you're seeing today, which is you keep it off your books because it looks like death. We had the opposite. Was in the '70s...was that they started the R&D partnerships?

Durbin: '70s and early '80s.

Schoenberg: OK, so here you were. You were spending money developing a product and the amount of dollars you were spending was very large relative to both your earnings and your net worth. So it was a material item. And if you did it yourself, it was an expense for that accounting period. If it was done by a group that was related to you but in some way could be defined as independent, it was capitalized.

Durbin: This is still going on. If you look at a couple of deals: PeopleSoft's deal with spinning out their R&D organization, and Rational setting up a company in conjunction with a VC to fund the web conversion of their portfolio products. Both of those have done exactly that to move the expense into this somewhat arm's length relationship and then buy it back and capitalize it when they buy it back.

Schoenberg: That's correct. Another thing. When you run a company you always get to the issue of, well, I could save three cents for the next quarter. [*Laughter*] Or I could recognize the expense earlier. So you ask the question, "When do I need it the most?" And you discover you don't know. I eventually came to the conclusion that I'm doing it straight-up because you know who gets the most confused by playing these games? Not my shareholders. Me. *I* get confused because I don't know what I've done after awhile.

Miller: Larry, I'm going to have to run to our Software Division Board meeting. They're talking about accelerated depreciation and tax credits. [*Laughter*] Thank you all very much.

Durbin: What was amazing was that Tesseract was selling software to companies which, when they bought the product, capitalized an asset that was more than we had on our balance sheet.

Campbell-Kelly: Question. You make accounting sound a lot harder than writing software. [*Laughter*] How much of a distraction was it? Did it create a lot of friction in the development of the software industry?

Durbin: Yeah, I think it did. I didn't know much about accounting. I knew that debits were to the window and credits to the door when I got into this. [*Laughter*]

Schoenberg: He was in a right-handed room. [*Laughter*]

Durbin: And, it was not something that I really wanted to get involved in. But my CFO brought these issues forward and all of a sudden these software accounting issues became survival issues. The accountants changed their mind about how we could treat the development of our software and the bank was going to call my credit line. I mean, that was how critical these issues were. All of a sudden I was on top of these issues big time and spending a lot more time dealing with them than I really wanted to. I wanted to be involved in software development and working on the next product and so forth. It ended up taking a lot of time and I ended up becoming expert on this very small aspect of accounting.

Jerger: I agree, but if what you're asking is, "Did it ever forestall someone from going ahead and developing new stuff?" I expect not. We went ahead and developed the stuff. We got angry as the devil about it and we went nuts trying to deal with it. But you had to develop new products, so you did. You never said, "Oh well, because of the accounting problem, I'm not going to do it."

Durbin: But it did affect investment.

Jerger: Oh, yeah, it affected investment.

Durbin: For us, it slowed down the ability to raise money, big time. And that's the issue that drove me crazy.

Campbell: It had a big impact on investment decisions. For example, the impact on the decision to open a new office or buy a company was extraordinary. Both Larry and I, for example, did several dozen acquisitions. You could spend three million dollars in cash to open an office and get it to cash flow breakeven, or you could write a check to someone who had a business in that city and buy a cash flow breakeven business.

One would think these were the same. The three million dollars you would spend to open an office was current expense in the five quarters or so before you got to breakeven status—a terrible cost. You could only afford to do two or three a year. But you could write checks for three million dollars to ten companies in the same month, and it didn't cost you a penny because that was all capitalized.

So, between writing the same three million dollar check and applying it in two different ways, there were totally different accounting treatments. And the investment community, which wanted to measure consistent earnings, would punish one and applaud the other and it wasn't logical. It wasn't necessarily good business practice.

Schoenberg: Martin, I think in some degree that this response is overstated. It's overstated because one person says that he had a problem with getting money. Dave Campbell talks about the investment community. Well, the question is, "What percentage of people who were developing software were constrained by either one of these factors?" I think that overall it was probably not a huge percentage. That is, many companies were either of a size or didn't have the public pressures—there wasn't the same kind of demand for short-term performance twenty years ago as there is now—so that they weren't affected. I think you're hearing from people who were more on the cusp. I don't think the impact was as general as they said, but I *would* disagree with Doug's statement because I know absolutely, as someone who ran a company, that we decided not to develop products because of the accounting implication.

Jerger: I don't believe that.

Schoenberg: Well, I simply said no to the development.

Jerger: The difference could be that you were a lot bigger company at that point than we were.

Durbin: For you and me, Doug, it was survival. We only built products that we absolutely had to have anyway.

Schoenberg: I'd like to add that it does not mean that the product was not developed. It means I refused to develop it in the context in which it was presented to me. I might have done something akin to what Dave talked about. I might have done something about setting it up as a separate entity. So I'm not implying that it stifled innovation. I'm implying that for those companies for which the reported numbers were significant, it definitely stopped some things from happening.

Durbin: I talked a long time with the CFO at MSA and he felt very strongly that the accounting practices were inhibiting them. And, clearly, MSA lost ground to new companies like PeopleSoft and Tesseract that came and took their markets away from them. And he said it was partly because of their inability to make the investments at the time that they should have.

Schoenberg: One of the other items on the list was valuation. How valuation of software companies was impacted by accounting issues. Well, I think we're really discussing that. I personally think that one of the big differences is small versus large companies, established versus non-established, and whether you had a mix of products and services. At AGS, by the time we were done, we had a lot of software products as well as the services, and it was much easier to handle. You set a budget of so much a year for this sort of thing and you didn't think about it again. That money was just gone.

But I do believe it was a major factor in acquisitions on both sides. It not only meant it was cheaper to buy than to build, but if people are buying companies, then people will create companies to be bought. And the cycle goes round and round.

Campbell: People could create private companies to be bought and public companies could buy them. That was one of the differences.

Schoenberg: Right. I always felt when I evaluated a product internally that no one included in that cost a multiplier for the probability of success. Have you ever wondered in software product companies who paid for the products that failed? You can never find who paid for the failures. They just sort of disappear from the face of the earth.

Durbin: And 80% failed.

Schoenberg: At least. OK, does anyone else have some other issues? I guess we don't have anyone here to talk about the service bureau issues. I don't remember very much about them. I think their problems related to the fact that they were very small companies and it was an educational process. I think one of the things that all of us who were involved with ADAPSO in the early days can be very proud of is the amount of time and energy we put into helping other companies start competing against us. It was not uncommon for someone to get up and tell a competitor how to run a business. It's a pretty extraordinary idea.

I had a conversation with one of the historians here about the difference between people who joined the trade association and those that *didn't* join the trade association. The people who joined the trade association were essentially people who saw the world as not a zero sum game. They said to themselves, helping this guy is not hurting me, it's increasing the total pie. Whereas the people who didn't join tended to be people who saw the world as zero sum. If I help you, it's coming out of my pocket. I bet this is generically true with trade associations.

Campbell: But one of the things that was unique about this industry was that our real competitor was the customer doing it for themselves. And so to the extent that we could make the customer comfortable with giving an outside company responsibility for creating their payroll system, for creating their database, whatever, that was a major hurdle for us to overcome. So we all really did benefit from helping everyone trust that there was a real industry, that these were real companies, and that turning responsibility for a $1,000,000 or $5,000,000 project over to an pretty small outside firm was an appropriate action to take. That was a big deal for us which made it sensible for us all to help each other.

Schoenberg: And, of course, the ultimate reason you help someone is because you think some day it will be you. I helped Dave with the sales tax, but I wasn't just trying to help him survive, I was saying, my god, I could be next.

Campbell: When we had that sales tax meeting in New York, I invited a group of people that I knew would all be affected. And I literally handed out Xeroxed copies of the tax invoice to the company and said, "Guys they got me, they're going to get you." We raised $100,000 at that meeting. And then we spent the money to fight the legislation and two years later we won. It was a long, long fight.

Durbin: We had the same fight in California. Because once New York had done this, then all the other states decided it was a good idea and they implemented some of the drafts of the New York legislation so it was even worse.

Campbell: There were actually words missing in some of the drafts that got picked up by other states. It was an amazing exercise in how legislation gets passed because, although you can question how much accounting impacts a business, taxes can be passed at any time and they truly influence business behavior.

Durbin: Well, the idea of making this *retroactive* for years!   My heart fluttered when I found out.

Jerger: He was absolutely apoplectic when he heard that.

Durbin: Oh, yeah, when I saw Dave's invoice, I went, "Oh my god, if they did that here…"

Schoenberg: Well, it is amazing that tax is as large a line item as most of us ever find on a financial statement and yet very few people pay much attention to it.

Well, let's see, what we can bring together from this.   I think the feeling that I always had was that it wasn't financial issues that were driving companies, which is, I guess, what Doug's been constantly trying to say.

Jerger: As a former accountant.

Schoenberg: The reason is he doesn't want to be liable. [*Laughter*]   But as in all things that we ever deal with, when something is a problem because it's irrational, it comes out in ways you cannot possibly imagine or think about.   I just had an experience with a company I won't mention because this is going to be public record, but we were at a 100% club meeting and the most senior people who ran operating units got up to talk.   And each one of them said he couldn't have been there without the help of his CFO, and my stomach turned.   My stomach actually turned.   I said, "Oh my God!"   I think it was only meant as social courtesy but imagine if it was meant literally.   It's a *terrifying* thought.   And so we can't really hide from the implications of allowing other people to control how we report our numbers to ourselves.

You know, my whole thing is that I don't produce accounting reports for the outside world.   I produce them to help run the company.   And that's how accounting should be.   It should help you run the company, not be some goofy idea of how someone else should read them.   I studied the background on accounting rules when I went to the FASB.   Accounting rules were set up originally to help *creditors* not owners.   To help creditors determine whether or not they could get their money back.   It was done by foreign governments. So you can understand in that context why being conservative, or careful, I guess is a better word, would be a useful thing. They weren't meant to literally quantify the process that you were going through. That principle never changed even though the use of it totally changed,

Jerger: I get *CFO* magazine. If you read that, you see that they are promoting being part of the operating effort. So I'm not sure that what those people said was just a social courtesy. The CFO really impacts a lot sometimes. It annoys me as I flip through the magazine that they are doing too much that affects how a company decides to do things from an operating perspective. But they're also kind of stuck with it.

Schoenberg: You know of all the current problems with Arthur Andersen. I'm head of an audit committee where Arthur Andersen is the auditor and my first response was, "Listen, it's the goddamn company's numbers, not the auditors' numbers, don't give me this crap." But they've explained to me that, in some cases, the auditors have actually suggested procedures that might be beneficial to the company. I personally had never heard that before. I never had an accountant come to me and tell me, "You know, if you did this you'd get a different treatment." Never in my life.

Jerger: They're probably afraid to. [*Laughter*]

Durbin: Larry, to address the point that you were making earlier, I think it's a very, very important point that in the early period the accounting rules were of no help to somebody who was trying to manage the company and look to accountability. I have a product here. What was my investment in that, what is my return on that? How do I hold product managers accountable for the money they're spending on R&D? These are the kinds of things that I wanted to look at as a CEO and the accounting policies were completely contrary to that. My CFO said, "Well, we can do this for our internal management, but for reporting, we're going to have to do something completely different." So, the way you're looking at the business and the way anybody is going to look at it from the outside are going to be diametrically opposed.

Schoenberg: Well, our time is up. Thank you all very much. I learned plenty and I hope we recorded something that we can use in the future.

Telecommunications Issues Workshop

Moderators: Joe Markoski and David Allison

Rapporteur: Joan Krammer

Participants: Tim Bergin   Dave Sherman
                               Mike Nugent   Bob Weissman
                               Warner Sinback

Markoski: I'm Joe Markoski. I'm the moderator of this session on telecommunications issues. David Allison is co-moderator. He is from the Smithsonian. And Joan Krammer is rapporteur for the session.

The rules are that you need to identify yourself and your company for the tape, so let me go around the table very quickly so we can state who we are and who we worked for at the relevant periods of time. Again, my name is Joe Markoski. I initially was with Wilkinson, Cragen and Barker and then with Squire, Sanders and Dempsey. From 1976 to 1996, I served as telecommunications counsel to ADAPSO and then ITAA.

Sherman: I'm Dave Sherman. I was general counsel for GE Information Services during the relevant period. Today, I finally found my calling. I'm retired and do nothing. [*Laughter*]

Allison: I'm David Allison, a curator at the Smithsonian.

Bergin: I'm Tim Bergin. I teach Computer Science at American University and I am the editor-in-chief of the *Annals of the History of Computing*.

Nugent: I'm Mike Nugent. I had two jobs, actually, during that time. I was staff attorney for ADAPSO for part of that time and then represented Electronic Data Systems on the ADAPSO Telecommunications Committee.

Sinback: I'm Warner Sinback. During the entire period that we are talking about here, I worked for General Electric. I founded GE Information Services in 1965, which was the first online information service company in the world.

Markoski: The goal of the session is to develop useful information about why the programs that ADAPSO pursued during the relevant period, which in this case is the '60s, '70s and '80s, were important to the member companies. To give us some focus as to what ADAPSO did during the relevant period, I've put together a summary for us to review. Then we can talk about the specific issues as to the who's and why's.

The first thing that struck me, and as evidenced by the small size of this group today, is that telecommunications issues were a very small part of ADAPSO's activities. There were, at any one point in time, only a handful of companies that were actively involved in the committee. I think maybe, in its heyday, you might have had ten companies involved. Within ADAPSO, it was driven by what was first called the Computer Timesharing Section, which was next named the Remote Processing Services Section, and then later renamed the Network-Based Information Services Section. I think it's now called the Internet Commerce and Communications Division. So it was a small group and it was also not a very popular activity within ADAPSO because it wasn't considered mainstream for the association. One quote that still sticks in my mind is a former ADAPSO President calling it "that big turkey." [*Laughter*]

And also the thing that struck me is that, for the issues we focused on, ADAPSO really was a voice by itself. CCIA was active for awhile but they fell by the wayside. CBEMA was active for awhile but they fell by the wayside. There was an ad hoc users committee but it really didn't focus on the same issues. Every once in awhile we'd have a coincidence of views. So, over the years, it really was ADAPSO that was fighting the battles.

The second thing that came to mind was that, for a small group, the association was very effective. If you think that the Internet is the success of the industry in terms of what it has done and what it has brought, one of the reasons the Internet is the way that it is today is largely because ADAPSO's goal was to keep online services unregulated, and the Internet is unregulated. The Internet is not dominated by any of the phone companies, which was something we were always concerned about—telephone companies extending their monopoly beyond communications. Probably *the* most important thing, based on looking around the world, is that access to the Internet is priced on a flat rate basis in this country. Most other places, it's not, and it hasn't had nearly the penetration it's had in the U.S. ADAPSO spent a lot of time and money on that issue—not flat rate access to the Internet, but the principles that led to it. Both within the United States and elsewhere, we fought the efforts of the telecommunications carriers to replace flat rate private line services with usage-sensitive data services. If we had not had leased lines, there probably would not have been the

Internet, at least as we know it now, or it would have been a carrier offering as opposed to what it has become.

One of the reasons I think telecom was never a mainstream activity for ADAPSO is everyone thought it was about the telephone companies. In reality, ADAPSO's telecom activities had nothing to do with telephone companies. ADAPSO's goal was to keep the industry from being regulated. That issue was fought at the FCC in the First, Second and Third Computer Inquiries when the carriers were trying to expand the scope of regulated communications to include a lot of what ADAPSO member companies did. And, as soon as we won that, they came back and opened another FCC proceeding, the Protocol Processing Inquiry, which is basically what Internet access is today. The carriers wanted that regulated, and we successfully fought that. Then the states wanted to regulate information services and we fought a lot of battles with the various states to stop that.

The next issue we pursued was fair competition which was, basically, to keep the telephone companies from cross-subsidizing their competitive computer service offerings, or reserving communications facilities for their services and denying them to other companies. One of the debates I remember was with AT&T, which was an ADAPSO member. The AT&T representative said, "Why are you trying to keep us out of the business?" And Dave Sherman said, "You're standing on my air hose, that's why." And that's the way we viewed it at that point in time.

Those issues came up in the Computer Inquiries regarding how we could get access to the network when the FCC was developing open-network architecture. When the Bell System was broken up, the issue was the line-of-business restrictions on the Bell companies, and what ultimately became the Telecommunications Act in 1996, which actually started in 1976. That was a twenty-year endeavor to enact that legislation.

We preserved not only cost-based leased lines, but also cost-based local access, because one of the things that the telephone industry as a whole wanted to do was to make information service providers buy facilities by the minute. And if you paid for facilities by the minute, it would either kill the demand for services or just make it so much more expensive that purchasers would reach the limit of their willingness to spend money.

With Phil Onstad of Control Data Corporation, the people from GE, and others, we fought efforts by foreign incumbent monopoly telephone companies to eliminate international leased lines which they saw as a threat to their revenue. The Germans went so far as to say, I think this was to GE, that they had to terminate their leased line in a single computer in Germany and do all their data processing in Germany. Which was a fairly transparent restriction on the efforts of US companies to do business over there. And we fought those kinds of actions with all of the carriers around the world.

We were dealing with essentially the same issues over and over again—sometimes concurrently, sometimes not. It was a situation in which the same issue would show up in multiple FCC proceedings and it was, in one sense, a war of attrition. We had to go toe-to-toe with the telephone industry. If we didn't, we were going to lose. So it really wasn't, in the view of the member companies, an optional policy exercise. If we didn't do it, we'd be regulated, we'd be paying usage-sensitive prices, or whatever the various threats were. So that's some background on what ADAPSO was doing on these issues.

We've been asked to identify which ADAPSO companies were in the lead on these issues for future researchers who want to check them out.

Sherman: Well, that relates back to the question of where did the RPSS/NBIS group fit within the larger organization of ADAPSO. The vast majority of the member companies of ADAPSO were small companies. The big companies that paid the bulk of the dues to the organization became members of ADAPSO because they were interested in these competitive and regulatory issues that most of the rest of the organization cared very little about. Many of the other companies were members for the purpose of cross-fertilization, making deals among themselves, having an excuse to go on a tax-subsidized vacation to attend management conferences, etc. They had no interest at all in these regulatory issues but they needed us because we paid the bulk of the dues. We represented the major companies: AT&T, GE, IBM, EDS, CDC, Tymshare.

Nugent: These were the companies that used the phone lines to deliver products and services to customers versus the smaller companies which were developing software.

Sherman: We were a very small percentage of the ADAPSO member companies. There were about six different sections of ADAPSO as I recall. Ours was probably the smallest section in terms of membership. But, we probably paid about 80% of the dues and supported the operations of the organization.

Allison: You mentioned some of the companies, but it would be useful to note which were the real leaders in that section.

Markoski: I have a list here of companies that at various times had different roles: ADP represented by Fred Lafer and Joe Gallo. AT&T. Boeing, through Boeing Computer Services. Control Data Corporation represented by Phil Onstad, Steve Beach and Bill Warner. Comshare was one of the leading forces of the telecommunications activity in the early '70s, represented by Rick Crandall and John Duffendack. Computer Sciences Corporation, when they had a network. Roger Allen was its representative. EDS: Nugent, Jeff Heller, John Lynn. Fujitsu kind of came in and out. They never really got active. GE: Sherman and Sinback. Honeywell came in for awhile: Helen Golding. IBM: Maryanne Angel. Bill Warner also represented IBM at a later point. National Data Corporation: George Shea, Mike Ingram. Bob Weissman has just joined us. His old company National CSS, represented by Les Srager used to participate in these activities. Reynolds & Reynolds popped in for awhile with Ronald Harwith. Sperry Univac. Tymshare with Tom O'Rourke, Warren Burton, Joanne Couche, Warren Prince.

Nugent: Lance Swann.

Markoski: Lance Swann was with CSC. Xerox Computer Services came in. But, I think the ones that were the most active probably would have been ADP, AT&T, Boeing, CDC, EDS, GE, IBM, and National Data. Tymshare at one point was extraordinarily active, so it varied over time.

Nugent: As some of the access rate issues came up, smaller companies that were dependent on the phone line to deliver services were worried about the rates going up, or they were worried about the ability to interconnect to particular users, so they joined with the large companies in ADAPSO.

Weissman: As you recall in the '70s, one of the major issues was the Bell System's effort to expand the use of message units because of the impact that would have on the cost of communications. I remember that as a big issue.

Sinback: When they saw the potential impact on their costs, the little companies got interested and then as soon as that issue was settled they went away.

Markoski: That really was a problem within ADAPSO because when ADAPSO was dealing with the banking industry disputes, a lot of service bureaus were affected, and you could get those smaller companies involved. Bernie Goldstein mentioned in this morning's session on banking litigation that the insurance agents could hit a button and get ten thousand people calling Capitol Hill screaming about the banks and insurance. ADAPSO never could do that because it didn't have the numbers and, except for the issue that was just raised with respect to access charges becoming usage-sensitive, these issues didn't affect that many people. So the one thing that we could never do was to have Capitol Hill bombarded with phone calls from angry constituents.

Sinback: The one time that we really surprised the FCC, we loaded their mail baskets with stuff for the better part of two weeks. We inundated them when the issue came up of paying usage-sensitive charges for access. There were enough people whose ox was going to be gored by that ruling that we were able to get a large group to respond and it made a hell of an impression.

Weissman: Another area where it was hard to get traction because of the narrow scope of the interest group were issues being created out of CCITT. There were a relatively small number of ADAPSO member companies, less than five or six as I recall, who had global packet networks and were very interested in what was happening at CCITT. Phil Onstad was, in effect, the de facto representative of ADAPSO at CCITT because he went on behalf of Control Data, but he would report back to us what was going on and what was on their agenda.

Sinback: It was the nearest thing to an international regulatory body for telecommunications.

Markoski: We started that battle in 1976. As each one of our companies wanted to go to Hong Kong or Singapore or Germany or Japan or the UK, either the incumbent phone company in the other country, or the US international long-distance carriers, did what they could to try and get rid of leased lines. They wanted us all to move on to their usage-sensitive services.

Sinback: Well, they maintained the right covered in their usage contract to control the usage to which a telephone circuit was put. If it was anything other than voice they immediately raised objections. And so we had to fight for these companies. We fought in the international body which was

CCITT, but then we also had to fight this individually with the countries. I spent thousands and thousands of hours fighting with Japan, China, Singapore, and Taiwan. I could run down a list of fifty countries and each one of them was an individual battle and in some of them we had to go to great lengths. The PTT's in most countries were responsible for postal service as well as for telecom service, so the minute email showed its face, they had a very strong interest based on their responsibility for the mail. In Belgium, for example, we had to finally go to the European court and file a complaint against the Belgians to permit us to use the telephone circuits in Belgium for electronic mail. And we won the case. They were admonished by the European court and instructed that they were to make the circuits available for us. But that wasn't the only case. In Singapore, we had a running battle for several years before we finally won. Hong Kong was another one that we fought for at least two years.

Sherman: Italy as well.

Sinback: The Italian government was a pain in the neck.

Markoski: The Italian government actually adopted a rule that would get rid of leased lines or make the price usage-sensitive. So it wasn't a subterfuge of moving us from one service to another. They actually wanted the international regulatory system changed.

Sinback: The battle that we had in the United States with AT&T was really replicated many times internationally and, of course, it was not a simple thing to win against AT&T. Their original approach to the use of their circuits was the same as the international people. They said, "You can't use our circuits for that, it's just not permissible." Well, the question is, what *is* permissible then?

When we first started timesharing in 1965, the telephone companies were amazed. The first one was Mountain States Telephone in Phoenix. Our usage of the circuits constituted what they felt was a threat to the way they managed telecommunications. If they had a hundred ordinary subscribers for telephone service, they configured their central office in a way that was based on the probability of how many people of that hundred would call at the same time and based on an average holding time between one and two minutes. It was actually 1.45 minutes. So this meant that they could configure their central office to handle twenty simultaneous calls with no problems.

Well, when timesharing came along, people signed on from a terminal through an acoustic coupler and they would stay on for an hour and a half. All of a sudden all of the calculations that the telephone company used to manage the process were thrown out because they had to now take into account this added kind of service. For example, we brought our very first system up on Labor Day of 1965. We had worked with Mountain States Telephone Company for the better part of two months, trying to explain to their engineers what was going to happen. They looked at us and said, "We know how to run this thing so you guys stop trying to tell us what to do." We had our computer center right in the center of Phoenix and the day we brought our system up we pretty much destroyed business communications in the middle of Phoenix for a whole morning. And they suddenly realized that what we were talking about really was something that was different from what they did before.

So AT&T, through Bell Labs, developed something that I believe they called a timesharing assembly. When we came to them for the second system, which we put in Schenectady, New York, they configured the New York Telephone offices there to handle it. Then we installed systems in a number of cities.

Nugent: That was when AT&T controlled local and long distance service.

Sinback: That's right. But the interesting thing was the marketing people at AT&T now sat back and said, "They're using our system for free, and they're making money off our system. So how do we get at them?"

The first case, I believe, was in Kentucky. They filed a tariff with the state regulatory body in Kentucky for what they called a timesharing assembly. Business lines at that time were costing us about fifteen dollars a month average across the country. This timesharing assembly tariff raised that price to about sixty dollars a month per line—an enormous increase. Well, AT&T was everywhere in the U.S. and we knew if it happened one place, it was going to happen all over. So we appealed to the regulatory body in the State of Kentucky to overturn this ruling and lost. The only step left for us was to go to court which we did and we won.

Sherman: That wasn't ADAPSO, that was GE.

Sinback: That was GE but this is all tied in with the movement in ADAPSO to follow these issues. Subsequently, they tried in several other states and lost and, finally, the whole thing sort of fell by its own weight.

Markoski: If you were to look back at these issues, which do you think would be the most significant ones that we were involved in?

Sinback: Well, that's certainly one. We would never have developed the industry if AT&T had succeeded in what they were doing because the economics were not there.

Weissman: There was another issue related to AT&T. In the mid-'70s, AT&T developed and began to license Unix. Part of the history of ADAPSO was coalescing forces to deal with 800-pound gorillas like the banks and IBM. Now AT&T showed up as a potential serious competitor on the software side. Obviously, that effort never really developed into a full-fledged software business but there were a lot of cycles burned within ADAPSO during that period.

Nugent: Because they wanted to offer that software to the public at rates that were pretty cheap. It raised the whole question of AT&T, the phone company, offering computer services and software using a rate payer funded subsidy to do that.

Weissman: I think that what happened was that the AT&T got diverted. First in defending itself against, and then dealing with the inevitability of, the break-up, and the focus just shifted. The opportunity, if there was one there for AT&T, was lost.

Markoski: One of the things we talked about at the banking session this morning which really ties in with this, was that the ADAPSO approach was pretty much uniform across all of these debates or fights. The argument never was that the phone companies shouldn't be in the timesharing business or shouldn't be in the remote processing business. It was that, if they were in the business, they couldn't unfairly exploit their monopoly, or buy their facilities wholesale when we had to buy them retail for the underlying transmissions.

Sinback: A level playing field.

Markoski: Just give me a level playing field to compete on.

Allison: AT&T was there in the ADAPSO debates?

Markoski: Yes, they were.

Allison: How did that factor in? Was there a debate within ADAPSO? Did ADAPSO go out with a unified voice or how did they state their position?

Markoski: Let's see if we can pinpoint when they joined. I think it was before the breakup.

Weissman: It was in the mid-'70s, I think.

Markoski: Okay, mid-'70s, so things were fairly contentious then.

Sinback: Well, their first thought, I feel reasonably sure, was that they would come in and change the position of ADAPSO. In the Telecom Committee, for example, their first representatives were very contentious. I'll give you one example. Our policy in ADAPSO always was: when the committee makes up its mind and takes a position, it's everybody's position. There are no minority votes. So the first time a contentious issue came up after they joined the committee, they said, "Well, fine, we understand the position you've taken. But as a paying member, we want a footnote that says AT&T did not concur with this. " I was chairman of the committee at the time and I refused. I was asked what my authority was to refuse it, and I said, "Well, it's in the bylaws that we've adopted that this is the way that we operate." The reason that we adopted this, by the way, was that CBEMA had been paralyzed by that kind of maneuver and I think that's why AT&T thought it would succeed. So they said, "Well, we don't buy that rule. We want to take this to the Board of Directors of ADAPSO." They did. And they lost.

Sherman: Not without a hell of a fight.

Sinback: Oh, it was a hell of a fight.

Sherman: Because AT&T paid a disproportionately large amount of membership dues, and a lot of the other member companies within ADAPSO who weren't interested in these issues were trying to...

Weissman: Keep them in the tent, keep the dues in the tent.

Sherman: Exactly.

Weissman: Talk just a moment about the sociology of that. I don't remember what the date was but it was at a conference in Hawaii. I set up a meeting between the rep from AT&T and Ed Kane, who at that time was the representative from IBM. I'd spoken to Ed and said, "This guy doesn't know how to deal with this trade association. We would like to keep him here but he's going to need to understand how it works. I would appreciate it if you privately just explained to him how a big company does it successfully." That effort failed. [*Laughter*] Ed failed. I failed. But we made an effort to try to get them to adjust their perspective. As Warner said, it was very clear to us early on that they were coming in with the view that they would become the 800-pound gorilla and that their dues would allow them to shape the agenda and the decisions.

[Ed. Note: The conference referred to took place in October, 1980.]

Sinback: Which they had been successfully doing in other places.

Allison: And so, for the record, how did it finally play out?

Markoski: What ultimately happened is they accepted the rule that there were no footnotes. They would argue like hell about their position but they figured out after awhile that there were certain things that we just weren't going to back off on. We weren't going to back off on no regulation of computer services. We weren't going to back off the requirement that they had to enter the industry through a separate subsidiary. But on the margin they could keep us from being gratuitously insulting, which we were sometimes known for. [*Laughter*]

Sherman: It wasn't gratuitous. [*Lots of laughter*]

Markoski: And there were things, on the margin, that were really important for them that were not important to the other members. I think that the way it really started working is that they replaced the representative. They sent a nice guy, Bob Lejeune, and we always tried to let him go home with something. He could always go back and say, "You know, they were going to do such-and-such and I persuaded them not to."

Allison: So they stayed and continued to pay the high dues, the whole bit.

Various voices: Yes, yes.

Allison: And worked the margins and felt like even just doing that was valuable to them.

Markoski: Then once the Bell System was divided, they were on the same side of the fence as everybody else because they were facing competition in the long distance business. I mean, perspective is everything. They actually found it to be a very good vehicle for them to get their agenda pressed when they didn't want it to be just another AT&T issue. They could hide behind ADAPSO as all member companies did. You don't always want to be in the front. So it really did work out pretty well.

Allison: Did MCI come into the business, have any impact on this?

Sinback: MCI was very active at one point in the committee.

Nugent: Bill McGowan.

Sinback: McGowan had very strong views on competition in long distance but they weren't in this business. They weren't in the value-added service business at that point so they didn't have the real incentive to do as much as the others.

Nugent: Their primary competition with AT&T was not in voice transmission, it was in the private data transmission business.

Sinback: They were interested in the regulatory side of the thing rather than permission for value-added services.

Markoski: If you look at the pictures out in the hallway, you'll see there are a lot of pictures of congressional testimony. Nine out of ten of those testimony or congressional hearings were on telecommunications issues. There's one up there with Steve Beach and Bill McGowan, the founder of MCI. There's another one up there with representatives of manufacturers and competitive long distance carriers. ADAPSO worked very closely with similarly situated organizations in other industries, the competitive telephone industry, for example.

Allison: We heard this morning that, on the banking issue, ADAPSO had some pretty important friends on the hill, particularly on the House side. How did Congress respond? Did they take positions on this? Were there different congressmen with different positions?

Sinback: We had some pretty important friends up there on the telecom regulatory side also.

Markoski: Ed Markey from Massachusetts.

Sinback: The congressman from California who lost his job

Markoski: That's where I cut my teeth in the Congress. He brought me in like a lamb to slaughter.

Sherman: Lionel Van Deerlin.

Bergin: Who were your enemies? What members of Congress did you consider to be on the other side of the fence from you? If these were your friends, who were your enemies? Anybody in particular?

Nugent: I wouldn't say ADAPSO had any particular enemies who targeted us. We were not that big a target.

Markoski: The Telecom Act of 1996 started in 1976 and that's when AT&T was pushing the Bell Bill to end the antitrust lawsuit. It was in 1981, I think, when ADAPSO really got active because that is when Ed Markey was a freshman, Congressman Matsui was a freshman, and a couple of other freshmen...

Sherman: A lot of our battles weren't fought in Congress but at the regulatory level with the FCC. I think probably more of our efforts were involved with the FCC than with legislation.

Allison: And was the Commission more evenly split? Did you have to work with individual members?

Sinback: We had to work with individual members, basically. Congress, I don't think, was ever heavy-handed in either direction. The one policy position the FCC took way back was that competition, if it was available, should replace regulation. That was a basic policy that they followed and still are following, for that matter. That was a real change when they adopted that. Who was the chairman of the commission?

Markoski: Ferris.

Sinback: Ferris was the guy. They had monthly breakfasts where the heads of various regulatory agencies got together and Ferris was the guy who came to that group with the idea that things that had been regarded as a necessary monopoly because of their configuration and the economics and so forth, maybe no longer qualified, that competition may be possible and they should think about this.

Nugent: Fowler was the Chairman during the whole debate about what is regulated and what isn't. They were trying to bring into the regulated sphere certain things that were closely related to data processing. I would say that Fowler was the worst of all of those guys, don't you think?

Markoski: Probably.

Nugent: Probably the most antagonistic.

Sinback: Yes, he was, but that policy shift in the FCC is what really led to deregulation and the break-up of AT&T and so forth.

Allison: Who were the major players in these policy debates other than ADAPSO and the other trade associations you mentioned earlier? Did individual companies participate? Were there coalitions?

Sinback: There wasn't tremendous participation from big companies. There were half a dozen.

Nugent: GTE Telenet was there.

Markoski: Generally the way it lined up was: you had the interexchange carriers pretty much as a block; the Bell Companies and the local exchange carriers were a block; and the large users tended to operate together. There weren't too many information service provider organizations. Those companies were basically represented by ADAPSO. If it was really important, an individual company might participate. IBM always participated but they were flush with money. They participated in ADAPSO, but they were also there on their own on specific issues.

But, yeah, we always tried to align ourselves with other people or, at least get other people to not unnecessarily trip over our toes, because what is regulated and unregulated is a very technical issue. It didn't look like a big deal but, if we had lost that battle, Internet access would be regulated telephone service today. The issue was whether what goes in looks like what comes out. If there was any change in it, it was on our side of the line, and if it was just a pure pipe, it was on the telephone company side of the line. Once you got pregnant by blurring that, you lost.

So we would fight all that stuff tooth and nail. That was what Mike was referring to. Fowler, during this period, wanted to let the phone companies into this business because it was high tech. The phone companies didn't want to offer it on an unregulated basis because then they couldn't subsidize it. They wanted it to be regulated. So there really were some very fundamental disagreements about how the world should look.

Sinback: But these simple tests were very useful because, if you looked at a bit stream going in and coming out, it was very easy to argue with the telephone company whether it was exactly the same at the end of the transmission. Has it changed in any way? And if it has, it's value-added, so therefore you can't regulate it.

Sherman: We made that argument over and over and over again on every floor we could imagine.

Nugent: If the Internet had been treated like a regulated service, it would have meant that only those who were common carriers could provide it, which would have made for a profoundly different Internet.

Sinback: Well, the Internet would never really have happened.

Markoski: From my perspective, and I suppose that of the historians, the irony is that the people who I think benefited the most from the Internet were software people, who were the ones who had the least interest in all of these issues at the time.

Bergin: How did they benefit more than others?

Markoski: My view is that if the Internet didn't exist, people wouldn't be using PC's the way that they are using them now because they'd be just stand-alone computing devices. But with the Internet, people are buying every software application you can think of and going online with it.

Sherman: It created a larger market.

Bergin: Yeah, but I'm not following the logic. I'm not disagreeing, I'm just not following the logic because the people who jumped on the Internet early were using freeware. Netscape was free.

Weissman: I don't know if I'm saying what Joe is saying but I think that what the Internet did was to change the computing network topology. The fact of the Internet created a communications capability which companies have made use of by building software which allows that communications component to become a fundamental part of the computing environment. If that component wasn't there, it would still be like the topology of the '70s and '80s with data here and customers there and lines in between. Software was what enabled the change to happen and software has also taken advantage of its existence. The whole enterprise software market would not have developed as it has if that topology wasn't available.   Software companies couldn't build it because they don't have the capital to do it. But they have taken advantage of its existence. Building extranets and VPNs and everything else that came out of that change in communications has enabled these markets to form.

Bergin: I would still disagree, because up through '93, '94 most global corporations had very robust networks whether they built them or leased them or put them together in various and sundry ways. If you're talking about the explosion of every Tom, Dick and Harry getting on there and doing email on the Internet, that has nothing to do with software companies.

Weissman: During that period I was running Dun & Bradstreet, which had a very robust global network with tens of thousands of online customers. The economics of that kind of structure was very different than what is available today. There were major markets and major market segments where you could not justify the infrastructure costs to deliver online. So, yeah, there were high-speed lines running data to a customer like General Motors and you squirt data down to him and back and forth. But the guy at the other end of the spectrum, the other end of the market space, didn't have a PC, didn't have an Internet, didn't have a private network connection and couldn't afford to put one in. That's the economics that changed. Whether the Internet resulted from that, or the Internet caused that infrastructure to go in with all the problems in telecommunications today as a result, it's there. And it has enabled these companies to expand, in addition to all those dot-coms who said, "I'm going to take advantage of its existence and try to do something with it."

Sinback: There is a principle in the Internet that is probably the most important principle and that is the packet-switched network. The comparison between that technology and the ordinary leased line technology that Weissman was just talking about is *phenomenal* in terms of the economics. It's hundreds of times more efficient cost-wise to have the packet-switched technology. So that technology in the Internet became a great facilitator for a lot of things, one of which is the software side. There are many others.

Weissman: When public packet networks became a real part of the market, which was the early '80s as I recall...

Markoski: Telenet.

Weissman: Telenet, right. The market price per hour of a 1200 baud connection, whatever was the standard at that time, was in the four to six dollar-an-hour range. Okay? Now compare that with the effective cost per hour for a 28K, 56K connection on the Internet. It is at least one order of magnitude cheaper, maybe two orders of magnitude. It changes the economics of lots of services hugely.

Bergin: Does it follow that corporations like Dun & Bradstreet have then abandoned their private networks?

Weissman: In 1994, I sold the global packet network of Dun & Bradstreet to Eunetcom which was a consortium of the German and the French PTTs, because tariffs had changed and there was the availability of other technologies which made it cheaper for us to get reliable service in other ways. Eunetcom bought it because they wanted to get into the global data communications business but they didn't want our backbone of Tandem computers. They wanted the 400 or 500 people we had employed around the world servicing that network so that they could get into a new service area.

Bergin: So they bought the experience and the knowledge that came with it.

Weissman: Exactly.

Markoski: IBM got rid of its network. GE's gotten rid of its network.

Sinback: If you look back at the beginning of the period we are talking about, the early '60s, and you compare the cost of communications per bit, and compare that to today, the difference is just *phenomenal*. The cost of communication has fallen to the point where today, in many applications, it's trivial. It's in the rounding error. Whereas back in the early time I'm talking about, it was an enormous part. When we first started out with our information service, the cost of telecommunications was 30% or 40% of the cost of the service.

Weissman: To put that in absolute terms, at National CSS in 1973, CPU, storage, I/O, and connect were all charged separately to a timesharing user. My recollection is that we got twenty dollars an hour for connect and, in 1973, that was 300 baud, with an acoustical coupler. Twenty bucks an hour. In 1973 dollars.

Allison: Let me push a little bit on Joe's assumption that if the regulatory battle hadn't been won, things would have a different pattern. Do you think that there is no other model? Assuming that you'd lost that case, would AT&T have continued to hold up its prices? Were there no other innovations or other pressures on them that would have provided another path to get some of the innovations that came in later such as packet-switching?

Markoski: I think you have to identify whether you're talking about it being regulated or unregulated, or about flat rate pricing. I think you have to separate the issues because I can come up with a different answer depending on which one you're talking about.

Allison: I was thinking about the regulated/unregulated issue.

Markoski: Okay. Let's think out loud. If you were at the Bell System, and could offer the Internet or you could keep on selling leased lines and dial-up at twice the cost and no one else could offer the Internet, would you have introduced it? Why did the Bell System have black telephones for so long?

Weissman: Let's move forward to the current day. Take a look at the people who control the local loop today. If there is a consensus among the pundits and the forecasters, it is that what is required is broadband connectivity. It drove a lot of people to over-invest and it's caused a few bankruptcies here and there, but it hasn't changed the message that for the future we must have broadband. Now, contrast that with the local loop providers' response to DSL, which is certainly not brand new.

Markoski: Over-priced.

Weissman: It is consistently overpriced, underserviced.

Markoski: Quirky.

Bergin: And largely unavailable.

Nugent: And look how they are still trying to put access charges on it.

Weissman: In an environment where people are saying, "If you build it they will come." There *is* a demand for broadband.

Allison: Do you think they will finally be challenged by wireless instead of the normal way of opening up competition?

Weissman: Well I'm an old RF engineer so I really don't want to get started on that. [*Laughter*] I think they will be challenged by other technologies. Certainly they *are* being challenged today. When you look at the number of installs of DSL versus the number of installs of cable modems, cable has been much more aggressive in capturing that market.

Sinback: But going back to one of the earlier points. If you assume that deregulation had not occurred and everything stayed the same, as a monopoly, the idea of competing with that was just economically impossible. The cost of the installed base to compete was just absolutely prohibitive. It just never would have happened.

Allison: That's really the early MCI story, isn't it?

Sinback: It is. And, as Bob said, these people are still acting exactly like monopolists even though they're deregulated.

They're out here digging up the streets. You can't get anywhere in Virginia now because Verizon is in the way digging holes in the street to put down these huge fiber optic cables for which there is no market. It's sad, because what they've been accustomed to is: if you put it in the ground it's going to provide an enormous return on investment. That's no longer true and so it's really turned the whole industry on its head. Except that they don't realize yet that they are on their head, which is just as sad as can be.

For example, one of the things that was available to the telephone companies very early on, even before AT&T was broken up, was that it was possible to transmit at least 50 kilobits and maybe 100 kilobits on the twisted pair wires that come into your house. And yet they never exploited that and they had the pairs coming into every house. All they had to do was to exploit it. Today, DSL really doesn't offer a hell of a lot more than a twisted pair. And yet, it's fifty dollars a month. Amazing story.

Nugent: I'd like to make a couple of points on the international side. ADAPSO, through Control Data's Phil Onstad, was very active in fighting for the right of its members to terminate our lines in our own premises overseas, and not have to terminate them in the central office of the phone company over there. That was a big deal because if you terminated at the phone company, you would then have to get a big line to get to your facilities. Warner talked about there being a restriction on what you could actually send over the lines in other countries, such as electronic mail. You couldn't even get private satellite service. So if you were in India and needed to get from point A to point B and the phone company wasn't doing it for you, you couldn't even set up your private satellite system. So ADAPSO, through various filings through various members, spent a lot of time in the international arena fighting for user rights regarding access to and use of telecom lines and service.

Weissman: There was another issue that we dealt with in the late '70s and early '80s. People began to talk about networking as more than connecting big mainframes down a leased line. That meant talking about distributed computing which raised the issue of co-location, of getting the right to place processors within the network, if you will. That was successfully resisted by AT&T and by the individual phone companies and the industry moved on and has dealt with that topology question in other ways. That was another case where ADAPSO spent its energy trying to cause some change. And again, that was another case where the only members within ADAPSO who were concerned were the biggest companies. And even those companies didn't really have quite the passion needed to pursue it because none of us had business plans ready to go. We could just see this as a future potential which we would use if it was available, but it wasn't as though we were going to die if we didn't have it. Certainly the software companies and the professional services companies couldn't have cared less.

Allison: I'm going to ask you guys a somewhat oddball question. I've often thought that the Internet and the whole international telecommunications structure developed the way that it did in significant part because of the relatively peaceful nature, at least in the Western world, of this time period. Do you think if it had been a different situation in terms of international tension and political strife that this would have been a very different kind of picture? Or do you think technology would have played out the same?

Weissman: I'm sitting here trying to think of evidence of it being different and I'm not coming up with anything. Certainly the relationship between the United States and Europe was good during this period. But it wasn't good with everybody. It wasn't good with the Eastern Bloc, it wasn't good with Russia. It wasn't good with China.

Allison: The pattern in Russia and China, weren't they significantly different?

Weissman: Well, if you want to talk about the infrastructure within a country, yes, I think we can certainly say they're different. But I thought you were asking about the global connect piece.

Allison: Yes, that's right

Weissman: I don't think the global connection was materially affected by those differences.

Nugent: And you had CCITT which is a body of the U.N. and they typically meet no matter what.

Sinback: A hundred and twenty countries.

Nugent: It's even more now. I think it's a hundred and sixty now. The CCITT meets for weeks at a time, made up as it is of professional phone company representatives and government representatives. They discuss these issues and they fight these battles. It's the same issues. The CCITT will come up with recommendations which then tend to get baked into the laws or the practices of the various countries. So these issues of co-location and usage of leased lines and termination of leased lines and pricing were fought out there at the CCITT.

Weissman: They are kind of supernational but they are like the conferences held every four or five years to deal with spectrum issues, where there are some rules of conduct, if you will.

Allison: We tend to think about politics shifting technology but it's really technology shifting politics. I mean in the sense that some of the advantages that come out of this willingness to cooperate and put politics aside, eventually that turns around and shakes the politics of the country.

Sinback: I don't think there is any doubt that the telecommunications revolution affected the fall of the Soviet Union in a big way, a *huge* way.

Allison: Yeah, and changing China, too.

Sherman: How about access to global applications? You had potential users in Russia, for instance, but you didn't have a network access point in Russia because you couldn't provide one there. Those users in Russia would have to get access through their own means to your service, someplace where you did have a network access point, perhaps in Finland, for instance. They found ways of getting to the service, but you were doing the service in Finland, not in Russia.

Weissman: And in Austria, and in Germany.

Sinback: As a matter of fact, we did a survey one time. We had footprints in our network for every user that came in and all we had to do was go back and dig through the data to find them. And long before the Soviet Union fell, we found that we had *a hell of a lot* of users coming in from Finland. And we didn't offer service in Finland. [*Laughter*] And they were regular users. These were people that came in two or three days a week, every week, and it's obvious that they had made an arrangement of some kind. In all the peripheral countries, we had users that were finding their way to our service.

Weissman: If you recall, during those years the Soviet government was still establishing five-year plans for hardware processors. They were trying to build their own processors and it was not politically correct to use an IBM processor or a GE processor and yet the Russian computers didn't work very well. So scientists and software people in those countries got creative.

Markoski: One thing I want to mention is privacy. The privacy battles of ADAPSO began almost twenty years ago. A lot of the issues being fought now were actually articulated back then. And the reason is because the

European Data Protection Directive was floated in the mid-'70s and this group, through Phil Onstad, saw the way it was worded as a real threat to the flow of international commerce. Invisible barriers to invisible trade, it was called. There would be requirements in the name of privacy that we had to process data within a country, we couldn't process it in the US.

Weissman: In fact, in the early '80s, the Bundespost put out a directive which said that personal data and other kinds of data, could not be processed outside the country. So you could not communicate that data online. You delivered a tape to the German border and handed it to somebody who would take it so it could be processed.

Nugent: And this was in the name of privacy.

Weissman: Yes, in the name of privacy.

Sherman: It was a question of where you could store the data.

Weissman: CDC had a problem with the Swedish government.

Markoski: The Swedes always used to say that the plans for the fire alarms in Malmö, Sweden were kept in a computer in Cleveland, Ohio, because they subscribed to Control Data's service. And they said that that was wrong.

Sherman: That wasn't a privacy issue, that was a security issue.

Markoski: That was a security issue, yeah.

Sinback: What happened is a funny story. A reporter was going to do a feature story on fire fighting and went to a fire station in Malmö, Sweden. While he was there working on his story, an alarm came in and he was very interested to see how they responded. A bunch of them ran and got their helmets and equipment, but one guy ran to a teletype terminal and furiously typed something in and then tore off a piece of paper and jumped on the fire truck and out it went. So when they came back, the reporter said, "I'm really terribly curious. I noticed you rushed over to this terminal and you typed and then you took the paper that was printed out." "Oh," the guy said, "those were the directions to the house where the alarm came from, how to get there, you know, directions, street by street." And the reporter said, "Well, where is the computer that's connected to?" "Oh," he says, "we have this service in the United States in a place called Brook Park, Ohio."

[*Laughter*]   So the guy wrote up the story and one of the Ministers in Sweden read this and said, "Oh my god, our fire fighting is all dependent on some computer in Cleveland, Ohio?"

Nugent: One of the other privacy issues that ADAPSO was involved with was the update of the wiretap laws for the digital world.   What are the laws governing interception of electronic data? What are the laws governing access to stored data?   What happens when law enforcement wants to go in and get data?   The rules in existence applied to the old voice transmission world but not to the data transmission world.   ADAPSO really spent a lot of time with others, including the ACLU and a hodgepodge of what you think would be atypical interest groups, to help update the wiretap laws in the digital world.   So that was another example of privacy issues being dealt with first at ADAPSO by this group.

Sinback: We had to make sure they didn't word it so broadly that it would put us out of business.

Bergin: If someone were trying to learn about issues that we've been discussing this last hour and a half, are there any references that you could provide?

Weissman: Those 25 volumes that Luanne Johnson referred to in her talk last night that contain Milt Wessel's files, I would assume are fairly comprehensive.

[*Ed. Note: An announcement was made the previous evening that these files were being donated to the archives at the Charles Babbage Institute.*]

Bergin: Yes, but I meant something condensed somewhere.

Markoski: Well, on the international issues, yes, because these guys helped me write a law review article on the international issues. It's in the *Cornell International Law Journal*, and summarized all the international leased-line battles and the restrictions. On the domestic battles...

Sinback: I've never seen anything.

Markoski: There is a textbook with the laws but it doesn't give you the dynamics.

Nugent: I don't think anyone has ever had the time to write about it.

Bergin: Which is what I guess has got to happen. Somebody's got to sit down and write some of this because no one is going to go out to CBI and go through 25 boxes.

Markoski: And the reality is that a lot of the people involved are dead.

Weissman: I think the answer is you've got to find an eager young doctoral candidate who is looking for a thesis subject and give him those 25 volumes.

Sherman: With respect to things like the amendment to the wire tap law, there is legislative history and committee reports that are available.

Sinback: And congressional testimony.

Allison: Yes, congressional testimony.

Bergin: But I was just hoping that there was a nice article somewhere that explains a lot of this.

Markoski: One of the things ADAPSO used to do was get some Congressman to hold a hearing on these issues because those hearings are published. We'd use it as a platform to air all these problems.

Allison: Actually, a shortcut to archival research, on more subjects than we know, is to go to the records of congressional hearings. It's definitely true on military history, which I used to do a lot of, and I think it's true in this field too. And you go from that back to your original sources. It's still work but not as much.

Weissman: The only weakness with that is the fact that for a long period of time we were really under the radar screen. We were not consistently having congressional hearings.

Allison: I haven't used FCC records. I assume they would exist but I don't know about archival access to them.

Nugent: If you read Computer III for instance, it will take you all through Computer I and II, and it's a real nice history of various efforts.

Weissman: Three is pretty comprehensive. And three really dealt with the telecommunications issues much more heavily than one and two.

Sherman: He's talking about the FCC proceedings called Computer Inquiry I, Computer Inquiry II and Computer Inquiry III. I think No. I was in about 1969.

Weissman: Yeah, that was the original one, and the second one was '73 or something like that, and the third one was '79.

Krammer: If I might ask a question. It's been quite fascinating listening to what people have been saying. A hundred years from now, how would you sum up this period of telecom? What would you want people to know?

Weissman: It marked the change from a regulated monopoly to the democratization, if you will, of communications. If you take a look at the telecommunications world today, it is much richer by any measure, not only in terms of bandwidth and function points but competitive mix, access, usability. And a hundred years from now I think that will be the essential point. The rest of this were skirmishes along the way to creating that.

Sherman: Except that we weren't communications providers. We used communications for the purpose of providing the computer-based services that we made available to US businesses, world businesses.

Sinback: And the other major contribution was the technical developments that flowed out of World War II into this stream of movement toward competition and away from regulation. The merger of those two things created a tremendous period of change.

Weissman: Communication science had halcyon years from 1950 forward.

Allison: As we said earlier, that deregulation pattern is still going on, it's not really done.

Weissman: To your question, Joan, if someone goes back a hundred years from now and asks how would you characterize this change in telecommunications, you would say that it moved from a monopoly environment to a much richer environment, in terms of technology, competitiveness, and cost structures. Order of magnitude changes, important ones.

148

Markoski: Our time is up, thank you everybody.

Intellectual Property Issues Workshop

Moderators: Ronald Palenski and Bill Aspray

Rapporteur: Joan Krammer

Participants: Norma Goetz   Lee Keet
                        Martin Goetz   Nancy Keet
                        Tom Haigh   Oscar Schachter

Palenski: I'm Ron Palenski. I'm a former General Counsel of ADAPSO, and I'm going to moderate the session.

Goetz: I'm Marty Goetz, formerly president of Applied Data Research. I'm a private investor.

N. Goetz: I'm Norma Goetz, Marty Goetz's wife. Been there, been through all of this.

Schachter: I'm Oscar Schachter. I was an active member of ADAPSO with Advanced Computer Techniques Corporation for about twenty years and am now in private practice as an attorney doing mostly intellectual property licensing work with software companies.

Keet: I'm Lee Keet. At the time that we're discussing, I was President of the software products group at Dun & Bradstreet, formerly of National CSS before its acquisition in 1979 by Dun & Bradstreet. Since 1984, I've been President of Vanguard Atlantic Limited, a venture fund.

N. Keet: I'm Nancy Keet. I've been on the sidelines watching all of this unfold.

Krammer: Joan Krammer, rapporteur for the session. My involvement is through the Smithsonian and I'm here to make summary notes.

Aspray: I'm Bill Aspray. I'm the executive director of Computing Research Association and, I guess, the Vice-Moderator, in case there's any vice.

Palenski: Marty, you were Chairman of the Software Protection Committee during what period?

Goetz: From 1972 to 1980, I was Chairman of the Software Protection Committee of ADAPSO. And according to the research I've recently done for my memoir, Lee Keet became Chairman in '80.

Palenski: If you don't mind, I'll ask you some of the questions that have occurred to me throughout the years. I put this timeline together, if for no other reason than, perhaps, to jog memories.

To me, there seems to have been two major areas of intellectual property law that were relevant, at least from a federal statutory viewpoint, back in the '60s and the '70s: patents and copyrights. There seems to have been, for example, a lot of churning in the patent area back in about '65-'66. There was a commission established by then-President Johnson to take a look at the question of patentability of computer programs and, at least as I understand it, the commission recommended against it, primarily because of the administrative burdens in collecting evidence of prior art.

In addition, there was the phenomenon that the patentability of computer software was disfavored by the U.S. Patent and Trademark Office, but more favorably received by the Court of Customs and Patents Appeals. Thus, software-related patent applications were frequently rejected by the Patent Office but would be appealed to the Court of Customs and Patent Appeals, which tended to be more sympathetic towards patent protection. Then some of these cases went up to the Supreme Court and, until Diamond v. Diehr in 1981 or thereabouts, the Supreme Court had never upheld any of these. So, a lot of churn in the patent area.

In the copyright area, the Copyright Office would register programs under the Rule of Doubt beginning about 1964, but it wasn't until 1978 that you had a clear statement in the Copyright Act that computer programs were copyrightable.

Marty, because of your familiarity with the patent issues, I'm wondering if you might talk a little bit about which early ADAPSO companies were involved in the software protection effort? What were some of the discussions you had, decisions you made, and things that you did?

Goetz: When I got involved in ADAPSO with software protection, my interest was in how you protect your software assets. At that time there was a suit against IBM and we were interested in lots of things besides intellectual property per se. And that's why it was called the Software Protection Committee as opposed to the Intellectual Property Committee.

I got involved in the mid '60s when, by chance, I ended up getting the first software patent. There were two very famous cases, one that evolved in the '60s called the Prater versus Wei case, which is well written up. And a second case in early 1972 which was called the Benson case. Both of those cases preceded Dann versus Johnson. Since about 1965, when I got the first patent, there had been a controversy as to whether software contained patentable subject matter. There was a lot of confusion because people thought of it as getting a patent for a program, which was not the case, because my patent, for instance, was for a sorting process.

So there was always confusion whether you should copyright or patent your programs and they really were separate issues. For at least fifteen years, from 1965 through 1980, the patentability of software was in question. There was also trade secret as another possible method of protection.

I got involved with the Software Protection Committee after the presidential commission that you alluded to. IBM was pushing their position which, at that time, was that they didn't believe that software should be patentable. They weren't selling programs, they were putting programs in the public domain. IBM, which for many years got the most patents of any company in the United States, or in the world, was against the patenting of software.

There were some initial guidelines back in 1965 on how to patent software but it kept changing depending on the patent commissioner, and then on the cases that came up. So for fifteen years there was lots of confusion.

Meanwhile, unbundling happened and lots of companies were being formed. I got involved in the software protection area but patenting was only one of my interests. My primary interest was how to effectively compete against IBM.

Palenski: What position was the association advocating at that time with respect to patents?

Goetz: Well, before I became part of ADAPSO, I was involved with an association called AISC which had, I believe, supported the Prater v. Wei case. I brought that effort with me when I joined ADAPSO, which at the time was in the process of being an amicus in the Benson case.

ADAPSO was generally supportive of the patentability of software but it wasn't universal. There were some companies within ADAPSO, IBM and others, that thought patenting was not appropriate and supported other forms of protection. In particular, Lee Keet was very much for trade secret protection as opposed to patent protection.

Schachter: Did IBM eventually change their position on the patentability of software? Do they now apply for software patents?

Goetz: IBM was filing for patents continuously, at least when the window to do so was open—it closed for awhile in the '70s—but they were consistent in being opposed to the patentability of software. In fact, in the late '60s or very early '70s, they came up with a registration system as an alternative to patenting, somewhere between a patent and a copyright. But, while they were against it, they were still filing lots of patents and continue to do so.

Aspray: You talked about things that were happening in the courts and about the Presidential Commission in the Executive Branch. Was there anything going on in the Legislative Branch that was trying to shape what was happening?

Goetz: Yes, there were some committees that were formed. I don't remember them.

Aspray: Any major pieces of legislation?

Goetz: There was no legislation until the late 1970s.

Palenski: In 1976, Congress adopted a new Copyright Act that became effective in 1978. Before that, the 1909 Copyright Act was in effect. From what I can tell from looking at Marty's records and from what I recall, the association did file briefs in most of the major patent cases that came before the Supreme Court: Gottschalk v. Benson, Dann v. Johnson, and then Parker v. Flook.

The ADAPSO position, as I recall, was that a process which is otherwise patentable if implemented in hardware ought to be equally patentable if implemented in software. So the association really didn't talk in terms of "software patents" but used the more traditional patent terminology.

Goetz: In the late '60s and early '70s, software companies started to file for patents. Boole & Babbage, a software products company, filed an early software patent. Today there are hundreds of software companies filing for patents. Perhaps too many. Business method patents are still considered very controversial. A business method is quite different from a really unique process and, unfortunately, all of the cases that came before the Supreme Court were not representative. They really were marginal, like a computerized system to set off an alarm. They didn't represent the type of things that software companies were trying to protect.

Palenski: What were some of the companies involved in the software protection efforts back in the late '60s and early '70s?

Goetz: I think Oscar Schachter's company, ACT, was.

Schachter: It was one of the reasons we joined ADAPSO in the early '70s. Software protection was one of the key issues that motivated us to join. We were primarily interested in traditional trade secret protection, probably as much from a lack of funds as anything else. Secondarily, we were interested in the copyright protectability of software. We weren't really focused on patentability of software.

Goetz: One of the problems was that software was always sort of looked on as a second-class citizen. It started out being a free service put in the public domain. And, really, part of what we were trying to do was to get stature. Every other industry seemed to have patent protection but here was an industry where you couldn't get patent protection. We were fighting IBM competitively at the time. So if IBM was against something, we were for it automatically. [*Laughter*]

That didn't turn out to be the case in the copyright area but it seemed like, wherever we were going, IBM was on the other side.

Aspray: Were there particular kinds of software companies for which this was a more important issue?

Keet: There were no application software companies, as I recall, on the committee either when you were running it, Marty, or when I was running it. Most of them were system software companies.

I was a member of the committee for a number of years before I took over the chairmanship and, as I recall, the members were all systems software companies.

Aspray: Did the application companies have some different mode of doing business or some other kind of protection mechanism so that they didn't have to use patents and copyrights?

Keet: A lot of the debate in the early years grew out of a lack of understanding or knowledge of where the courts and the legal system would go. There was a lot of discussion about needing additional protections because we weren't sure we were going to really get the protection that many of us thought were embedded in copyright or, potentially, in patents. There was a large debate about how so much software is not obvious, doesn't implement an algorithm, etc. My position all along was that there was going to be a very narrow window of opportunity for somebody to find something that was truly patentable software.

But our discussions really revolved around how to protect the distribution of our software, how to protect it against theft by customers, protect it against theft by rogue employees, and theft by our distributors. The application software companies in those days were much more service companies than they were packaged-goods companies and, therefore, they were working more closely with their customers. In retrospect, the protection we relied on the most was the business-to-business contract. It turned out to be the ultimate protection until people started to package their software for easier distribution, which coincided with the PC revolution.

At the end of my tenure as chairman of the committee, we had Jon Shirley, the President of Microsoft, involved. The PC guys couldn't get the same contract protections. They weren't delivering hands-on services so they weren't there to observe if somebody was using their product illegally. Their interest, therefore, was much more in how to protect a mass-produced piece of goods.

So there was a transition to needing to know what the legal protections would be, instead of focusing on alternative ways of protecting ourselves. Are we going to enjoy copyright protection for what we've done? Are we totally reliant on trade secrets and contracts? Is Marty going to prevail and everybody's going to be able to get a patent? It was confusion.

Goetz: Definite confusion and, of course, to the extent that one could get a patent, a very small number of programs would meet the criteria. It was very unclear how you would stop someone from using your program. It was unclear whether copyright law was actually valid. It was never tested in the courts. So, back in the early '70s, the focus was on making sure your contract was valid. In fact, that was one of the reasons companies were licensing rather than selling the software because you'd lose lots of rights if you sold it.

Schachter: Just to add a footnote to what kinds of companies were patenting software. The systems software companies were a lot closer to the machines, so to speak. They were actually driving the machine. Theirs was a process that was making the machine work in a particular way and I think that they could more easily formulate the words that would allow them to patent a particular process. The application companies were one step removed from the machine and from the system software and, therefore, had difficulty in formulating the kind of terminology that allowed them to patent software—until you get into the business process patents that we have today. So that may have been another reason why the early companies were all pretty much system software companies.

Keet: I'd like to add that we didn't even know ourselves what category to put software into. There was a lot of discussion about whether this was analogous to the piano roll. And, therefore, do we fall into that category? Or is this analogous to a machine component or part, and do we fall into that category? In other words, we were trying to find the bucket that we belonged in because we were inventing stuff and we didn't really have any history to look back to. And we weren't getting tremendously good advice from the attorneys because some of them had a particular penchant for patents and others thought that we really needed to rely on trade secret protection. And there were some who were saying that it's unique and we need sui generis legislation. I'm trying to remember the name of an attorney... Was it Pamela Samuelson?

Palenski: Well, there is an attorney by that name. Formerly on the faculty of the University of Pittsburgh Law School, she's now teaching at Stanford University Law School.

Keet: She was leading the charge in the early '80s. She was leading the charge for: Forget it, guys, copyright doesn't apply, patent doesn't apply, we need a legislative act to protect software. I remember some very heated meetings where we had people yelling patents, we had people yelling copyright, we had people yelling trade secrets, we had people yelling contracts, we had people yelling sui generis. And I'm sitting there thinking, why did I take this job? [*Laughter*]

Palenski: Part of the issue was that, under the 1909 Act, which wasn't superseded until 1978, there was a Supreme Court case, White Smith versus Apollo. It ruled that pianola rolls, another digital medium of recordation, were not copyrightable because they did not communicate with a human being but, rather, a machine and, hence, were not "writings" in the Constitutional sense. And even after Congress passed the new Copyright Act under Congressman Kastenmeier's leadership in 1976, it wasn't until Apple v. Franklin was decided by the Third Circuit that that argument was laid to rest, even though that case never went up to the Supreme Court. I can still remember the amicus briefs asking how something could be copyrightable if it wasn't designed to talk to a human, if it was designed to talk to a machine. So even though, beginning in about 1964, the U.S. Copyright Office would register programs, it was under the Rule of Doubt. Which means, essentially, we'll register this stuff for you, but, in the event of a litigation, you have to prove it's copyrightable.

The process to change that began in 1976. The CONTU Commission was set up to study the issue of copyright protection for computer programs. The computer program amendments to the Copyright Act, which implemented the CONTU recommendations, weren't enacted into law until December 1980. So you had some sixteen years where, with respect to copyright, things were very much up in the air.

Keet: Even after the implementation of the act, it was in doubt. Which is why we put a proposal before Kastenmeier in January of 1983. Software was not an enumerated art in the act that resulted from the CONTU commission. We felt that we needed it to be enumerated. I believe that the proposal for the improved protection of software resulted in a bill that was put before Congress, which was—help me, Ron—HR 6983?

Palenski: Yes.

Keet: It was simply a proposal to make a very, very modest change to the 1976 Copyright Act, to enumerate software as one of the copyrightable forms of expression.

Schachter: Originally, I believe, the Copyright Office would not accept object code as copyrightable. You had to provide source code and you had to provide the full scope of the program—which meant it would be publicly accessible. So no one was particularly interested in using that method of protection. It wasn't until they adopted later rulings which allowed you to file just pieces of the program, and to excise any real trade secrets even in those pieces, that people started feeling comfortable about registering software for copyright protection.

Goetz: I got indoctrinated very early by Mort Jacobs, my patent attorney, who had previously worked at the Patent Office and then had worked for RCA and then was in private practice. He kept saying, "Use the existing laws, don't wait for Congress to make something happen." Certainly, as I look back, to get Congress to enact a new law when you've got opposing sides is almost impossible. The CONTU committee got them to change two sentences in the copyright law to say explicitly that software is copyrightable material. That was sort of the extent of it. It was important for them to say that, to get that into law, but to get a new law would have been very difficult. And then you've got the people on the patent side who say, "Look, the patent system has been great for the last two hundred years and doesn't need to be changed." Of course, in the early 1900's, some famous person said there's nothing more to patent. Do you know who that was?

Keet: It was the then head of the Patent Office who said that everything that could be patented had been patented already.

Anyway, this proposal was to broaden the definition of what a computer program was so that it would include the schematics, the logic flows, and so on. That was the definition that was originally put forward in the World Intellectual Property Organization proposals. But when they enacted the '76 copyright law and the subsequent modification in 1980, we felt they had it too narrowly defined and, therefore, the courts could interpret the forms of expression that created software, such as source codes or block diagrams and so on, as not protected.

But then there were the court cases that came along and the courts, I have learned over the decades, get it right eventually. And that's what happened, they got it right.

Palenski: "Eventually" being the operative word.

Keet: Yeah, but the point is they respond to the needs of our society in a continuous fashion whereas Congress responds in a static fashion. Our industry is very dynamic and, therefore, a lot of those court cases actually went beyond what we could have done in a static bill because they had to make the decision to divide the baby or whatever. They had to say, "Is this right or is this wrong?" I was an expert witness in a number of cases and they always hinged on some piece of minutia that required a judge or a jury to think through what was the intent, and whether the law applies rather than what you would get by statute. So I've become a bigot on the other side of the issue, saying that we probably should have been using the existing laws more aggressively at the time.

Palenski: One impression I have, and maybe you can either affirm or deny it, was that IBM was a major proponent of copyright particularly because of the existence of the international conventions. So if you brought computer software under the ambit of copyright, then you would have automatically achieved international protection because of the Berne Convention and the Universal Copyright Convention.

Keet: I can't emphasize enough that when Microsoft and other PC companies joined ADAPSO that was their view also. They wanted enforcement of copyright. They felt that they could deal with the piracy issue as copyright infringement. Piracy means a lot of different things to different people. I never had a customer steal software from me. We always relied on trade secrets and contracts, and there were always top-level companies behind them. I think that was probably true for most of us in the business. I did have a distributor steal from me once by making illegal copies of our software and selling them without telling us. It was the only case I ever had where somebody actually did that.

But with something like Microsoft Windows, there were whole shops being set up to stamp out copies and sell them by the tens of thousands at low prices. That's where those guys wanted to go. They wanted to use the power of international law and put some muscle behind it so they could go to the government of Singapore and say, "You've got a factory here that's stamping out illegal copies and you're in violation of world conventions." They didn't want to say, "You're in violation of US law."

Goetz: The only reason that IBM was slow to support copyright was that they were originally calling all their programs a service that they were giving away and putting in the public domain. So it didn't really make sense for them to say it's copyrightable. As soon as IBM unbundled, they started copyrighting their programs that were not in the public domain and I think just about every company used the copyright system. Perhaps a few didn't, but it didn't stop them from using trade secrets which were state laws as well.

Of course, then you didn't have consumer software and all the thievery. As Lee said, there was very, very little unauthorized use of programs by corporations. Now, of course, there is actually a lot of unauthorized use of PC software. So the Microsofts of this world do go after corporations.

There were other ways of trying to protect software: by having software locks, a special device that you would put into your computer; having software keys that would be triggered with an internal identification. There were all kinds of techniques to stop illegal copying but many of them proved to be impractical.

Schachter: It created a lot of controversy in the industry when software companies tried to use those software locks and software keys to prevent copying.

Aspray: Why was this controversial?

Schachter: Well, the users were up in arms about it. If they wanted to move a piece of software from an obsoleted PC to another PC, they couldn't because it was registered for a particular PC. So the large corporate end users were very much against this.

I'd like to raise another topic, the question of published versus unpublished copyrights. A lot of companies relied on the protection as an unpublished copyright rather than going to the copyright office to actually register their copyright.

Palenski: Until the 1976 Act, there was a dual copyright system. In order to get federal copyright protection, a work had to be published with notice of copyright—the "c" in a circle symbol. The effectiveness or the applicability of copyright with respect to programs was in doubt and, therefore, companies relied on trade secrets. If you had to publish to get copyright protection, would you be foregoing your trade secret protection? And then there was also a separate state copyright system, also called "common law copyright". One thing the '76 Copyright Act did was to abolish the state copyright system so that you have a unified system now. The current Copyright Act protects both published and unpublished works, but that wasn't the law of the land until 1976.

Schachter: And that became very important because one of the problems that I had with copyright registration is that the day you register a piece of software for copyright, your client is changing it. And a month later, the likelihood is that some of the code has been changed. Do you keep on filing updates of the software? How frequently do you have to file those updates?

So the use of trade secrets and unpublished copyrights is probably more prevalent in the industry. I don't know if anyone has done a survey of how many software companies actually file for registration with the copyright office for every piece of software that they write and how many of them don't rely on actual registration.

Goetz: Well, ADR, for example, never filed. We would always have a copyright stamp on our manuals and on our source code, on just about everything, but we never registered it with the Copyright Office.

Schachter: Yeah, ACT never did. I recently had an interesting case of a bank loan being made to a software company. They wanted to have a lien on all of the assets of the software company—trade secrets, copyrights, etc. And they were alarmed that the principal software of the company had not been registered in the Copyright Office. Although the company had an unpublished copyright and trade secret rights in the asset and were willing to give them a lien on that, the bank insisted that we file all of those pieces of software in the Copyright Office so that they would have a lien on a registered copyright. They said the bank just doesn't like to have liens on unregistered, unpublished works.

Keet: It's also important to point out that before the '76 Act, there was a standard that said that you had to put your copyright mark on every printable page of a copyrighted work. We went to great lengths to generate a copyright notice in the delivered code to the customers because of the copyright mark requirement. Our attorney advised us that we had to show the copyright mark not just on the manual but on the actual delivered code and it should be on every page of the printout.

Fortunately, we had a source code generator and we modified it to put the copyright notice all the way through all of the source code. It was a mess. You would be reading along in the source code and there would be a copyright notice as a comment. It was just a bizarre time. The word I would use is paranoia. We, as an industry, I think, were paranoid about things that didn't happen. We thought that there was going to be a lot of thievery. We wanted to anticipate it because we put so much of our money and intellectual energy and effort into building these things, and we didn't want them stolen.

It wasn't until the PC industry came along that it actually turned into a huge problem. I can't emphasize that enough. I don't think you can find somebody from the era of the '60s or '70s that will tell you that they had a big problem with thievery.

Goetz: We didn't have any problem with the copyright because we didn't distribute our source code. So it was pretty clean for us. We delivered a tape to the user which had our object code, and on the tape and on the label it said copyright with a date. Our manuals had the copyright notice on the inside cover and that was about it. If anything got printed out on a printer, we didn't worry about it. So it was nice and clean. We didn't know if it really protected us but it didn't become a burden within the company at all.

Keet: IBM never put a copyright mark on its software. I published a lot of software while I was at IBM, including some products that became tremendously widely used like the Bill of Material Processor. We put a copyright mark on the manuals. These were Type II and Type III programs and the documents would say "Copyright IBM Corporation" with the date. But the programs themselves never had a copyright notice.

Goetz: But that was in the '60s.

Keet: Yes, this was in the early '60s.

Goetz: They weren't copyrighting their programs because all of their programs were in the public domain, or most of them were.

Keet: I believe that the manuals said—we'd have to go back and find some of these in the Charles Babbage Institute archives—that the programs were the property of IBM and were provided to the customer for their exclusive use. But they never said these are copyrighted nor was there a copyright mark on the program.

Palenski: Under White-Smith v. Apollo, the pianola roll case, the copyrightability of programs in the '60s would have been up in the air—because the Supreme Court said if it doesn't talk to a human, it can't be copyrightable.

Keet: I'm just trying to paint the picture of a lot of confusion, a lot of paranoia, because we didn't know whether we were marching out there to sell our stuff to a bunch of thieves or good guys. It turns out they were all good guys.

Goetz: It was a very unclear era. There were the questions of whether software was tangible or intangible and what was software. Of course, IBM was giving it all away for free, and then suddenly they're selling it. What were they selling and how do you protect it? There was the question of: Is software taxable, is it tangible? There was a great deal of confusion all wrapped up with the intellectual property issues.

Keet: On the Contracts Committee, in which I participated and so did you, as I recall, Marty, we were trying to determine what should be the standard form of contract, or what is a good legal form for delivery of this product to a customer, and how do you protect it with trade secrets and so on in the contract. That took place simultaneously with these intellectual property issues.

Palenski: In contract law, one of the big questions at the time was whether software was a "good" under Article 2 of the Uniform Commercial Code, which is the commercial law that has been adopted in all States except Louisiana. Or whether it was some sort of "service" or something else and fell outside of the UCC. For tax purposes, the question was whether software was tangible and, therefore, its transfer subject to state and local property taxation or sales and use taxation. Interestingly, the industry was whipsawed by government on the nature and taxability of software. On one hand, the Federal government took the position that software was intangible and, therefore, did not qualify for things like accelerated depreciation, the investment tax credit, and other favorable federal tax treatment. But the states, in their desire for revenue, were taking the position that software was tangible and, therefore, its transfer or sale was subject to sales and use taxation.

Keet: The UCC gave implied warranties for fitness and use for a particular purpose, as I recall the words, but we in the industry were trying to separate the transfer of the license for the software from our service agreements. The reason for that was, speaking for my company, we were trying to create hell-and-high-water leases for the underlying product. A hell-and-high-water lease is a lease where the customer agrees not to assert any defenses that he might have or to offset any payments that might be due against other claims. We actually had two documents. One was a service agreement and a warranty that was document B. And we had the software term license or lease, which was document A. The reason we separated them was we could take that pile of document A's and go to a bank and get financing for them because we had General Motors saying I will pay x dollars per month for the next thirty-six months no matter what. And the other document where we said we would provide service to General Motors was our liability and General Motors had to think that we were strong enough to stand behind that without being able to go against the financing lease.

Schachter: Was that the first case of off-balance sheet liabilities preceding Enron?

Keet: Oh, gee, did I start Enron? [*Laughter*]

Well, we would not have survived without those financing leases. I was very involved in these ADAPSO committees because of the very things we're talking about. If the UCC provisions applied under state law then we wouldn't have been able to separate the warranty. The position we took was, if it's a business-to-business transaction among sophisticated parties, that's not subject to the UCC laws. But the states individually did not necessarily agree with that position and therefore our financing was in jeopardy depending on the state in which we were writing those contracts. I just raise that because this was all tied together. You can't separate contracts from taxability, from financial issues, and from software protection. We were just struggling to figure out the business model that would allow us to keep our companies alive because there were only two sources of capital. One of them was from entrepreneur investors meaning friends, family, relatives, and anybody else you could steal a wallet from. The other was your customers, which meant you had to get sales and collect the money. We were really working hard to try to figure out how to make those collections come faster, make the amount of money we were getting bigger, and to finance it once we got a commitment.

Krammer: What I'm curious about is the comment that there was a problem anticipated that didn't materialize during that time period.

Goetz: We were selling to major corporations and then, maybe, smaller corporations but zero software to consumers. There was a contract and these were corporations where you're dealing with the data processing manager. He's not going to cheat because he could just end up losing his job. So there was very little thievery. On the other hand, you wanted to protect the program from your competitors. You didn't want your competitors to take it, change it and then go out and resell it. But from the user perspective there was very little thievery. In fact, ADR was never aware of any company that was using our software without being authorized to use it.

Keet: There was a problem which we discussed a lot in these committees of what you do about employees' non-compete agreements which were gradually being obviated by the courts, especially on the West Coast. California eventually made them totally useless. There were problems and lawsuits when an employee would go away and start another company to produce a competitive product and the competitive product looked awfully similar to the product that his previous employer had been producing. We had a lot of discussions about what we should be doing about that, what kinds of agreements could we get with the employees that would let us protect our property, and if we could rely on copyright, trade secrets, etc. for that kind of protection. So that's where the problems did occur.

Krammer: But I'm also curious to hear what other surprises happened. Going back to your comment that you were anticipating that something would happen and it didn't. What other surprises were there in that time period?

Keet: Well, we had a distributor in Germany which was a subsidiary of a larger German company based in Munich and the guy who was running it turned out to be an out-and-out crook. We distributed source code, unlike ADR, and our source code was customized to each customer. One of the things that we did was put the customer name into the source code so that when they actually compiled it and started the system it would say "XYZ Steel Company" on it. And we got a complaint back at our headquarters, bypassing the distributor, saying our distributor can't seem to get the right name on our software. [*Laughter*]

That's when we found out that there were lots more copies of Task/Master in Germany than we actually knew about. That was the most egregious case of theft and, in that case, nothing would have protected us because it was like going out and finding your car. You might have every lock in the world on that car but if it's gone, it's gone.

Aspray: Coming back to Lee's comment about employees. Did ADAPSO or other trade organizations put out white papers or guidelines that suggested to companies what their model agreement should be or their model practice should be in these areas?

Goetz: We had employee agreements and they would generally protect us to the extent possible. The question was how they would hold up in your state which was always an issue. I don't recall ADAPSO getting too involved with employee agreements.

Schachter: I don't think we had a model employee contract. I think most software companies, after a period of time, adopted what is typically called now a professional practices agreement that they have virtually every employee in the company sign. It deals largely with confidentiality of materials, confidentiality of customer material, and the ownership of the work that you do. It clearly covers all inventions etc. etc. that you develop while you are working for the company. Some companies also have a non-compete agreement, but, as Lee said before, those are very much subject to state law.

I'm interested in returning to an earlier topic which relates to selling your software to large companies and, therefore, protection wasn't an issue, because you had contract protection. In the mid-'90s, there were a number of cases where companies were, in fact, allowing the distribution of illegal copies of PC software throughout the company, and the SPA went after them on that.

Today we have the situation where much business software for mainframes or for large servers is priced on the basis of the number of users on the system. You don't have to make copies of the software. You just put someone else on the system and—voilà—they're a user and they have a copy of the software available to them without your having copied it. Software companies are struggling to protect themselves against the situation where you license the software for fifty users and suddenly there are a hundred users on the system. You can put locks into the software but that gets to be very impractical. The end user says, "I don't want to have to come back to you, and revise my contract every time I want to add five more users." Since most companies have access to their customers' computers for maintenance purposes, they're developing methods of actually policing the number of users which a large customer has using its software.

Keet: To the earlier question, one of the best things that ADAPSO did was create open forums where people would sit around and do exactly what we're doing here and trade experiences and ideas. On the employee issue, we had a lot of discussion about what others were doing and, from that, I learned the idea of putting in your employee handbook or in some other document what the rules and regulations are for the company. We got the employee to acknowledge that and made it into a contract by having the employee sign a postcard-size form on hiring. And also any time the employee got a promotion or a raise or a change of status, because there has to be consideration on both sides to make it into an agreement. We specified that violation of trade secrets or theft or misuse of copyrighted materials would constitute egregious damage to the company, etc. Did ADAPSO publish anything on that? No, but it was pretty well accepted practice. I always used it in our company. Subsequently, since I started Vanguard, we've used it in every single company we funded right to this day. It has become kind of an evolved industry standard, but it came out of those discussions at ADAPSO, I want to emphasize, even though ADAPSO didn't publish a contract.

One of the things we're not focusing on at this conference as much as we should, in my opinion, was how the business practices evolved. We've spent a lot of time talking about ADAPSO and trade associations, which is appropriate. But if you go back to those early discussions, a lot of them had nothing to do with the formal committees or sessions. It was sitting around saying, "How much are you paying your sales guys? What's the compensation plan? How much do you expect a top guy to make? What are you doing in the way of marketing? What journals work for advertising? Where do you get your sales people?" And so on. All of that information swapping when there was no standard to go against.

Schachter: Nothing on pricing, of course. [*Laughter*]

Palenski: So long as everyone made his or her own independent decision that was fine, you could talk about whatever you wanted.

Keet: We all made our independent decisions. And everybody had different prices anyway, so just getting the guidelines was all you wanted. But things like distributor agreements: Do you give your distributor 50%, 60%, 40%? Can they make money at 50%? Because we wanted them to make some money. And then we would share what we thought were the cost bases. We weren't trying to be collusive and put together a single policy. We were trying to figure out how to put together the business practices. That's where the real interesting history is in my opinion. There was no model you could follow. You didn't go out there and just adopt the model of an automotive parts manufacturer and say it applied to software. We didn't have anywhere to go. We didn't know what it was going to cost to distribute and support software in Europe. How much money do you have to give to a French company to translate the manuals into French, to provide telephone support and on-site support and to deal with you across the Atlantic? What kind of a percentage split did you have to give them?

We felt our way all along on those issues. We were doing exactly the same thing on intellectual property. We didn't know where we were going and we weren't getting a lot of guidance from the other industries out there. Their experiences didn't seem to apply much to us.

Krammer: The question that I want to put to the group is: If someone was looking back fifty years from now, what would you want to tell them?

Goetz: I'd say the interesting point is that there is a healthy independent software industry out there. It's important that there be one fifty years from now. We ended up looking to protect ourselves because there was a large company then, IBM. And there's a large company now, Microsoft. The issues are in a certain sense intellectual property issues. Must they provide interface information or is that a trade secret? Intellectual property issues for software are still out there. They affect the growth of the independent software vendors. There're thousands of them out there. There were thousands in the '70s and '80s and the issue is to have a viable software industry. So I'd say we hope, if we look back fifty years from now, that there will still be a viable software industry not dominated by a couple of companies like, for instance, the auto industry.

Keet: I have a little different cut on it than that, Marty, because I think we are moving in the direction of the auto industry and there will be fewer companies. I think if you went back and looked at the history of the automobile industry, you would find that in the '20s and early '30s there were companies selling isinglass windows, and Fisher Bodyworks was a separate company that would build you a custom body on a General Motors chassis. And you had choices for your electrical systems. You didn't have Delco and Remy belonging to General Motors, they were independent companies. The consolidation of that industry was in order to better serve the consumer by giving them one-stop shopping, reliability, a place to go to get everything serviced. I think that's the direction that the software industry is going and I believe that there will be more software under the covers of larger integrated systems and that they will be sold by companies like General Motors and Chrysler.

I think that it would be awfully interesting to see from the standpoint of the evolution of an industry like the automobile industry how that consolidation was affected by companies like Delco and Remy and Fisher Bodyworks. Because they created the opportunity for that consolidation and hence for a very rapid movement forward in technological progress where the technological progress changed from being the invention of the individual component parts to the integration of the component parts into something that became very easy to use. You don't think about it anymore with a car. You get in, you turn the key, you expect it's going to run. You expect it's going to run for a couple hundred thousand miles. You don't really think about needing a radio or whatever the other components are and I believe that's the direction we're going.

Krammer: What would you say, in a few key points, about this early period then?

Keet: Well, it was a period of invention. You know, when I started there weren't compilers. I was there when ALGOL-60 was introduced and it was a miracle. You could actually sit down and write a program in a reasonably high language and get the machine to execute. And then you could take that program to another machine and compile it and have it execute on that other machine.

We can talk about the bad things IBM did, but IBM created the base standard and the technical underpinnings and the marketing umbrella under which many of us flourished. The fact that there was a single architectural standard gave us a great customer base to sell to. The fact that this is a big country with lots of people who all speak the same language, across a fairly homogenous base with common contractual and legal systems was tremendously important.

And so, I would say it was a period where everything was being invented simultaneously. If you had tried to invent an automobile in 1908, you would have had a very, very hard time. You could have built one but you needed people out there to give you all the components. Somebody had to build the transmission and somebody else had to build the motor and somebody else had to put the siding on the thing and somebody gave you the running boards and somebody else built the wheels and that's what we were doing. If any one company had tried to do it all, it couldn't have. I think we're in a phase of consolidation and one of the reasons I think the history is important is because once the industry is consolidated, people will forget, will not realize that it didn't just spring magically out of dust.

At TSI, we wrote a telecommunications monitor system. That was our base stock in trade. You wouldn't think of doing that now. That has to be part of the underpinnings of the operating system.

Goetz: Maybe at the next session this afternoon we can continue the discussion of whether the automobile industry is the right model. Maybe it gives us a model which the software industry in the next fifty years *shouldn't* look like. It may turn out that it will look like the auto industry but would that be better for the world or would lots of small innovative companies be better? Lee may be right. It may happen but will that necessarily be good for the world or for innovation and invention and progress?

Schachter: I'm concerned that in the direction that we're going, the ability of a Microsoft to be born in an IBM era is not going to happen in the next era. The possibility of another Microsoft being born while Microsoft is so dominant is not going to happen. Lee's scenario is the one that is going to prevail. And that is going to, I think, kill innovation.

Keet: Well, if you believe what was said in one of the speeches this morning, the industry has doubled in eleven years. If I'm remembering my rule of 69's right, it says that the average percentage growth rate is less than 7% and, if we are as an industry growing less than 7% per annum, the innovation and the growth from a financial incentive basis in an entrepreneurial or capitalistic society is going to be consolidation. So I think that there may be an inevitable economic law regardless of whether you're proselytizing on...

Goetz: I'm certainly not anti-General Motors but there was a phrase when GM dominated the automobile industry: What's good for General Motors is good for the world. Unfortunately, it took the Japanese to make GM realize that they better improve their cars and do a lot of other things to compete. So I think competition is important whether it be twenty companies or two thousand.

Keet: I want to add one more point in response to Joan's question There was a lot of stuff that had to be invented back in the '50s and '60s and '70s because it didn't exist and, if you didn't have it, you couldn't build a system. Building systems today is much more a matter of adding bells and whistles. That isn't to say that these bells and whistles aren't good, but they aren't fundamental underpinning stuff that you absolutely have to have and that, to me, is characteristic of a technology era as it matures.

Once the underpinnings are there, consolidation is where consumers see the value. And they pay the bills. So I believe that we're in the consolidation phase of an industry and that fifty years from now software will not be viewed as a separate business. And, that's why we want to preserve its history, because it was an important separate business.

Aspray: Separate from?

Keet: Completely integrated solutions. The example I'll give you is there is more computing power in your automobile today than there was in the entire world thirty years ago. The increase in the processing power in the last thirty years—this is a real number—is thirty-three thousand to one. And the next thirty years is going to be thirty-three thousand to one and you're going to have computers and software everywhere. I mean *everywhere*. It's going to be in your pen, it's going to be in your refrigerator, it's...

Goetz: I'm going to take the other side. Large corporations, small corporations had problems twenty, thirty years ago building applications. They still have problems. The need for better software is still there. What's happening is they decide they're going to outsource because their IT department can't deliver. They outsource and they find out the outsourcer can't deliver. There is still a radical need for more and better software. If you look at the power of hardware, there's no question that it's increasing.

But if you look at the typical large corporation, one that is spending millions and millions of dollars each year, they continue to be in a panic state. They've been in it for twenty or thirty years. They survive, they get by, but no one is really happy with building large software systems, mission-critical systems. And I think that problem may be with us twenty or thirty years from now.

Aspray: I have a question about expert advice during the 1960s and '70s. We heard that there weren't many good models in other industries about how to handle these intellectual property issues. So as a software company you went out and hired legal counsel. Where did you go to find them? How good were they? Who were the kinds of people that were good choices and what were the kinds of typical choices?

Goetz: Well, I believe ADR got lucky and happened to find someone at a conference that was into software pretty early. You know, lawyers adept at intellectual property existed long before software.

Aspray: Were intellectual property issues dealt with by your principal internal legal counsel? And if so, what would you look for when you were hiring such a person? Did you look for somebody that came from the traditional computer industry or somebody that came from the Patent Office or just what was the background?

Schachter: If we're talking about the '60s and even the '70s, if you wanted to hire someone who was specifically an intellectual property lawyer in the patent or copyright area, there were no lawyers who were trained in software, or there were very few. Since, as Lee said, most of the work needed to be done by your contract, you needed to make sure you had a tight contract which both protected your software and protected you in whatever other way contracts traditionally protect you in terms of making sure you got paid and things of that kind. I would say that most people went out and hired contract lawyers, people who had a background in contracts and business law. Intellectual property really was the domain of a lawyer in a very large software or hardware company. The average software company would go outside for that particular expertise.

Keet: We hired a local law firm. The company was based in Connecticut and we hired the biggest law firm in New England at the time, Cummings & Lockwood, and got a really good contracts guy, Howard "Woody" Knight, who drafted all of our contracts. He was a great lawyer, but he didn't know a lot about patents. He knew enough to know that he didn't know enough to help us and he put us in touch with another firm in Connecticut that specialized in patents. They gave us the advice that we didn't have anything that was patentable. They also gave us copyright advice, but basically we worked through the contracts guy and in the end it was the right answer. The contracts were the way to go.

Then people came along through the trade association, like Ron and others, who knew a lot about these issues. And we then had everybody in touch with everybody else. They'd come to the meetings and would get advice. Everybody started to exchange information, but I would say that it was in the late '70s when that really got going.

Palenski: Interestingly, this morning I was looking for a tape that Fred Lafer, Milt Wessel, Herb Marx, the people who founded the Computer Law Association, made on that group's 25th anniversary. Actually, that group, which today numbers some 2,000 members from around the world, sprang from meetings at ADAPSO. It was an attempt on the part of the lawyers who were trying to serve this community to meet and to share information and insights.

Goetz: There were many lawyers back in the '60s and probably the '50s that were patent, copyright, trade secret lawyers, intellectual property lawyers.   They didn't have a lot of experience with software, but they adapted quickly as most lawyers do.

Palenski: There are lawyers out there today who are trying to reinvent themselves as biotech lawyers.

I can't believe it, but our time is up.

Aspray: Thank you all.

Workshop Photos

Accounting Issues Workshop

Conferences Workshop

Bruce Coleman, Ed Bride, Art Esch, Bob Weissman, Rich Carpenter and Larry Welke in the Conferences Workshop

Banking Litigation and Issues of the 1960s Workshop

Julie Johnston in the Issues of the 1960s Workshop

Intellectual Property Workshop

Ron Palenski in the Intellectual Property Workshop

Contracts Reference Directory Workshop

IBM Relations Workshop

Moderators: Oscar Schachter and Paul Ceruzzi

Rapporteur: John Gracza

Participants: Martin Campbell-Kelly Luanne Johnson
                       Norma Goetz   Kim Jones
                       Martin Goetz   Lee Keet
                       Bernie Goldstein   Amy Schachter
                       Burt Grad

Schachter: This is the session on IBM Relations and my name is Oscar Schachter. I think I know most of you. I'll be the moderator. Paul Ceruzzi to my right here is the co-moderator. Paul, why don't you say a couple words about yourself.

Ceruzzi: I'm Paul Ceruzzi and I'm a curator at the National Air and Space Museum, part of the Smithsonian Institution in Washington D.C. I have a special interest in computing primarily relating to aerospace but also to computing in general. Of course, IBM has had a very big presence in the aerospace computing field. Maybe some of you don't know that, but they have. I'm interested in computing topics generally, including what has been going on this weekend, which I've found extremely fascinating.

Schachter: Our Rapporteur today is John Grazca.

Gracza: I was on the staff at ADAPSO from '87 to about '92-'93. I spent a number of years working for the software group.

Schachter: We're going to try to cover the relations that IBM had with the software industry from the earliest period that we're aware of, which is the mid-'60s, through the end of the '80s. I did not get involved until the early '70s and, at that point, the issues that were just starting to come to the fore were in the software products area. IBM had recently, in 1969, unbundled its software and hardware. There were still many issues remaining even after that unbundling, as we'll see.

Prior to that time, IBM had divested itself of the Service Bureau Corporation, which had been a wholly-owned subsidiary, although it was separately run and managed as a result of a 1956 consent decree. But in the mid-1960s, IBM was starting to look at re-entering the data processing market through timesharing and other means. If anyone has some memory or knowledge of that period that would be very helpful. Bernie?

Goldstein: If there is a birth date for the industry, it's probably with the 1956 consent decree. IBM, in that era, played a very influential role in the development of the industry. IBM's salesmen were extremely aggressive and would frequently sell hardware to users with the justification they could sell excess computer capacity to cover their costs or even to make a profit. And selling excess time or access to computers was the origin of many early firms that eventually became players in the computer services business. IBM eventually lost its monopoly position in the industry, but at that time, they were a monopolist.

I think the best illustration I have of IBM's position in the marketplace is that, if you wanted to upgrade your computer, you would pay an additional price of 20% or so more than what you were paying. IBM would send an engineer into your facility and *remove* part of the machine. There were governors placed in the machine to limit its processing capacity and, therefore, you paid 20% more *for less*, as you upgraded your computing equipment to make it run faster. I don't know who else would have the power to do that in a marketplace except a monopolist. I can't imagine somebody who had to deal in a more competitive environment being able to do that.

One of the things they did that helped build their position was develop training programs. Remember, the original computers in the marketplace were Univac computers. If a client had a problem developing a program, Univac would send in experts in who would do that for the client. IBM took the same budget and spent it on schools to train customers how to do it themselves. So Univac developed technological cripples in terms of people using their hardware while IBM developed disciples. It was those disciples who eventually moved around to other positions, supported by the extremely well done educational programs, who helped build IBM's position in the marketplace. If you put a 75% market share together with those vignettes of what it means when you have that 75% market share, you can begin to understand how dominant this company was in the marketplace. It doesn't take much imagination to see business managers or a board of directors sitting around deciding what hardware they are going to buy and deciding that the least risky is the hardware that represents 75% of the marketplace.

So IBM put giant American companies out of the business. It destroyed RCA's attempt to be part of the business, largely destroyed General

Electric's attempt to be part of the business. This was *enormous* strength and *enormous* market position. That's the era we lived through prior to IBM's conflicts with the software product companies.

Schachter: How did IBM affect processing services companies in the mid-'60s?

Goldstein: Well, the effect was that a monopolist can engage in monopoly pricing. We could not afford to buy the machines because virtually all of us were underfinanced and had limited resources.   We rented, so we were marked up twice, if you will. Number one, by the higher price that a monopolist could charge to take his product to market, and, number two, by the fact that we had to pay the rental price and not the capital price on some depreciation scale.

Schachter: So you were renting time from some large corporation?

Goldstein: Sometimes we were, but that comment also applies to renting equipment and putting it in your own computer center.

Grad: Let me ask a question here about processing services companies in the '60s.   Was SBC itself a major factor in the concern about IBM during the '60s?

Goldstein: I would say no.   I had the impression that, in the IBM Corporation, SBC was sort of a Siberia. If you weren't in the hardware side of the business or the research side of the business, you were sent to SBC. Sent to Siberia. So there was a Darwinian selection process, I think, in the IBM organization that didn't bring the most aggressive management to SBC.

Grad: But Frank Lautenberg of ADP said in his speech last evening that IBM was their largest competitor and yet ADP ended up being a very large customer of IBM. He talked about his complaints to Vin Learson at IBM: How can you compete with me when I am one of your best customers?

Goldstein: Well, Frank played in a different league at that time. Frank was in the big leagues of this industry while the rest of us were in the little leagues. IBM's attitude to SBC can perhaps best be illustrated by their private settlement of Control Data's antitrust action against them. The reward that Control Data got was SBC. IBM said, "Here take it, it's yours."

So I don't think IBM gave a lot of weight to SBC when they made that decision as a mechanism of settling that action.

Goetz: Who pushed for SBC to be separate in the 1956 consent decree? Was it companies like yours that were saying make them separate?

Grad: The 1956 consent decree had nothing to do with computers, it had to do with punched cards.

Goetz: Why did the Justice Department ask them to separate it from the rest of their business?

Grad: Because Remington Rand had only 10% of the business. The punched card business was the issue. The decree told IBM you can't control 90% of the punched card delivery business anymore. You can't say that other people's punched cards won't work on your machines anymore. You've got to separate the service bureau from the rest of your business because that's feeding customers across to your hardware business. As I understand it, that was all part of that 1956 decree. It was later interpreted to include computers, but to my knowledge that wasn't explicit in the consent decree in '56. Does anybody know?

Schachter: That's a fascinating bit of history, because I think all of us are under the impression that the consent decree in '56 primarily had to do with separating the Service Bureau Corporation from the rest of IBM.

Goldstein: It was one of the Bill of Particulars.

Goetz: Wasn't ADAPSO pushing for it?

Goldstein: No, ADAPSO didn't have a role in that.

Grad: ADAPSO didn't exist. It was founded in '61. This is '56. SBC was one of the founding members of ADAPSO, wasn't it?

Schachter: And that points out that IBM's role in ADAPSO has been schizophrenic. We've had fights with them on the one hand and, at the same time, they've been very supportive of the industry. When ADAPSO needed them on a tax issue or a software protection issue, etc., they were there. They were very supportive of many of the positions of the small software companies.

Keet: That was much later, though.

Schachter: Yes, that was later.

Keet: They got dragged into ADAPSO kicking and screaming as a result of the activities that Marty started and a lot of us participated in. I think they decided they had better have a representative watching us.

Goldstein: Someone on the inside seeing what's going on.

Grad: That's correct. Bill Lynch was SBC's representative in the early '60s and then Steve Beach joined in the mid-'60s. He was a lawyer from SBC. I think what we're looking for is whether there is any institutional memory as to what the issues with IBM were in the '60s. It sounds like there weren't any heavy-duty issues with IBM, except as a competitor, in the early '60s. It's in the later '60s with software that the issues start to heat up. Is that correct? Did you see it that way, Bernie?

Goldstein: I think that's reasonable except that they had the power of pricing their equipment in a very special way, the power of a monopolist.

Keet: I'd like to correct the record here, if I'm understanding it right. Steve Beach and others represented the Service Bureau Corporation, not IBM.

Goldstein: That's correct.

Keet: I don't think IBM was involved in ADAPSO at all until the '80s.

Goetz: No, no. When I came in '72, Tommy Spain from IBM was there as a member of ADAPSO.

Grad: And I was brought in as an ADAPSO member from IBM in 1972.

Keet: I stand corrected.

Goetz: They had a vendor relations group within IBM and, I think, the ADAPSO representatives were part of it.

Grad: Industry relations was the term they actually used. In 1971, about the time that the Software Industry Association came into ADAPSO, Bill Lynch suggested that, since I was the director of development for one of the software areas, I should join ADAPSO as an IBM representative to try and counteract what Marty was doing.

Goetz: I joined ADAPSO when the Association of Independent Software Companies became part of it in 1972. In January or February of that year, ADAPSO had a meeting in Dallas where they had what they called an IBM Mock Trial. Bernie Goldstein spoke and chastised IBM at that time. When ADR became a member later that year, there was already an economic policy group in ADAPSO that had been formed to try to influence the Justice Department in the IBM trial. That group started at the beginning of '72 when they had the mock trial.

Schachter: The first written record I could find, thanks to Marty who provided it, is an ADAPSO monthly bulletin to the members in 1972 stating that ADAPSO had intervened in the IBM antitrust action to try to open up the file records.

Goldstein: It was being tried before Judge Edelstein. The secrecy rules did not allow for the dissemination of the progress of the trial or the positions taken by the principals at the trial. ADAPSO entered a friend-of-the-court filing to open those proceedings.

Schachter: And, in fact, they were opened.

Goldstein: Yes.

Schachter: That was the first interaction that I could find.

Grad: I think a number of individual companies may have provided information to the Justice Department or prepared position papers. I know, Marty, that you were certainly one, but there were others.

Goetz: As a member of AISC prior to joining ADAPSO, I visited the Justice Department with some members of ADAPSO, Larry Welke and others.

Goldstein: AISC was an independent software organization. I think you had fifteen thousand dollars of cash and we did the deal for cash. [*Laughter*]

Grad: So was SIA. They were both independent organizations.

Keet: When did SIA come in, was that the same year?

Goetz: They came in before, at the end of '71. Larry Welke belonged to the software group and brought it into ADAPSO in '71. AISC came in about a year later.

Grad: And that's when I got involved as IBM's representative to the Software Section. Lynch was still responsible for overall relations. I'm showing in my notes that Ed Kane was involved and Grant Leschin and well as Tommy Spain, all from IBM.

Schachter: What years were those?

Grad: This is in '75; they had been involved for some years but I don't know exactly when they started.

Goetz: Well, I know Tommy Spain was there and Grant probably shortly thereafter.

Grad: At some point, a Manufacturers Relations Committee was established and I don't remember when. Does anybody recall when that was set up? It was operational in June of '75 according to the minutes that I have here.

Goetz: Do you have anything that might show who was in attendance?

Grad: We have Lloyd Baldwin of Cincom Systems, and Jerry Dreyer from ADAPSO. Bruce Coleman of Boole & Babbage was the active leader at the time. He was the president of SIA. I have detailed notes from a Manufacturers Relations Committee meeting. That was the original name, I think, that we agreed on.

Schachter: Right, we didn't want to single out IBM. But was there anything other than IBM that was discussed at those meetings that you see in the notes?

Grad: I don't see it here. I have a note from Tom Farewell, who was on the staff of ADAPSO at the time, about getting other companies such as GE, Xerox, Honeywell and Burroughs involved. But as a practical matter, the name of our session here is IBM Relations because that was 99% of it. I remember that at one point we had a big problem with DEC because they wouldn't give us access. They wouldn't play by even IBM's rules. But it didn't affect many people. It affected just a few companies.

Schachter: Why don't we go back in history to '69 because there were several seminal events that took place in '69. One was the decision by IBM, which they made evidently at the end of '68, to unbundle software and hardware. And secondly, the ADR suit against IBM. If Marty could talk to the ADR suit, and Burt could talk to the unbundling within IBM because he was involved in that, that would set the stage for what happened in the '70s.

Goetz: The ADR suit, which was in April of '69, was about four months after the Justice Department brought their suit. We had been competing with IBM against their free software for about four years, so we had a four-year history of having skirmishes with IBM. But it wasn't until they had a new product called TSO, a timesharing option that they announced they were going to bundle with their operating system, that we went into court. Prior to that we didn't really feel that we had a court action. We settled that suit about a year later. I do think that ADR and other companies helped push IBM to unbundle voluntarily by using the press and others to tell them it was unfair competition. Originally, the Justice Department suit was a hardware suit. It was the Big Seven against IBM in the mainframe hardware market. But there were leasing companies that were having problems with IBM's method of pricing their hardware, as did companies that were manufacturing peripheral devices. We got the Justice Department interested in our issue as a software company. There were about four different private companies pursuing IBM, along with the Justice Department.

Grad: The most significant suit as far as IBM was concerned was the Control Data suit in terms of its scope and the skill with which CDC pursued it. I was on IBM's unbundling task force and this is my recollection. We weren't allowed to carry out any papers so I don't have any documentation, only what I can remember.

It got stirred up, apparently, by Burke Marshall and Nicholas Katzenbach, IBM attorneys, telling Tom Watson, Jr., IBM's chairman at the time, that systems engineering was a tie-in sale and that there was no way they could ever win a suit on a tie-in sale on systems engineering. That was the primary impetus for unbundling. But if they made the decision to unbundle systems engineering, they also had to unbundle education and field engineering where they were getting pressure from independent firms that wanted to be able to maintain any manufacturer's equipment. IBM announced the decision to unbundle in '68 and hoped that would avoid a Justice Department suit. At least, that's what Marshall and Katzenbach had told them: If you go ahead and do it on your own you probably won't get sued by the government. Again, this is anecdotal. It's what I was told.

We set up the unbundling taskforce in December of '68. I went to work on the software aspect of it from the Data Processing Division and, of course, in January of '69 there was a big shock when the suit happened anyway. As most of you know, the government didn't push it suit very hard for quite awhile.

Schachter: For twelve years.

Grad: No, for just the first three years, there was not much happening. It seemed like the government was depending upon Control Data to push ahead. But Control Data's suit was not about software or about services; that wasn't where their concern was. They were pushing on IBM's so-called "fighting" machines and early announcements and those kinds of things. They were very good.

Marty's suit came in April of '69. By that point, we had pretty much decided that everything on the applications side was going to be unbundled and we were arguing among ourselves about systems software. The systems people didn't want to unbundle any of the systems software but the view from the attorneys and others was that they had to do something. So they drew the line so that utilities, sorts, the flowcharter, all kinds of utility programs including languages, were unbundled. But the main systems software, OS, DOS, all those things were kept bundled.

Schachter: But even when some software was unbundled it was given away free.

Grad: No. It was just a timing issue. They were totally unbundled but the timing was that, as of January 1, 1970, you'd have to pay for any software you obtained. You were given six months notice because the announcement was made on June 23,1969. Those who already had these programs got to keep them without charge but any new customer had to pay. There were arguments about what had been promised, what hadn't been promised, whether a salesman had done something or not done something, and there were a number of special cases. But as it ended up, there was no big fight about software inside IBM except for systems software. The real fight was about systems engineering. *Everybody* got pissed about that. Every customer was unhappy about it and IBM adjusted their position and changed the rules. The story is that David Kearns, who was then a vice president in

IBM's Data Processing Division, lost his job at IBM and went to Xerox because he was responsible for the decisions and how they were implemented in systems engineering. I don't know if it's true or not. That was the story.

Goetz: When I joined ADAPSO, we were concerned about IBM's business practices and some of the problems that the hardware companies were having in terms of fighting machines, pre-announcements, and so forth. I know that Lee Keet early on was very concerned about some IBM pre-announcements that froze his market. ADR was concerned about tie-ins because we had just settled our suit and they had tied in TSO to their operating system. We weren't going to fight that but we were concerned about additional tie-ins. So there were lots of issues. When I joined in '72, ADAPSO was already in the process of preparing a position paper for the Justice Department in case there was ever any kind of settlement or consent decree. I became president of the Software Section in '73 and, at that point, there was universal agreement within ADAPSO to have a position paper. The only thing that was controversial was that we said in the 1973 position paper that IBM should have a separate software company. And that's where some people disagreed. Informatics, in particular, said, "Let the sleeping giant sleep." [*Laughter*] But as far as their business practices were concerned, we were all in agreement. We wanted them to toe the line.

Grad: An interesting comment just to add to that. I was IBM's representative on the IBM Relations Committee and I was very active in SIA, which was what the Software Section was called then. Because I was running a software group within IBM, I remember thinking, "Wouldn't it be wonderful if it *was* a totally separate corporation." All the damn rules about releasing programs were killing me inside IBM. I couldn't develop programs for back-level operating systems. I couldn't run on anybody else's software systems. I couldn't tie in with anything. I thought it would be wonderful if I was running a separate operation. I didn't say that out loud, of course. But IBM business conduct guidelines were revised partly as a result of the Manufacturers Relations Committee. ADAPSO had an effect. I can tell you that. ADAPSO affected IBM's business practices.

Schachter: We're glad to hear that.

Grad: One of the things it affected was an awareness within IBM. People in IBM ignored the software world. They paid no attention to it.

Goldstein: Well, yes, and that carried throughout the IBM organization. There is a program on the radio in New York that asks you to identify the turning point in a baseball game and, if you guess right, you get a prize. The turning point for IBM was when they entered into the contract with Microsoft and what they did to themselves then.

Grad: But that's the '80s, isn't it? That's '81. We can get to that but what I'm concerned about is capturing this period of time because IBM did not succeed as an application program provider. It just didn't.

Ceruzzi: What about CICS?

Grad: That's a system program. It was my product, it came out of the Data Processing Division. Lee keeps telling me how lousy it was because he had a much better product that he was competing against it with.

Schachter: He's probably right. [*Laughter*]

Grad: I won't argue.

Ceruzzi: So explain for the tape the difference between a system program and an application with regard to CICS.

Grad: Mr. Keet, would you like to do that?

Keet: Well, CICS was a telecommunications monitor, which is a sub-operating system. It runs under the control of the operating system but it divides up the resources within a protected program space. It runs in a separate partition, to use the word that applied to the System/360 and the operating systems of those days. And it provides a master scheduler, a stack, dispatch and control mechanism so that a program can host multiple terminals. Each of those threads, to bring another term in here, can have its own control mechanisms, its own space, and can also exercise control over rewrites of files so they don't trample on each other.

Ceruzzi: But, in practical terms, it was used by customers to do online transactions.

Keet: No, no. It was the shell into which the customer wrote his applications. It was not an application. It hosted the application and there were rules you followed so that when you wrote the application, you could be assured of various services that allowed multiple terminals attached to that application to execute independently of one another.

Jones: A good analogy today is if you think of collapsing all of the client Windows computers and saying, "Now they are all running in the mainframe in one space." That's what CICS was.

Grad: We used the term "transaction processing system". You could write your transaction applications, what it was going to do with each of these transactions coming from dumb terminals, 2260s, and later 3270s. And it would handle that application cleanly for you. But it was a systems program.

Ceruzzi: Was this something that was understood in the trial?

Goetz: It wasn't an issue in the trial because IBM unbundled it. It's a sub-operating system and, logically, they could have said, this is part of the operating system. But they didn't.

Grad: There's a reason why they didn't. The product divisions which were doing the operating systems didn't believe in any of this stuff. We built this with customers. CICS was built with Commonwealth Edison of Chicago. And IMS, the database management system, was built with one of the aerospace companies. The Data Processing Division did those because the product division said, "No, we don't have time or money to do that." So we also built all the VM programs. All of what became the enduring programs came out of the Data Processing Division, so they were never considered to be systems programs.

Schachter: And after unbundling, those were separately charged for.

Grad: Yes, we had seventeen programs that we unbundled. CICS, IMS, and GIS were among them. They unbundled one language. But the ones that made money were CICS and IMS. Everything else was second rate. We had PALIS for the property and liability insurance industry and ALIS for the life insurance industry. But they were nothing. It's interesting, from a standardization standpoint, that all the application-building companies, when they built their online applications, ended up using CICS, for whatever reason.

Keet: Not true. That's absolutely not true. We had more than 20% of the market in 1978 when IBM announced a tie-in—an *uncontested* tie-in. The master scheduler of CICS henceforth would be the control mechanisms for the DL1 database system for the smaller systems. I went to IBM and told them that this was a tie-in. There were people there from the ADAPSO IBM group, including Ed Kane and Grant Leschin from Industry Relations, and a bunch of others, and they all nodded their heads and said, "Yes, it's a tie-in. It's linked. What do you want us to do?" And I said, "What are my choices?"

And they said, "Well, it's clear that you can sue us." They gave me the impression that they acknowledged that I had an open-and-shut case. They said that IBM didn't damage our market intentionally. Which I do believe, incidentally. They said, "We'd love to make it up to you. Would you like some contract programming work?" [*Laughter*]

The third choice was to walk away. Fortunately, at that point, we had other products that we were thinking of porting to CICS because it did have a dominant market share and I made the decision to just walk away, not to sue IBM and not to take the tainted dog bone that they were throwing.

Part of the problem was that IBM used its market muscle to tell the guys making the decisions that they needed to stay 100% in the IBM camp if they wanted to be favored customers. We were there fighting over the scraps, the customers that had said no to IBM and were buying independent software. We were competing with companies like ADR which had a database system and had added on a telecommunications monitor and were selling the two combined.

Schachter: So they had bundled two products. [*Laughter*]

Keet: We didn't take them to court.

Goetz: Lee, for the record, we sold them separately.

Keet: I know you did. When somebody wanted to buy an independent telecommunications monitor, we won most of those sales. We had a really dominant position until IBM made that tie-in decision.

Ceruzzi: And what was the name of your product?

Keet: Task/Master. It was one of the first. We introduced a predecessor product named Graphics in 1969. We changed the name to Task/Master and introduced a multitasking version in 1970. We sold it aggressively from '70 to '78 and a lot of the customers were on non-perpetual recurring licenses so when IBM killed our new sales, we still had a very good revenue stream. It was another reason we could walk away. But it wasn't true that CICS was a good product or everybody would have bought it because they love Burt. [*Laughter*]

Schachter: Why don't we go back to '72. At the end of '72, the economic policy group met in New York and prepared a position paper which was adopted by ADAPSO in 1973. It's so interesting to read the five points of proposed relief. In 1987, ADAPSO adopted its last position paper with regard to IBM. It has virtually the same five points, with an additional two points added to cover additional IBM practices. So it's hard to say exactly how much effect we had on IBM. I believe that we slowed them down, that we made them think twice about what they were going to do, but that, in large part, we didn't stop them from doing much. Marty, I don't know if you would agree.

Goetz: I think we slowed them down. I think the plan was really to just slow them down. In retrospect, I think it was just that IBM was basically a hardware company. They were thinking of what was good for their customers and what was easiest for them, not about stepping on some software company. I think when we made them aware of the problems they created, they became more sensitive and, in that sense, ADAPSO was very effective.

Keet: What happened in my experience was that there were so many of us they had contact with as a result of ADAPSO that a lot of people in IBM came to appreciate us. I know I said to them bluntly that I was selling a hell of a lot more hardware for IBM as an ex-IBMer making software than I ever sold as a salesman selling IBM hardware. I think that they eventually saw that we were good for their business, not bad for their business. I think some of the enlightenment came through these constant encounters.

Grad: I think Lee's point is very significant. Those of us inside IBM who were interested in software felt that we were being stepped on all the time by the hardware people because we had to justify software in terms of hardware sales, not in terms of a stand-alone business case on software. We kept saying, "The best thing that can happen is that all the software companies use IBM systems, IBM tools, IBM whatever, and that their software runs on IBM hardware. That's the way to win." We didn't get much of a reception until very late in the '70s. I'm trying to remember when the "love-in" took place that Sam Albert organized where they invited a whole bunch of software executives to partner with them.

That may have been later, probably early '80s, but I see here in my notes that in '75, IBM hosted a very large meeting for all of the people in ADAPSO to give them a complete education on what IBM was doing. It was obviously a sales pitch.

Goetz: They did that every two or three years. It was sort of a love-hate relationship.

Grad: But there was a meeting called a "love-in". I think that's the time at which they finally realized what Lee was saying. That it was really to their interest to have these people on their side and that they, in effect, made IBM totally dominant because all the applications were being built under IBM systems.

Schachter: But there did come a time, as lawyers like to say, when even that became an issue because the ability of software companies to provide applications and provide tools for IBM operating systems depended on having interface information that was complete and available early on in the development process. They didn't get the information until the product was already released. That became a major issue when IBM started adopting an OCO policy.

Grad: When did the big level playing field project start?

Jones: Was it about '84?

Grad: Was it that late? I'm trying to tie it in time-wise.

Jones: It probably did come up in the late '70s but in a different context.

Schachter: But even in the '73 position paper, Point No. 4 was that the IBM software organization would be required to release comprehensive software interface specifications to all interested independent software companies at the same time it released them to its hardware organization. I don't know if that ever happened but...

Grad: To its hardware organization or to its internal software people?

Schachter: In later variations of this, it became its internal software development organization. In the first iteration it was to its hardware organization. We didn't distinguish between them either, I guess, at that time.

Grad: A lot of the growth in the big software companies in the '70s was in database, data communications, that kind of stuff. A lot of the money from the bigger companies came from that area. They were arguing that IBM was taking advantage of internal knowledge and that they couldn't get the interface information they needed. Also they couldn't get guarantees that the interfaces were locked. There was a set of those issues. My recollection is that was in the late '70s but I could be dead wrong.

Jones: I think it was continuous.

Schachter: There was never a feeling that we had the same information that the IBM organization had internally. I guess, as time went on, IBM started to protect itself against Fujitsu and the plug-compatible competitors like Amdahl, and it just became more and more problematic. Until in the '80s they adopted the OCO policy.

Grad: I'm trying to remember. I know that I was instructed, even though my applications people in IBM had early access to interface information, that using it was very dangerous because it wasn't locked. And if I took a chance and built against that, I took the risk of losing money. They were concerned that if they published it and then changed it, all the software companies were going to be coming after IBM claiming that they changed the rules. So they said they couldn't do that. The response from the software companies was that they shouldn't let the internal software people have it either. That was the counter-offer.

Goetz: They wanted to be on an equal footing.

Grad: And that was the whole level playing field issue that came up later.

Goetz: But I don't think IBM ever explicitly changed their business practices. They were sensitive to the things that ADAPSO said, but they never said, "Okay, we're going to change our policies."

Grad: I think you're wrong. I think there was a point in time at which they explicitly issued rules on timing: that they would not give their internal people access to software information that they didn't publish externally. I remember that. I don't know when, but I remember that happening at some point in time.

Keet: I remember them stating in a meeting that we had with them that they were considering doing that, but I do not remember ever seeing a policy issued.

Ceruzzi: In practical terms, what would prevent them from violating that?

Grad: Internal rules. In a big company like that, you publish rules to operate to. A salesman out in the field might do some very, very nasty things. He could violate everything that's in the book and, if he got caught publicly, they'd scream at him. If he made his quota and did well and no one caught him, the issue disappeared.

Ceruzzi: This is the exact same issue that's on the table today with Microsoft releasing the APIs. And at one point Steve Ballmer got up and said, "Well, you know we talk to each other inside the building, you can't make us shut up." That shocked everyone.

Grad: That's Gates and Ballmer. That was part of their stupidity.

Ceruzzi: It was stupidity but they were telling the truth.

Campbell-Kelly: How much did the System Application Architecture make the interfaces publicly available?

Grad: They were available.

Campbell-Kelly: Did that not resolve these kind of issues?

Grad: It wasn't that simple.

Keet: And it was a lot later.

Grad: The software companies' argument was: We've got the published interface, but meanwhile you're developing more capability, you're adding new functions, you're doing things in your systems programs.

I remember Syncsort complaining to IBM because IBM had added some new hardware feature and was announcing a new sort program that was going to run much, much faster because it was using this feature. But they wouldn't make the function public. IBM said that the reason was that they weren't guaranteeing that they would continue to use the function. A terrible argument. So Aso Tavitian, CEO of Syncsort, went after them. First of all, he proved that they were lying in their ads and that, in fact, the sort did not run any faster; the test cases that they used were just flat wrong. He got them to withdraw the statement that this was a faster feature. But he also insisted, "If you're going to put it in, you've got to publish it." Aso won that round. This may have been the mid-'80s or even later, but Syncsort was on their case over and over again because they kept claiming things about their sort program that he thought weren't true and they couldn't prove.

I don't know if that answered your question. IBM published very high-level interfaces. That's not where we were fighting. The battles were different.

Schachter: Let's go to one of the other battles that happened in the early '80s which was re-bundling, when IBM decided to bundle fourteen of its products into what was called SSX.

Goetz: Yeah, this ended up being a problem that ADR had because IBM had a lot of small users that had a small operating system. In retrospect, I don't think they did it to hurt ADR, or to hurt Pansophic which had something somewhat similar.

Schachter: You've mellowed a lot. [*Laughter*]

Goetz: Nevertheless, it was hurting our sales significantly. They bundled fourteen products, including the operating system, and sold it as one product to their small users. It was called the Small System Executive/VSE system and was an operating system that was a subset of VSE. We complained because we competed against one of the individual products. ADAPSO was very sympathetic because no one wanted to see re-bundling. We didn't want to see it happen on the bigger machines. So ADAPSO supported our position. That was a case of IBM overtly bundling but for a very limited market.

Keet: What we now call suites. [*Laughter*]

Grad: And everybody does it.

Goetz: But the suite included the operating system, so it's more than an office suite.

Grad: What operating system was included?

Goetz: DOS.

Schachter: IBM did modify the policy, I think.

Goetz: They eventually modified it so that if the user didn't want one of the products, it would be deleted from the tape that they would get, and they would pay less rent. So that was a very minor victory. I don't think IBM did it to hurt ADR, but it was, in fact, hurting ADR. So we complained and we got IBM to at least listen to our case. It was quite different than the mid to late-'80s when they bundled a mini version of their DB2 database into the OS2 operating system when Microsoft was building IBM OS2. There I think they were concerned about losing a piece of the database marketplace. They knew what they were doing and didn't care that they would perhaps hurt a lot of database companies. But I would say, for the most part, IBM was very hardware-oriented and really wanted to work closely with software companies. It really helped them sell their hardware. Everybody was building software for IBM's computers.

Grad: Oscar, you were running the IBM Relations or Manufacturers Relations Committee for quite awhile.

Schachter: Right.

Grad: How many years, do you remember?

Schachter: I think I started in '76, '77, sometime around that period. I was chairman until Marty became chairman in '87. At that point I became president of the Software Products Section and Marty took over what we were then calling the IBM Interface Committee. We kept changing the name from Manufacturers Relations to IBM Relations and then to IBM Interface Committee because the interfaces became a major issue at that point.

Grad: There was a committee that Kim Jones and I worked on. Roger Sisson, an independent consultant, was a third member of that committee. There were a lot of people involved writing papers relating to IBM policies. Kim, do you have any idea what timeframe that was?

Jones: It was probably the late '80s.

Grad: Was that a specific outgrowth of the IBM Relations Committee?

Jones: It was an outgrowth of the announcement of SAA.

Keet: Wasn't Rich Carpenter of Index Technology on that committee? And Jim Emerson of Pansophic?

Grad: Yes, Jim certainly was. A few of us did the writing but there were a lot of other people involved. We'd have meetings at each of the conferences and there were a lot of comments made.

Jones: I know we reported back to the Software Section board.

Schachter: The last position paper was in September of '87 and, to some extent, it was a reaffirmation and updating of the '83 position paper which had the seven points that were first defined in '73. As you read through the seven points in that paper, you can substitute Microsoft for IBM and make an intelligible statement out of it. For example: To the greatest extent possible each product or service offered should be narrowly defined, unbundled from all other products and services, and separately described, priced and offered to customers. Any product which has ever been offered on a separately-priced basis must continue to be offered on a separately-priced basis. Certainly Microsoft has violated that. Each product or service has to be costed to include all costs of conceiving, constructing, acquiring, packaging, maintaining and supporting the product. And the next point was that, after including all of those costs, it also needs to be fully priced to include a reasonable profit. I don't think we ever really got terribly involved with IBM in that arena.

Goetz: We never challenged them, we just wanted to make sure they fully priced their software because they had all the same salesmen selling hardware and software.

Grad: The way they did pricing, it worked that way mechanically. You couldn't avoid it because the overhead was spread based upon revenue. The only argument you could make is that if the salesman spent a lot of time trying to sell and didn't succeed, he didn't charge it against the project. He charged it on a percentage basis.

Schachter: The next point in the position paper, which we haven't talked about, is: Products or services shall not be announced until there is an operational prototype.

Keet: It would have wiped out our industry if we had to follow that rule. [*Laughter*]

Grad: None of you were going to follow those rules, that's for sure.

Schachter: What's totally operational?   It happens all the time that it's announced, it's released, it's put on the machine and it's still not totally operational. [*Laughter*]

Grad: It's interesting, because I remember some of our discussions in our meetings at the Software Section Board and with the IBM Relations Committee when I asked, "Would you be willing to live by the rules you just wrote down?" And, of course, the answer was no.

Goetz: We always felt special rules for special times.   [*Laughter*]   And that's conventional practice because, for instance, bundling is not illegal unless you monopolize one of the products.

Grad: That was always Marty's answer at the time, that IBM is different. You have to have special rules.   We were proposing these rules for all manufacturers at the time, though, not just for IBM, right?

Goetz: The reason that particular point about an operational prototype is in there was because IBM had taken a position, because of the Control Data suit, that they wouldn't announce a piece of hardware until they had a prototype. So we said, "Fine, if they have to do it for hardware, let them do it for software."

Grad: That's right, I'd forgotten that.

Schachter: Early announcements had the effect of freezing the market at various times. Was that purposeful? Were they trying to let their customers know what was coming down the road?   What was their motivation for those early announcements of products?

Goetz: Well, Lee Keet said he was hit hard when CICS/DL1 was announced.   IBM's position was always that they wanted to let their customers plan ahead.   Lee, what did you think when they announced CICS/DL1?

Keet: Well, I would make a distinction between IBM's public announcements and what its sales force did. This was an account control issue and those were the operative words in IBM: maintain account control. CICS versus Task/Master, or IMS versus another database management system, were account control issues. The salesmen were basically given a license to kill. They were made 007's or 008's, or whatever, and they would do anything. I always thought that IBM, at its core, like Microsoft, thought that they wore the white hats. And they behaved fairly ethically at the core. But at the periphery, depending on which sales guy you were dealing with, they could be the dirtiest, ugliest, most aggressive fighters in the world and they'd use any tool at their disposal. I know. I sold for IBM for three years. [*Laughter*]

Schachter: In the '70s, were they using that tactic because they were concerned about CDC? Were they using it in the '80s because they were concerned about Fujitsu?

Keet: In my experience, they were using it because they didn't want a foreign piece of system software in an account because they felt that was a wedge to challenge account control. If a piece of system software of importance could be installed, could be maintained, could host applications with different standards than those IBM was supporting, then that was a chink in the armor. And from that point on, that account could move aggressively in the direction of independent suppliers. At least, that is what the sales force thought. I'm not complaining about it, it was just that you were fighting a very, very strong competitor who could turn very ugly.

Jones: Wasn't it part of the sales culture in a way, Lee? We haven't mentioned the term that I always associated with IBM sales at that time which was FUD—fear, uncertainty and doubt. Cultivating that in the client base was just part of the sales culture.

Keet: Those of us who survived had to fight FUD by making ourselves look larger. What's the animal that puffs itself up? We had to do things to make ourselves more impressive and that's why Larry Welke had such a positive impact. He helped us look more professional and bigger than we were. He would publish reviews of software. It was like the *New Yorker* magazine. If it was not a good restaurant, don't write the review. So we always got good reviews. He gave $1 million, $5 million, $10 million awards on a mechanical calculation basis that let you count your sister-in-law's kids. [*Laughter*]

Schachter: This is off the record, by the way. [*Laughter*]

Keet: No, it's not . And we did another thing which a lot of people do. These are the anecdotes that I think should be collected because they are about the business practices that people came up with to succeed. We prepared a checklist which compared Task/Master to CICS. It had almost 200 questions which you could weight yourself and that you could check yes or no. Of course, the questions were very biased, so you could never put a yes next to a CICS question, so it didn't matter what weight you gave them. [*Laughter*]

A journalist who was in a hurry for a date or a drink picked it up and said, "Would you guys just put in what you think are the important weightings?" So we put in the weights and, of course, checked yes on all for Task/Master. To make it look a little more legitimate, we put in two new questions that we checked yes for CICS. He published that and we had it reprinted and sent it out to everybody along with a blank one saying, "We know this may be a little biased in our favor, so here's a blank one. You fill in what you want." It gave us enough legitimacy that we could actually go up against those IBM guys who were saying things like, "Those are little guys. They're going to go out of business and you're going to have your whole future ruined as a result of making this terrible decision. Besides that, you won't be a friend of IBM and we won't service you as well in the future as we used to in the past because we know you made the decision not to be a friend of IBM." Those were the kinds of pitches the IBM salesmen made.

Grad: I don't know what effect it had on the sales people at IBM, but the '70s were a terrible period in terms of IBM sales. IBM hardware sales tanked during the '70s. The stock price tanked. I had some stock options that were so far underwater when I left in '78, that it wasn't even worth discussing or negotiating. It was a very tough period. I'm sure the sales people were under intense pressure. There was a new growth market in the software area but the IBM salesmen didn't make much money off of that. That was peanuts to them. Their goal was to sell hardware. CICS enabled them to sell hardware and, therefore, that became a gut issue. IMS sold hardware, so that became a gut issue. Most of the other stuff, selling some kind of utility program or something, couldn't have mattered less to the salesman. He wasn't getting any money out of it. He wasn't getting any money out of operating systems. Therefore, IBM was responsive in certain areas in these committee discussions because no one cared. In other areas, you got big stone walls.

Schachter: But it's interesting, Burt, on the interface questions, one of the arguments that IBM used—I remember this expression so clearly at a number of meetings that we had both at ADAPSO and at the IBM headquarters in Armonk—was: We don't want software companies grazing through our source code to see where there are holes so they can develop pieces of software to fill those holes. Do you remember that, Marty? That was an expression that I heard a number of times, "We don't want them grazing through our source code." So evidently they *were* somewhat concerned. Or they may have just used that as an argument.

Jones: That was the OCO argument.

Campbell-Kelly: Can I ask a question about operating systems? Marty, around 1977 or 1978, you wrote quite a number of provocative articles about the fact that IBM hadn't unbundled its operating systems and you argued that it was stifling innovation. You, and others, also alleged that it was probably soaking up processing cycles as well, that the operating systems were really inefficient. Around the late '70s, IBM did, in fact, start to charge for its operating systems, but it didn't open up a market for operating systems.

Goetz: Well, no, because by that time they dominated the market. But their main reason for doing it was that they started having the Japanese and Amdahl plug-compatible computer manufacturers coming in and taking the free operating system.

Ceruzzi: Didn't they steal it? Wasn't one of the Japanese companies convicted?

Goetz: Well, there was a suit against Hitachi and an agreement with Fujitsu. Basically, it was all IBM code. Amdahl was always all IBM code. There was too much code to write to be plug-compatible.

Grad: It was Fujitsu, I believe, which was convicted of stealing the code. IBM and the court came up with this very elaborate process for how they were going to be allowed to use it but only under monitored conditions.

The IBM clones caused big problems for IBM. The minute IBM unbundled system software, anybody could buy it and use it on any of the IBM work-alikes. Was Amdahl the first of the IBM work-alikes?

Several voices: Yes. Yes. Yes.

Grad: Yeah, so it was a pretty complicated situation. The claim Marty used to make was that they were purposely over-building the system software so it would take more machine cycles. I gave a speech after I left IBM when I talked about the totally illogical process by which IBM decided on CICS and IMS. I said that I was never told to slow the machine down, but I was never told to speed it up either. [*Laughter*]

Keet: Do you remember the Series 50 EAM machines? I used to install those things. They'd just change a gear in the machine and the price would change with the gear. It would just run slower or faster.

Grad: You're paying for performance—that seems like a reasonable thing to do. [*Laughter*]

Keet: Their EAM market was pretty well-saturated by that point and they wanted to get to the lower end of the market. They were introducing computers at the high end and they wanted to use this old stuff. So they changed a gear, literally one gear, so that a 407 line printer, instead of going chunk, chunk, chunk, chunk would go ka-chunk, ka-chunk, ka-chunk. And they sold it for less.

Ceruzzi: People must have known that they could swap that gear.

Grad: No, you couldn't touch the equipment. Under the contract, only IBM field engineers could touch the machine.

Ceruzzi: But people did.

Keet: Well, they did it in collusion with their field engineer or something.

Ceruzzi: There was a case where having the floating point option was a lot of extra money but it just involved installing a jumper wire. Word got around and people would just do it.

Jones: That was with the 360, I think.

Ceruzzi: Somebody at a university called a repairman said, "Our floating point option's not working." And he was told, "Well, you haven't paid for floating point for years." [*Laughter*]

Keet: Even in the computer era, the rents were based on meter readings. There were some notorious cases of tampering. There was one case of a branch manager who had been promoted to VP, where they found that the meters had been tampered with, with IBM's assistance, so the customer didn't have to pay the extra charges. It did happen.

Grad: Did we ever end up discussing things such as pricing issues or pricing practices on the IBM Relations Committee?

Schachter: Well, we had those two points I mentioned that the software had to be fully-costed and fully-priced.

Grad: But I don't think IBM would have discussed that with you, did they?

Goetz: We never had anyone talk about that.

Keet: Tommy Spain wouldn't talk about that. Well, he wouldn't talk about anything. He was the best negotiator I ever met in my life. But that was a big issue. He said, "No, we can't talk about pricing issues for very obvious reasons. And we can't talk about unbundling or re-bundling because that's an issue before the courts and we can't... " He had an excuse for every single thing.

Schachter: They pulled the lawyers out of the closet whenever they could. Whenever it wasn't convenient to answer a question, "Well, the lawyers won't let us talk about it."

Grad: Was Ed Kane actively involved? I'm trying to remember some of the people that were actively involved from IBM.

Goetz: Amby Carr.

Grad: But that was later, wasn't it?

Schachter: Grant Leschin was certainly involved during that period.

Keet: Tommy Spain came back for a meeting that John Imlay organized. We'd finally reached the point where we'd gotten their attention and a group of us went to a meeting that John organized in Atlanta. I can't remember who all was there because one of Tommy's great tactics was to drink everybody else under the table. [*Laughter*] We had a great party but I can't remember who was there. [*Laughter*] Tom could do it sequentially, which was really interesting. He could drink you under the table and then the next guy under the table and...

Ceruzzi: I thought they weren't supposed to drink.

Grad: Well, that's what makes Tom so unusual.

Keet: Tom had stepped back and let Ed Kane run the show for those middle years in the '80s. We didn't see a lot of Tom in the '80s. He came back for this meeting which was around '86 or '87.

Schachter: Is that the love-in you were talking about?

Keet: No, this was a small group.

Grad: Bernie Goldstein raised a question before he left today about the early '80s. I don't remember the IBM Relations Committee getting involved in the PC issues, do you?

Goetz: Yes. When IBM and Microsoft came out with OS2 in about '86, it became an ADAPSO issue because IBM said they were going to come out with a special version of OS2 called OS2 Extended which would include a DB2 database. We were fighting against DB2 at the mainframe level and they said, "Well, when you get your PC with OS2 Extended that has DB2 at that end, you will obviously want DB2 on your mainframe." And we said they should sell the database separately. Eventually, they decided they would withdraw OS2 Extended and then OS2 died.

Grad: How long did the Manufacturers Relations Committee continue?

Goetz: It continued into the early '90s because there was a DEC issue. DEC started bundling. I became chairman about '87 or '88 and served until about '92.

Grad: The level playing field issue. Was that specifically related to the Manufacturers Relations Committee, do you remember?

Jones: No, it was originally just a report to the board and then it expanded.

Grad: Wasn't it triggered by the IBM relations issues?

Jones: Yeah, but it was specific to the announcement of SAA and a concern that that was going to blossom into something new.

Grad: IBM had another thing besides SAA, another three initials – was it a communications interface?

Ceruzzi: SNA. System Network Architecture and System Application Architecture.

Grad: SAA came after SNA, didn't it?

Keet: Correct. SNA was part of the seven layer protocol implementation.

Grad: I don't remember how much these things were business-related and how much they were technically-related.

Keet: SAA was a business initiative in my opinion. SNA was a technical initiative.

Jones: My recollection of SAA is that we were concerned that there was going to be some stifling of creativity within the software industry and that IBM was so dominant that SAA would become the standard.

Grad: Was this the too-early standard issue that came up so many times? Don't let your standards get set until the technology has evolved sufficiently?

Jones: Well, yes, to some extent, and it was also very squishy. It was very high level and not well-formed and not even particularly well-thought-out. It was another one of those things that I think was viewed as potentially freezing people out.

Keet: Some of it was very detailed but not thought out, like screen designs.

Jones: Right, right.

Keet: You had to put commands in one spot and you had to put instructions in another and had to use this kind of iconography and blah, blah, blah. It was the rulebook. Everybody's application was going to look the same but they hadn't thought about it very much and, therefore, it would have stifled creativity.

Grad: That has always been a very tough issue with any of the external standards groups. Those same kinds of issues always come up. The comment we always made about IBM was that it was the sea we swam in. The good news is that it did give us a set of standards that gave us a large market to sell to.

Keet: Well, nobody would dispute the IBM umbrella. I think that we have to acknowledge that without IBM as an established dominant player this industry would not have been as successful.

Schachter: Imagine if there had been ten hardware companies each with 10% of the market.

Keet: Even back when it was IBM and the seven dwarfs, remember that?

Schachter: Right, but IBM still had 80% of the market, the seven dwarfs had 20%.

Grad: The 360 in the middle of the '60s is what totally shifted the balance.

Goetz: The application people would say it wasn't a big problem because they were building their applications in COBOL which would run on different manufacturers' computers.

Grad: That was fine for a batch program but the minute you moved over to CICS and made an online program out of it, you were into IBM-only because the others didn't have a CICS look-alike.

Jones: Unless you built in a proprietary language.

Keet: Or unless you used Task/Master. Which was written in COBOL.

Grad: It could have happened that way. The database world turned out that way. IMS did not dominate anywhere near the way that CICS did. IMS had maybe 20% of the market at most. IDMS, Adabas, all these others had big chunks of the market.

Keet: I'll take a bet that IMS had over half the market.

Goetz: At one point they had a majority of the market but it went down to about 40%. That's when they started getting concerned that IMS was losing market share and that's when they started coming out with DB2 very intently.

Grad: You're talking about the early '80s. I'm talking about the '70s.

Schachter: We need to wrap it up. Thank you all for being here. If everyone made the points you wanted to make, if everyone got their feelings out on the table, I think we've accomplished what we came here to accomplish. Thank you all for participating.

Big Eight Accounting Firms Workshop

Moderators: Dave Campbell and Thomas Haigh

Rapporteur: Elizabeth Virgo

Participants: Jay Goldberg   Ron Palenski
                                 Doug Jerger   Mary Jane Saunders
                                 Phil Frana

Campbell: Our charter here is to record observations or thoughts or experiences related to the topic. I haven't thought much about recording my thoughts for a hundred years from now, but that's what we're here to do. I also have one good takeaway for you. For years we lived with the term "The Big Eight" and then the number went down and we didn't have a good term to replace it. I think we now can adopt the term "The Final Four." [*Laughter*] That's your takeaway for the day.

We'll go around the table and have everyone introduce themselves and talk about their perspective on CPA relations. And then I'll speak a bit to the leadership questions that were provided.

My name is David Campbell and I am the Managing Director of a company called Innovation Advisors. During the late '70s and early '80s, I was running Computer Task Group and chaired the ADAPSO CPA Relations Committee. We entered into direct negotiations with some of the Big Eight firms which we'll talk about in some detail. Jay?

Goldberg: Jay Goldberg. I run a venture fund called Hudson Ventures. I was chairman of ADAPSO in 1987 and I ran the Professional Services Section of ADAPSO during the period when it was negotiating with the Big Eight. At that time, I ran a company called Software Design Associates.

Saunders: I'm Mary Jane Saunders. From '83 to '89, I was on the staff of ADAPSO and I'm now a lawyer in private practice.

Palenski: I'm Ron Palenski. I was on staff as counsel to ADAPSO from December of 1978 until October 1994, and CPA relations was one of my responsibilities.

Jerger: I'm Doug Jerger. During the '70s and '80s, I was with a company called Fortex Data Corporation and served as the Chairman of the CPA

Relations Committee, working with Ron. I ended up in that position because I was mad at Arthur Andersen, which is where I started working directly out of school. I was with them for ten years and I was bothered by the fact that they did consulting work for companies and were auditing those same firms.

We testified in front of Congress on this issue on August 1st, 1979. Ron and I spent a lot of time talking to Congressional staff and to the SEC. When we talked to the SEC in 1979, we said, "This is a problem." And they said, "Do you have any egregious examples of it? Or any examples at all?" And we said, "No, we don't, but when it hits the fan it's going to be terrible." It did. It is.

Later I was on the staff of ADAPSO, but that was in the '90s.

Haigh: I'm Thomas Haigh. I'm your historical co-moderator. I think we should try to cover the chronology of ADAPSO's involvement with the issue and how it progressed over time.

Beyond that, one question I'm really interested in is: What was it like competing against the Big Eight accounting firms and why have they been so enormously successful in this area? I have some figures here that show that in 1977 they had 70% of their revenue from audits, 18% from tax-related services and only 11% from management advisory services. Today, obviously, the consulting side in most of the firms is more profitable and shows more growth than the auditing and other traditional areas. So one of the things that I'm not able to explain as a historian is what it was they were doing that let them compete so effectively in consulting services and grow their revenues from them so successfully.

Virgo: I'm Elizabeth Virgo. I'm a consultant. I worked with Burt Grad for a long time on valuations and we had quite a few brushes with the Big Eight on behalf of our clients. And, ironically, I was asked by Deloitte Touche, as an independent consultant living in Bermuda, to be their consultant. So I had plenty of opportunity to bug them about this whole issue of independence.

Frana: I'm Philip Frana. I'm the National Science Foundation's Software History Project Manager at the Charles Babbage Institute and another historian.

Campbell: Larry Schoenberg of AGS Computers was active on this issue and I think Mike Nugent of the ADAPSO staff also worked on it.

My own experiences working on the issue were at the time when we were deciding whether to try to keep Arthur Andersen out of the business and/or out of ADAPSO. It was several years after Doug got involved and we were working with Jack Chesson, who was the staff guy for Congressman Dingell. Dingell may have been a nasty guy but he was our nasty guy. So we supported him and the same issue that was raised by the SEC came up: Can you find a smoking gun? Can you find a place where an audit was done inappropriately because of a consulting services contract?

We raised money across the various sections of ADAPSO and did a survey to provide a response to the smoking gun question. Candidly, in my assessment, we were not able to come back with a smoking gun. We went to every ADAPSO member and said, "If you know of a suspicious situation, just send in a name or a place and we'll try to research it. "

The people we were working with were John Fairfield and Robert Prince from Andersen. We were negotiating to keep them out of ADAPSO and they were negotiating what they would do if we let them in. As always, economics was part of it. They were willing to come in as full dues-paying members and they were large companies. Since dues were proportional to revenues, they were going to be making large dues payments. And they added that they would run educational programs at ADAPSO to share their expertise in project management and a whole variety of things. My sense was that we had raised money, taken our best shot, tried to find a smoking gun, and did not find anything that was going to be legally enforceable. And we caved. That's my sense of what happened in the mid-'80s. Do you have any different recollection, Jay?

Goldberg: Well, my view of the association in those days was that it should be inclusive. I always felt that having the Big Eight as members of the association would be an advantage in that it would at least allow a dialogue to take place. So I was very much in favor of having Andersen join. I think what we had hoped was the other seven would follow them and, if I remember correctly, they didn't. But Andersen became pretty actively involved and engaged.

Jerger: Yeah, Fairfield, whom I had known when I was at the firm, was the guy that we were dealing with mainly. We had a luncheon one time at one of the clubs in Chicago and he said, "Look, the only reason you guys are opposed to our doing consulting is you're concerned because we are better than you guys are." And I said, "Keep it separate from your auditing and from the Andersen name and we'll compete with you on any basis at all. And, by the way, why don't you join ADAPSO." Of course, he said, "Why would I? You're telling us you're going to attack us." So we gave him IBM as an example of a company that had been attacked by ADAPSO but thought it was beneficial to belong and that it could lead to a better understanding all around.

Campbell: In response to your questions, Tom, I'll throw in a little bit of data since the issue of independence of the audit function is so much on the floor today. Literally. This is Saturday, the 4th of May, 2002, and on Monday the Federal Government starts its trial against Arthur Andersen. And it really will end up with the demise of the firm. The firm probably won't exist by the end of this year.

The *Wall Street Journal* did a survey on this issue earlier this year. They surveyed 300+ of the S&P 500 and every one of the firms bought some non-audit services from their auditor, and the non-audit fees were three times the size of the audit fees. One other set of facts for the record is that Accenture, which is the new name of Andersen Consulting which was spun off from Arthur Andersen, has about a $20 billion market cap today. I think the amount that CAP Gemini paid when they bought E&Y's consulting practice was $10 billion. For KPMG's practice, I think the number was about $2.5 billion, and I think Price Waterhouse expects about an $8 billion valuation when they complete their IPO which they filed for last week. We will see the separation of these firms, but it's interesting that the troubles that befell Arthur Andersen happened after the separation of the consulting unit. And, frankly, if you are being paid $25 million to do an audit of a company, is that not inherently a fairly significant conflict?

Goldberg: Non-audit work is more than IT consulting.

Campbell: Right. There were a variety of other kinds of services. I flew in this week with an audit partner from PW. His comment was that having responsibility for the audit is the equivalent of having a hallway pass in high school. It allows you to go anywhere in a company and be treated with deference. And that is enough of an advantage in a competitive capitalistic system.

I think that they really did things that were pretty significant conflicts of interest. They would be on the assessment panel for a software product, for example, even though they might have a similar software product. How could a company like Doug's submit its software for assessment and give a Big Eight firm that was creating a competitive product access to the code? What protections were there? I don't know that we thought that any code had actually been stolen, but it certainly made people nervous at the time.

Jerger: I don't think they stole anything, but they got all the work because of that hall pass they had. After Arthur Andersen spun out Andersen Consulting, John Fairfield said, "Well, we separated the consulting business from the audit business. Jerger, you were right." And then I went to their offices. Arthur Andersen has brown doors as their logo, everyplace in the world. When I played on their softball team, we had brown doors on our T-shirts. So if you went to three floors of this building, it said Arthur Andersen on the brown doors, and if you went to the fourth floor, it said Andersen Consulting on the same brown doors. They made a big deal about the Chinese wall between the two identities, but that just wasn't the case.

Goldberg: To put it into a context, it's important to understand the era when this was taking place. In the early days of the software industry, most of the systems being sold were related to accounting. In today's world you don't think of it that way. You think about software as games or engineering or medicine. In the early days, the vast majority of software was accounting software. It got sold to or through the CFO, so the CFO was the decision maker in the acquisition of most software. That was the case even for system software because the data processing department typically reported to the CFO in a large company. And Andersen or KPMG had a relationship with the CFO to begin with. To me that set the stage for a conflict because the market was so centralized. In today's world I think it's probably less of an issue than it was in that era.

Jerger: Even if a CFO didn't have a close relationship with the accounting firm, let's say he had two competing bids, one from Jay's company, SDA, and one from Arthur Andersen. Let's see, there's big dollars involved and a lot of risk. Hmm, I think I'll go with Andersen because no one can criticize that decision. They were covering themselves, right?

Campbell: It was also true in those firms that their economic model was based on bringing young people in, getting very significant effort out of them, and then moving those people out in an aggressive but supportive way into their client companies. To this day they manage very strong relationships with an alumni network which is very active. None of our companies had that model. We were bringing young people in and keeping them because we were growing our businesses. So their normal business model populated the customer world with their alumni, very deliberately, because the ratio of people in the firm who would become partners was fairly small and the rest would be exported to their customers. Those were the people that helped influence buying decisions.

Jerger: At Andersen, you knew even before you started that the rule was it's up or out. So if you didn't go up, you went out quickly, and the alumni group was terrific, worked very efficiently.

Virgo: That hasn't changed, really. That is still what they do.

Campbell: Part of the issue is, what were the long-term impacts? They've grown, but our industry has also grown dramatically, so it's hard to measure it exactly. We'd have to go back to the late '70s or early '80s and measure the total amount of third-party professional IT services done by the Big Eight compared to that done by all other companies combined. And then compare that to the percentages today. They have grown dramatically, as you can see by their revenue, but there are now many multi-hundred-million dollar companies that didn't exist in 1975. The company I was running, Computer Task Group, went from revenues of $3 million to $300 million in the 25 years from 1975 to 2000. Andersen's revenues didn't grow a hundred-fold. They were much larger than CTG then and they are still much larger, but you'd have to measure a whole set of companies and their growth rates to determine the impact.

They had an extraordinary competitive advantage. It may not have been a hard conflict of interest in the sense that it influenced whether they gave a clean audit opinion or not, but they had a significant advantage because if you were a major public company, you effectively had to have one of those eight firms do your audit. That was just the tradition as it evolved. The SEC said you had to have a public firm audit your books—that had been mandated since 1934—and, as it evolved, you really needed one of these eight firms for all practical purposes. So, if you were a major public company, you were going to have one of that set of companies as an auditor and they also provided this other service. We all know how easy it is to add another service to the sale to the same customer. So they clearly had a competitive advantage. I don't know whether that constitutes a hard conflict of interest.

Goldberg: It's also possible that they enhanced the growth of the industry. We tend to look at it from the standpoint of competitive issues, but the fact is that a lot of large companies might not have embarked on major development projects had those efforts not been done by accounting firms. So, to some extent, I've got to believe that large companies had the confidence to do the stuff that they did because it was done by a Big Eight firm rather than a small independent software firm. We always looked at the negative aspect of it but I think there were actually some positive aspects in terms of legitimatizing the business, giving it a more professional appearance. If you were a consulting firm back in the '60s and early '70s, you were looked on as being a lesser form of life. It was like we were just temps, like Kelly Girls. The fact is that Andersen, and some of the larger companies like EDS, gave the industry much more of an air of professionalism and much more stature.

Campbell: I'll tell you a true personal story about my business strategy. One of the things that the SEC did in the mid-'70s was to require firms to report how much they spent on their audits. I was running a company that was about $4 - 5 million in revenue and I got the 10-Ks of my two largest clients, Bethlehem Steel and Marine Midland, to find out how much they paid their auditor. It turned out that they paid their auditor about the same amount they paid me to do information systems. The services were unrelated but the dollar amounts were the same. I had one office in Buffalo, New York, and said, "Hmm, Price Waterhouse is a $400 million dollar company and we're a four million dollar company, but I get just as much money out of these clients when I'm in the same city they're in. So if I'm in all the cities that PW is in, then I'll be a $400 million company." And on that very tenuous bit of logic... [*Laughter*] ...I thought, "What the hell, let's build the company. I can get money out of these big companies just like they can." And, frankly, it worked pretty well.

Goldberg: And here I thought you had a strategy. [*Laughter*]

Campbell: It is interesting for those of us on the professional service side of the business that these guys were great economic models. I mean, they were a model of how you could have a human resource-based company with a ratio of junior people, medium people, and senior people, charge certain rates for different levels of people and generate a sustainable profit and cash flow. Those were the models that we used when we became public companies. It wasn't a perfect model but it helped us know a little bit how you could grow and create branch office networks and so on. So I think in that way, too, they provided a useful sort of model.

Jerger: There were also some benefits to the software product companies because when the Big Eight started coming out with products—Andersen had some software products early on—it created credibility for buying software products. But, generally, you could beat them competitively because their products weren't that good.

Campbell: I had an interesting relationship with Andersen that I didn't think about as being related to this, but maybe, in a way, it reflects on it. I started a joint venture with Andersen Consulting when I was at BBN. We launched a company called ServiceNet.

Haigh: Could you give the timeframe, please?

Campbell: This would have been in 1996. In a way, it might have been one of the first ASPs—Application Service Providers. BBN was a technology company that had launched its own networks, and Andersen was seen as controlling the client and having great application expertise. So we started a joint venture called ServiceNet to bring those two things together. It failed. It got to $100 million in revenue almost immediately because Andersen turned over all its internal operation of Notes and data management and so on to ServiceNet to give it a running start. But we couldn't get their client business. The word among the Andersen partners was that everybody would be willing to be the *second* partner to have their clients go on to this new service.

In one pivotal meeting I had with George Shaheen, who was the managing partner of Andersen Consulting, I said, "George, you've simply got to tell your partners to..." And he said, "Stop. A partner doesn't tell partners anything. I can't tell them to bring their clients onto this application. They won't do it." In my mind, if they didn't have that level of influence over their customers, then it wasn't going to be successful. Because I thought *we* did. If we had the customers, we could have pulled them onto the service but he didn't feel he could influence his partners sufficiently to make it successful. And something interesting came out about the Andersen partners' relationships with their clients. That personal relationship would not allow a partner to do anything that would benefit the firm unless he thought it would provide certain benefits to the client. We ended up folding the joint venture.

What should happen now, relative to CPA relationship conflicts of interest? How does it get fixed? Ron, what experiences would you like to share from the past?

Palenski: Originally, I was hired to pursue some form of litigation against one or more of the Big Eight firms. There were other models within the association, other areas where there was concern about using leverage of some sort of government monopoly or government franchise to gain competitive advantage against competitors who didn't have the same thing. That was certainly the case in telecommunications which was, I think, the model for many of the programs—the theories, as well as the solutions—within the association. When Doug was running the committee and I was supporting it, the solution that we proffered to the SEC wasn't to keep them out of the business but make them run the business through an arm's length separate subsidiary with a different name and a clear firewall between those people who were providing management advisory services and the auditing function. Let them compete but compete on an equal basis.

As Jay said, for a number of years in the early '80s, we broke our pick trying to find the smoking gun. But, as Dave very clearly explained, what was at stake here wasn't so much some overt wrongful act but the free hall pass and that's just the way the chips fell. There's nothing wrong with having a relationship with your customer. That's a good thing to have. So, at the end of the day, it was Jay who led the association to the realization that we were busting our pick and not getting anywhere. If we weren't able to keep them out of the tent, maybe we'd be better off to bring them all the way into the tent. When I left the association in '94, Arthur Andersen was a very good corporate citizen of the association.

Goldberg: I think you could look at this both ways. You could look at these as issues that independent companies had with the Big Eight being in the industry in those days, or you could say that the Big Eight's activity in this business enhanced the industry and helped make it grow. And I think they are both true.

Campbell: In the material that Doug put together for this workshop is a reference to two guys, Edward Pringle of Coopers & Lybrand and Russ Peppet of Peat Marwick. Those were two of the firms which agreed to adopt codes of policy relative to fair competitive practices in software and to propagate those standards within the firms. At least three of the firms did that. They agreed how they were going to communicate with their own people about their policies on competitive practices. They still had a hall pass and a substantial unfair advantage, but it seems to me they tried to do things to eliminate blatant conflicts of interest.

Goldberg: If I remember right, some of the things that we wanted them to do, our own people wouldn't agree to do. For example, we asked that they not be both a selector of software and a bidder on the same project. Some of our members said, "Well, if I get the opportunity to do that I'm going to do it." [*Laughter*] Clearly there was some element of envy here which was not really rational.

Jerger: Pringle and Peppet were two upfront standup guys. I was impressed with the way they kept after their own companies on behalf of the opposition.

Goldberg: But the problem really was primarily with Andersen, if I remember right, because the other guys were doing consulting but not as much of it was IT-related. Wasn't Touche the one that wouldn't do IT consulting?

Jerger: Yeah, I think it was Touche. Andersen had the blackest hat from our perspective.

Campbell: Coopers & Lybrand and Peat Marwick really weren't the problem. Andersen was. People would, you know, roll off the school bus. They would hire hundreds of young people as programmers and they would bid on major projects. They were a direct competitor to those of us who were trying to build our own service companies.

Palenski: They had that whole facility at St. Charles, Illinois where they would literally bring in people from around the world for training. They still do, by the way. Everybody within the Andersen organization went through there at one point. I know the time that I visited there, they were up doing computer science projects into the wee hours of the morning.

Jerger: And then returned to their monks' stalls to sleep. [*Laughter*]

Campbell: The scale of their projects—where they'd have fifty or a hundred people working on them—was also sort of incomprehensible in the early stages of the industry. For us, five or ten people on a project was a large project. Then we'd hear that Andersen had a hundred people working on an implementation for a client, and maybe it helped us all expand our thinking to some extent.

Haigh: One of the things you identified as distinctive about their model was their practice of hiring large numbers of smart young people whose tenure with the company might be relatively short. It seems that a lot of the actual work on a project was going to be done by bright, motivated, but relatively inexperienced people. Do you think that had any implications for the kind of work that they could do effectively or for the quality of the work that they produced? Or is this something that other companies had to copy in order to compete successfully with them?

Goldberg: In the early '80s when Andersen was really expanding robustly, there was a feeling in the software industry that you could build your business around following their failures. They had any number of very, very large projects with big companies fail. I think most of us felt that the reason was that they would lead with a partner, somebody very, very smart, and then follow-up with dozens of people fresh out of their training program. So there were many instances of projects at large companies that did not go well. Customers spent tens of millions of dollars and then would bring in other firms to try to clean it up. I think the problem was probably excessive growth, and maybe a lack of standards and tools back in the early '80s. They corrected it over time.

Their model was a pyramid model and it was based on the premise, which we didn't have in our companies, that, in a partnership, because it took so many years it took to make partner you had to have a large number of junior people at the bottom of the pyramid. It was an accounting business model that they tried to implement in a technology business but it really doesn't work very well in a technology business, where you need many more senior people supporting a fewer number of junior people. I think that they changed that model over time but, in the early days, that was the model they used and it really didn't work very well. So they definitely had a quality problem although they had enormous demand for their services and enormous growth.

Campbell: It's interesting looking back on how people did large-scale software development projects because the schools didn't teach it. We got hired into the industry in the early '60s, most of us with math degrees or something like that, because there were no programming degrees. And even when universities started cranking out computer science graduates, they were trained in obscure languages and trained to teach other people how to teach obscure languages. Or people were trained to write compilers. No one got a college degree in how to build a better accounts receivable system, yet thousands and thousands of those were built. Building a huge, complex, multilayered, multiroutined, multicurrency, multinational, multilanguage system is a very complex endeavor. I don't know when it was that people started getting actual degrees in serious commercial software project development. Andersen started doing their own training very early on. We started doing some training at CTG in 1977. It wasn't easy to get people at the time who had any kind of formal education in how to do commercial software development.

Goldberg: One of the speakers this morning attributed a degree in computer science to Joe Piscopo in the late '60s. That didn't happen, because computer science degrees didn't exist in the '60s and didn't really exist in the '70s.

Haigh: I did his oral history and, when I quizzed him on that, he said that his degree was technically in applied mathematics but when his brother took the same courses two years later, they called it computer science.

Goldberg: But it was in the statistics department.

Haigh: Stanford had one of the very first freestanding computer science departments. That was in 1965.

Goldberg: But I would bet that was a graduate-level department.

Haigh: Stanford was graduate only until 1980. However, the very first department, at Purdue, was founded in 1962 and began a separate undergraduate degree program in 1967.

Campbell: However, computer science was numerical analysis, compiler design, parsing, string processing, algorithms and so on. Nobody cared much about what has ended up being a multibillion dollar business. I still can remember when IBM announced OS 360 and Watts Humphrey had two hundred programmers working on the software. I thought it was incomprehensible that you could have two hundred programmers build something that would work. Which I guess is still an open question thirty-eight years later. [*Laughter*]

How do you think the conflict of interest should be resolved now? It's a tremendous challenge. Accounting is complex. Accountants get paid a certain fee to attest to numbers that are management's numbers and the system's not working well. Has the system gotten too complex to make it work well?

One of the things that happened, I suppose, is that the investment community has gotten so much more attuned to the relative change in a quarter's performance that a decision has a much more dramatic impact than it did, than it should. As people keep trying to fine-tune things they get down to a gradation where they find the new rule doesn't work in application. For example, the revenue recognition rules of last year which said if there are any words in the agreement that say the customer doesn't pay until they are satisfied means that no revenue gets recognized. The cost gets recognized as it is incurred and then all the revenue gets recognized at one time. That is not the way any of us ran our businesses or managed them or reported them. I can understand that kind of reporting but it's not really quite right. It's not matching revenue and expenses. Someone tries to create rules that they think are better but they're not.

Jerger: So you have an over-engineered rule which causes confusion.

Campbell: I don't know what the solution is.

Going back to the CPA Relations Committee in the '70s and '80s, those of us who were in the business were young and we were leading companies fairly early in our careers. And one of the things we were trying to do was use the force of Congress to influence change. That was an amazing experience that might be worth chatting about. I can remember our conversations with Jack Chesson and all he knew was that it was good for him to attack the Big Eight. I remember him saying, "You guys come here and you're like real people and they show up in their limousines." And guys who showed up in limousines he didn't like. He wanted us to give him something he could use to attack the Big Eight. He was willing to take an outrageous stand because it would benefit his guy. It was my first exposure to the fact that if you got a staffer in support of your position, you had the Congressman. You could almost see your words in the memo to the staffer coming out of the Congressman's mouth on the floor. Wow, that was amazing.

Palenski: Some things haven't changed.

Jerger: He was like an attack dog when he got going but the good news was that he was our attack dog.

Campbell: But it was a little scary. He could turn on you. We didn't quite win. We got pretty close. Dingell ran hearings, didn't he?

Saunders: There are pictures of you testifying at those hearings on the board outside this room.

Palenski: That's the reason we got into the discussions with Fairfield and Pringle and Peppet. We at least got their attention. Maybe no regulation was changed or no law adopted but we got the accounting firms' attention, which in turn led to discussions, which led to a fairly productive relationship.

Frana: Do you think it was good or bad that they were in the business?

Campbell: I think it was good. I think it would have been better if they had had less ability to flourish. I think that they had a significant competitive advantage that we never got.

Goldberg: Clearly, they had a competitive advantage.

Frana: However, on balance...

Campbell: On balance, I think it was better that they were in the business.

Jerger: I also think that's the case. Having spent ten years with them, I think that what they are doing is wrong, flat-out wrong. But from my software perspective...

Goldberg: From the standpoint of the history of the computer software industry, I think they made great contributions to the development of the industry.

Campbell: From the standpoint of the investor community, can you have a firm that takes 75% of its revenue from a client for doing a variety of services, attest to the financial adequacy of that client's numbers and not be conflicted? My opinion is, in most cases, the answer is yes. I think there were some things that were somewhat unique to Andersen that made them more aggressive in this area than the other firms. I think there are other firms that walked away from business that Andersen stuck with. I think that it's not a total coincidence that Sunbeam and Waste Management and Enron happened. I believe that Andersen should not have given a clean audit opinion to the transactions that were approved at Enron. They ended up making decisions and signing documents as a partnership that I think they shouldn't have. And what led them to that? They were the smallest, I guess, of the auditing firms after the separation from Andersen Consulting.

Arthur Andersen was the strongest with Andersen Consulting, and the weakest once Andersen Consulting was split off and they were vulnerable. The Enron account may have been too material for the firm and that put them in a strong enough conflict of interest that it compromised their integrity.

Haigh: Back in the late 1950s, when the accounting profession was first getting to grips with the implications of computer technology, one of the worries that they expressed was that they didn't know how to audit computer systems. Where is the paper trail if they don't know how to program? Are they going to try and read the punch cards of the input and the output and work from that? I've seen a lot of sources discussing that problem and I know that somewhat later they became more heavily involved with computer services. I'm wondering if there was a connection, whether they thought they needed to be involved in this area in order to be able to continue to audit.

Campbell: They certainly had to develop computer programming skills to be able to do an audit of stored data. When it was no longer ledger books, they had to be able to go through automated systems, for sure.

Jerger: Yeah, I was with Andersen from '60 to '70, and about '62 or thereabouts they came out with a computer services checklist or some darn thing. It was a checklist you went through to find out how the client used computers. It was to help you figure out what the devil was going on because you couldn't see things the way you used to see them. So there was a tremendous learning effort within the firm to try to figure out how to deal with information that was generated in a new kind of way. They spent a lot of energy doing that and as a result they learned a lot. And they said, "Hey, we should do something in this area." Because it was clear at that point, even for neophytes like us who didn't know much about systems and programming, that there was a lot of nonsense going on in the DP department. We could never get any reports out, it took a long time to get information. So they said, "Ah-ha, there are opportunities here."

Campbell: Why were they never successful in the software products business? They tried a few times. They never really created a successful software product.

Goldberg: Probably you should generalize and think about how many professional services firms ever did. And I think the answer is that the cultural differences are so distinct that very few, if any, professional services companies, including the accounting firms, ever were able to transition from services to products.

Campbell: Even with their scale it wasn't possible.

Goldberg: I don't think that their difficulty in auditing technology was the driver behind building their IT practices. It doesn't ring true to me. Back in the late '50s, it was punch cards for the most part and the reports weren't that different. It wasn't that hard to do the audit. It wasn't very different from looking at sheets of paper at the end of the month when the reports came out. There were ways that people could fudge results, but it was the same process of generating journal entries and the journal entries would document it. There was a piece of paper translated into a punch card translated into a report. I don't think that's what led them to build these huge practices. I think they built some simple tools that solved that problem.

Jerger: But they did learn a lot and they are smart people so they figured...

Goldberg: And their customers were asking them for help. When you talk about IT in the '60s, it was the CFOs, the controllers, who were the buyers. They didn't know Computer Task Group or Software Design Associates or the other companies in the business. They *did* know their auditor. They had relationships with those guys and they said to them, "Can you help me build a payroll system? Can you help me build an accounts-payable system?"

Campbell: I think the first CIO was Max Hopper, right? Wasn't he the first person to have the title CIO? I'm trying to think when that would have been.

[Ed. Note: Hopper worked for American Airlines and received much publicity during the 1980s for his role in expanding its SABRE on-line reservation system.]

Haigh: The first serious attempt to propose CIO as a title was in a 1981 book by William R. Synnott and William H. Gruber called *Information Resource Management: Opportunities and Strategies for the 1980's.* [*Ed. Note: New York, John Wiley and Sons, 1981.*] But before that I think most companies used a title like VP of MIS. That's the first title that brings together technology and management under one roof.

Goldberg: But prior to that it was the CFO, because the only systems that people bought were payroll, accounts receivable, accounts payable, inventory, billing, etc.

Campbell: The data processing department was obviously under the influence of the accounting firms.

Haigh: So would it be fair to say that independent software services companies and the Big Eight accounting firms were both competing against the internal data processing organization to provide services?

Goldberg: Absolutely.

Jerger: Sure. One of the benefits of having the accounting firms in the business is that clients felt more comfortable going to them if they decided not to do it in-house. And once they got comfortable with the idea of working with an external organization, then at least there was a shot at competing against the accounting firms.

Goldberg: It legitimatized the business.

Haigh: And what obstacles would companies face when trying to convince the CFO that it would be better to give something to an outside firm than expect their internal data processing department to deal with it?

Campbell: The customer always wanted people who had two years experience in a not-yet-released technology. [*Laughter*] So that really was the way you would get started. You'd try to get people up to speed very fast and then move them around quickly. So that they'd be doing the first project utilizing new technology at each of several customers.

There was a point in time where the really great people couldn't advance in their careers in a typical company. Take a $500 million manufacturing company. A really great programmer is never going to go beyond being the No. 1 programmer. He's not going to become president of the company. In our companies, they could move from programmer to project leader to vice president of development to where they could run the business. So it was fun for us to give people much greater career opportunities. We were, therefore, able to hire better people or more ambitious people than the stodgy, locked-forever-in data processing department of a company.

Over time, the functions became more technical, so that you had to know database, IMS and CICS to build the application rather than just understanding the subtleties of annuity accounting. When it turned into more of a technological linkage project management activity than an understanding of the business function, we got more of the work and were able to compete better with the Big Eight.

Goldberg: These systems were all being built for the first time in the '60s. So if you were a DP manager building your first system on a 1401 computer in 1961, an outside vendor could come to you and say, "I built five accounts payable systems in the last six months. Here are the companies I built them for, here are their references, here's how it turned out." And the people in your company had never built one before. A lot of times people would choose the outside vendor. Forgetting about the technical issues, it was an experience issue. If a software company had success in a particular piece of business, it was able to sell that experience. So, even though there was a lot of reluctance, you could create a market based on your expertise. It was selling the first one that was so hard.

Jerger: The parallel in the software products business was that it was a reference sell. You had to get one dynamite customer and then really take care of them. And then you paraded them around everywhere you could as a reference. You could also compete against the in-house staff on price. The customer would balk at paying $200,000 for a product but you could easily show them that it would cost $2.8 million to do it themselves with a big risk that the project might fail. And you'd often get the business that way.

Campbell: As I remember, the Big Eight firms tended to have strengths and weaknesses within different industries. Price Waterhouse would be strong in oil and gas and someone else would be stronger in banking. It was partly because they had a lot of people in different geographic areas that they got the benefit of people who saw across a whole industry. Therefore, they could sell on the basis of industry expertise and so on and so forth. Jay, did that affect you in New York with banking or not? Did you see that as a factor?

Goldberg: We rarely competed against the Big Eight. We've been using the phrase "competition against the Big Eight" and I don't think it existed to any great extent. We would hear that a customer was building a system using a Big Eight firm. It was never a competitive bid. Rarely did one compete.

Campbell: That's a good point.

Goldberg: So there was business being given to them and there was business that was being competed for. We used the term that we competed with them but the truth is, in any given company, we didn't.

Campbell: We just never saw that business.

Goldberg: That business never went out to bid. It was a negotiation between the CFO and the accounting firm.

I think putting it in the context of the buyer is interesting. Because this was before there was a VP of MIS, so you had a CFO who had grown up through the accounting profession, either public or private, who knew nothing about computers. He was technically illiterate and had a controller working for him who was also technically illiterate. And then you had this *wave* of technology coming at them. They didn't have confidence that they really understood the technology or what they were buying. It was very natural for them to turn to somebody they trusted. And the guy that they trusted the most was their auditor.

Jerger: Did you ever have a prospect or a customer that you really felt sorry for because you just knew they didn't know what was going to happen?

Goldberg: Almost all of them. [*Laughter*]

In the early 1970s, my company built an accounts payable system for Fairchild Publications. Publishing firms, then and now, are noted for being relatively tight with G&A dollars and they were relatively tight with our dollars. The VP of Finance at the time was a guy named Phil McGovern. He and I had a great relationship. We finished the project and sixty days later I called him up and said, "Phil, you never paid us our final installment." And he said, "Well, come on down and we'll talk about it." I assumed there was some kind of big problem so I went down to his office. And with this great grin he said to me, "I wanted you to be the first one that I told: Your check is stuck in my system." [*Laughter*]

But that was the way they thought. They didn't think in terms of the technology. It was accounts payable to them and it was cutting checks and dealing with vendors, and the technology was a necessary evil. This was stuff that they had to do because everybody else was doing it and they were getting a lot of heat from their bosses about it. We would promise performance improvements. Our sales pitches always were, "If you buy our software, you'll need fewer people." I think even today those pitches are being made and there is very little evidence that any accounts payable department ever got smaller as a result of using anybody's software. But they certainly became more productive. There is no question about that.

Frana: Were they ever concerned about that? That the technology would make them obsolete?

Goldberg: Yes. There was *huge* resistance in those days. Automation was a new term, computers were new, and the employees within these companies were terrified. Not the CFOs, necessarily, but the people that you had to work with to get systems done thought that they would be replaced. They absolutely were afraid.

Jerger: We had an accounts receivable management system that we sold to big companies like Exxon, Hershey Chocolate, and Mars Candy. There was an automatic cash application and some reporting features that would save the companies lots of time. But one customer wasn't using it. We asked what was going on and were told that it was too hard to use. So we had a couple of guys go in and work with the people on the clerical staff and they found out that they were deliberately making it hard to use. But there was one woman who liked them and she admitted that the system worked so well when it was used right that they were afraid that some of them would lose their jobs. So they convinced her that that wasn't true and she convinced the others and from then on it worked fine. So we followed that rule from then on: Find a lady who likes you and convince her.

Campbell: In my mind, there was a linear progression of technology that was comprehensible up to a point and then we had a gap. We went from manual ledger cards to ledger cards that could be processed through a Royal McBee machine, to ledger machines, to punched cards. And from punched cards to magnetic tape, which were a different medium, but information was still in sequential sets of records that people could look at. And that was mentally linkable.

And then we went to disc systems where any piece of information could be accessed at any point in time. You were then able to do different kinds of processing and, I think, that was a step that an awful lot of the data processing managers couldn't or didn't want to make. They said, "We don't quite know what index sequential access management is or how to use it, so you guys do that stuff." I was an IBM System Engineer and IBM SE's were given away free in the '60s. Lease the machine and you get one of these guys for a year to help you figure it out. And we were like gods to those customers. I had had three weeks of training and could do something with the software. They thought it was magic and very few of them aspired to develop that level of capability. That gap in confidence created the opportunity for this industry.

Goldberg: Thank goodness.

Campbell: Yeah, thank goodness. The new technology was tricky to use but not all *that* tricky to use. But it wasn't a natural incremental step in the evolution of the technology.

Goldberg: And there were no people.

Campbell: Yeah, there were no people trained to do this.

Goldberg: AT&T embarked on the first real major training program with women. They would hire women right out of school—my wife, Mary was one of them—and they expected that you would work there two years and then get married and have a kid. The whole premise was that they got the money back in two years by training people how to write COBOL programs. But that was in the early '70s. In the '60s, there was nothing. There was no place you could go except for IBM. There were some commercial schools that were trying to provide training. But big companies weren't doing it. So when the 360 came out it was just like a vacuum. If you knew something about systems and programming, you just got sucked up. It created opportunities for all these firms to develop.

Campbell: A lot of the professional service firms got started in the five years after the 360 was announced.

Virgo: Can I change the subject?

Campbell: Sure, of course.

Virgo: We were talking in the Accounting Issues workshop this morning about the problems that the companies faced in getting financial support, especially from investors. Where does the Big Eight fit into that issue? Is that something useful to explore right now, including the whole issue of capitalization?

Campbell: I can give you a perspective on it. While we were trying to start companies from scratch, they were sitting inside $400 million revenue, very profitable companies. So they were able to finance this expansion of service very, very easily. Because it's a relatively simple business. You hire someone and pay them ten dollars an hour and charge $25 an hour and if you do enough of it, it works out. [*Laughter*] At the time, *we* were able to figure that out. That's how bright *we* were. [*Laughter*]

But it's much easier to add a service like that to an existing revenue stream so the advantage they had, in addition to access to the CFO, was that they had cash flow to grow. And they had a distributed office structure to serve people across industries. Adding a thousand person organization to an existing ten thousand person organization is a lot different from starting an organization from scratch and going from zero to a thousand.

Jerger: And they had been practicing for fifty to seventy-five years.

Virgo: I was actually thinking more about how well the audit side helped in those situations where there was some feeling of competition.

Campbell: There was no feeling of competition in the '60s and '70s. The feeling of competition came up in that audit people were paternalistic towards the consulting side, while the consulting side was really more profitable because it had ballooned in growth. There is a very finite amount of audit business in the United States. You take the ten thousand public companies times the audit fee per company. It's an extremely finite market without much growth, whereas the IT market is hundreds of times larger. The problems began to come up as the consulting businesses got larger. Initially, the people on the consulting side weren't CPAs and that was a major problem because they couldn't be partners in the firm. You could be contributing five million dollars in revenue, but you didn't have the right to be a partner. Finally they changed those rules. The conflicts started when the consulting side was larger and a greater source of profitability for the company.

Virgo: But going back to the role of the Big Eight and how they helped or did not help the software industry. Did they help in dealing with the issue of capitalization and trying to make the industry more bankable?

Campbell: I don't think they did, to be honest. There was a spike of activity in companies going public in the '60s and then that basically shut down for the '70s. The public market had the same kind of speculative fever in the '66 – '69 time period as it's had in the last few years. But in the '70s, software companies were almost unfinanceable. If you started a company in 1970 or later, you didn't see public markets until 1980. So the FASB rules weren't much of a factor in the '70s. They were more of a factor in the '80s. When were you having your issues with capitalization of software, Doug?

Jerger: '78. We started in '70, right after all those bubbles burst.

Goldberg: The Big Eight weren't in the software products business so they couldn't care less because all they were doing was professional services. The auditing firms were just struggling with the audit issues as opposed to trying to help or hurt the software products business. Revenue recognition issues, software capitalization issues, taxation issues were pretty complicated then because they really didn't understand the products business.

Virgo: Well, that's really what I expected you to say because in our dealings with them we found that if you were dealing with the audit side they had *no* comprehension of revenue recognition. And that made it very difficult because they were not going to bother about having any comprehension and so they said, "You just can't do that." And somebody like Larry Schoenberg would present an intellectually sound argument that we could and should.

Goldberg: And did.

Virgo: He did actually persuade one auditor who had been *adamant* that you couldn't do things that way.

Goldberg: But they weren't conflicted in that relationship because their firms had very little in the way of software products.

Virgo: I was looking for whether they were constructive and helping or actually obstructive.

Goldberg: Those were tough issues though, and in fact they haven't been resolved yet. If you look at the way that the pendulum has swung in those rules, even today there's the question: Should or should you not capitalize software? It's an issue that has been hanging around for thirty years and it's a pretty complicated issue. So I never felt that the accounting firms were doing anything wrong or bad. I just think that they are tough issues.

Campbell: But new problems continue to come up. There's a new accounting regulation recently adopted which requires firms like the ones we ran to include reimbursed travel expenses as revenue. I don't know a single person in the business that thinks that is the correct thing to do, but that just came down as a new accounting rule.

Jerger: I didn't see that. Geez.

Campbell: You gross it up. There is not a single person that I know running a business that would think of revenue that way. Not one. That is now defined as the correct revenue recognition accounting treatment. Reimbursed expenses are considered in both revenue and in expense.

Goldberg: Which may not seem significant, but it reduces your margin. It makes the business less attractive to Wall Street, because to the extent that you are increasing your top line and increasing your expenses, your net margin percentage goes down. If you used to be an 8% business, now you're a 7% business. So it makes your presentation look worse to the outside world and there is no real reason to do it.

Campbell: If you've got two competing businesses both billing $2000 a week for a person, the fact that one of them has a $1000 travel expense and therefore looks like a $3000 a week person is not significant to the quality of the person. It's really misrepresentative in revenue per employee calculations, as an example. This shows that even today, with all the things we should have learned, promulgations get made which seem to be just flat wrong.

Jerger: Who did they ask?

Campbell: They may have asked the audit firms. I don't know. The audit firms aren't public companies because they are partnerships. So they don't suffer from the impact of the reporting requirements as public entities do.

Haigh: Historically speaking, did skilled individuals ever move back and forth between Big Eight accounting firms and other computer-related services firms? Were they separate worlds?

Jerger: I think they went one direction.

Campbell: People left the accounting firms but nobody ever went to them.

Jerger: It was one direction. They went our way.

Campbell: It's unlikely that anyone ever went as a professional from one of the independent firms into the Big Eight. You went into the Big Eight as a college graduate.

Goldberg: You mean in the early days? Your question is did it happen in the '60s and '70s?

Haigh: Yeah.

Goldberg: Today there is free movement back and forth. I can't remember losing somebody to an accounting firm. But at the same time we rarely hired people from accounting firms as well.

Campbell: CTG did. You're reminding me of statistics we had when we were doing massive levels of recruiting, five hundred people a year, a thousand people a year. And the investment community would always say, "Where do your people come from?" So we kept statistics and we had a breakdown of how many came out of the Big Eight, how many came from other sources, etc. It was a reasonable percentage but, at that time, it was one way. I don't know if they would have been invited back.

Goldberg: They were a college-recruiting business. That was their model so they rarely would hire people from outside unless they had a specific need for a very senior person with specific knowledge. That occurred sometimes.

Campbell: They'd take a college recruit and put them through the system so they would learn to develop programs using set procedures. Those were the people who could be effective on those larger projects because they were all trained to do things one way.

Okay, does anyone have any wrap-up comments that they want to contribute?

What's the forecast? Since someone's going to be reading this in a hundred years, will Accenture remain the largest firm in the professional services business, do you think? If they are the largest right now in terms of what we call a straight IT consultant, do you think they will be fifty years from now?

Goldberg: I can't imagine. It's hard to picture that twenty-five or fifty years from now this business will look anything remotely like it does today.

Haigh: But in fifty years there will still be auditors, because there is a law that they have to be there. Will there still be IT services as they exist today? That's driven by market conditions and could turn into something totally different.

Campbell: I would guess that there will not be independent paid third-party auditors. I think either they won't exist or there will be federal auditors. The government will say, "We'll do it the same way we audit your tax return. You submit the data, we're going to sample, and we'll accept or deny." Because I think the current system where you pay your auditor $10 million isn't working and I don't know if it's the system you would create going forward. Maybe the companies should pay a fee into a central pool and from that pool they find an auditor. The current system is that I ask four companies to bid, and I pick one to give my $10 million to and they tell me whether I counted things correctly or not. That's a strange system, I think, so I wouldn't be surprised to see that changed. That's my forecast for 2100.

Jerger: He wants to go on the record just in case that possibly occurs.

Goldberg: You heard it here first. There have been auditors for a long time.

Jerger: I said seventy-five years. I think it's about a hundred and fifty years in the case of Peat Marwick, so they'll be around, I think.

Campbell: For a wrap-up statement: I think that auditing firms had unique relationships with the early commercial users of computers to help accelerate their willingness to use outside providers of service, which benefited the industry, and they took advantage of a unique access they had to capture a disproportionate share of the industry than they would have had otherwise.

Haigh: I think not competing directly with the Big Eight was a key issue.

Virgo: So do I.

234

Haigh: They may ultimately have used their access to increase the market for computer service firms.

Goldberg: I think they added a level of professionalism to an industry that wasn't perceived that well by the market in those days. I think they helped establish the market, for good or bad.

Haigh: So, in retrospect should ADAPSO have been so concerned about their entry into the field?

Campbell: Yes.

Goldberg: Yes.

Jerger: Yes. [*Laughter*]

Goldberg: They did have an unfair competitive position that was given to them, as David has said, by the government demanding that large public companies be audited. They had an unfair competitive advantage, so I think it was important that we tried to keep them out of the business. The fact that we failed, I think, is okay. I don't think it turned out so badly.

Jerger: So, we're saying it was absolutely appropriate to oppose them, but in retrospect they didn't hurt us too bad, if at all. In fact, in certain ways we benefited.

Goldberg: But I would say it's because we were lucky enough to be in an industry that had such explosive growth that there was room for all of us. In another industry with more limited growth, they would have owned it and the rest of us wouldn't have had any opportunity. The problem was made easier by the fact that the whole industry had enormous opportunity, which I don't think any of us understood at the time.

Campbell: But, I think also that their taking advantage of the industry came back to their disadvantage because of the conflicts which arose from the growth in non-audit fees. Which is contributing eventually to their demise. So, they helped create the industry, helped validate the industry, took unfair advantage of their special relationship and, at the end of the day, that's having an impact on their future.

All right, thanks everybody.

Industry Image Workshop

Moderators: Rick Crandall and David Grier

Rapporteur: Julia Johnston

Participants: Sam Albert   John Maguire
                      Lowell Dent   Mike Maples
                      Jerry Dreyer   Dave Sturtevant
                      Ed Bride

Crandall: I'm Rick Crandall, the moderator of this session, Julie Johnston is our rapporteur and our co-moderator is David Grier from George Washington University.

I'm a last minute stand-in. John Imlay, the former CEO of MSA, was going to be here and couldn't come at the last minute due to a flight cancellation. He initially said he wasn't going to come because he wouldn't be able to fly up until this morning, but I had him talked into it. I called him and said, "John, we're going to record ADAPSO's contributions to the industry's image at the time when we needed it and, of course, if you're not here I'll try to remember what you did. My memory might not be as good as yours but *I'll* be there." [*Laughter*]

Let's start by going around the room and getting names and companies and why we're here so that Julie can record all that.

Maguire: I'm John Maguire, Software AG, an active member of ADAPSO for a long, long time. I worked with John Imlay a lot, on the trips we took to call on the news media in New York City.

Dent: I'm T. Lowell Dent, Computer Power, Jacksonville, FL. I joined ADAPSO in either '62 or '63.

Dreyer: Jerry Dreyer. I joined ADAPSO as a chief staff executive in December 1966 and retired in 1986.

Bride: Ed Bride, *Computerworld* in the early '70s, and *Software News* and then *Software Magazine* from '81 to '91. I was responsible for keeping Dave Sturtevant busy, keeping the image untarnished.

Sturtevant: My name is Dave Sturtevant. I had the privilege of being Vice President of Public Communications of ADAPSO from 1979 to 1987. John Maguire and Jerry Dreyer and a few other people were on the committee that interviewed me and hired me.

Albert: I'm Sam Albert. I'm the President of Sam Albert Associates today, but for eighteen of my thirty years with IBM, I was responsible for the consultants, the CPAs, and the legal profession. In 1981, they gave me responsibility for the entire software and services industry. I was responsible for the revenue that came from this function, the marketing practices, the marketing strategy and the marketing programs for the software and services industry.

Grier: I'm David Grier. I am a professor of computer science and international affairs at GWU. I was also involved in the computer industry. During the '80s I was a systems designer for Burroughs Corporation and then I did software support. One of the things that interested me about this session—I don't want to steal Rick's thunder—but it seems to me that, from the start, the software industry has had to define what it was publicly, with very little in the way of guidelines as to how to do that, how to present itself. And the question starts from there: How did you do it and how did you recognize that there was even a need?

Maples: Mike Maples. I worked for IBM for a number of years and Microsoft for a number of years and I participated in ADAPSO, representing both of them. I started with ADAPSO probably in the late '70s or early '80s, through the mid-90's.

Johnston: I'm Julie Johnston. I was an ADAPSO staff member, Director of Research, early '80s.

Crandall: And I'm Rick Crandall. I was Founder and CEO of Comshare for many years until 1994. My first involvement with ADAPSO was when the Computer Timesharing Section was formed which I think was approximately '68.

Dreyer: '69.

Crandall: That then transformed into my broader participation in ADAPSO. I was President of ADAPSO in '78 and I was active on a lot of committees, particularly Image, Research and Statistics, and Strategic Planning.

So let's get started. We are mostly concerned with the period from the point when the Image Committee was formed in about 1977 through its most active period in '81 or '82. When ADAPSO was formed in the '60s, it was initially a service-bureau-based trade association. Then, when the Remote Processing Services Section was formed, ADAPSO also became an association for the timesharing companies. The software companies came in after that.

I don't remember the service bureau period very well but I do remember the significant growth period in timesharing, which was the late '60s and all through the '70s. There was significant press coverage associated with that very rapid growth but I don't remember any work being done in the trade association related to that. Most of the work that RPSS did in ADAPSO had to do with the problems it was having with the telephone companies and with communications regulatory practices and policies, and trying to get that whole arena opened up. Initially, AT&T and the whole telephone industry considered that anything we did that had to do with networking looked like reselling telecommunications, and that was illegal as far as they were concerned. But I won't spend any time on that.

The earliest date that I can remember associated with the subject of industry image was a meeting that John Imlay and I had in 1977. It was probably at the spring ADAPSO meeting and it was right after some conversations I'd had with Jerry Dreyer who indicated to me that I was going to be a shoo-in for ADAPSO President in 1978. Jerry was a master of orchestration during that time. In fact, I think he was the significant glue in keeping the disparate groups together in the organization by making things happen when they needed to happen, instead of relying completely on the democracy of the organization. I can't imagine this is the first time that has been said.

I was looking for what my strategy as President of the organization in 1978 would be and, in discussions with John Imlay, who is among the most image-conscious of anybody I know, I decided that one of the most powerful strategies that we could employ was improving the industry's image. The objective would be to get the marketplace to acknowledge that software was an industry in its own right, and was not just some adjunct to hardware. For example, the focus that IBM had on calling these companies ISVs, independent software vendors—presumably meaning independent from IBM—was a focus that we wanted to completely flip around. This was well before the PC and well before any of those developments that would assist with that image. So John and I agreed that if I was to become

President in 1978, he would become my Senior Vice President, or whatever the exact title was. And since that was the step for his becoming President the following year, we figured that between the two of us we'd have a two-year run to work on the image strategy.

We decided to make those two years of consistent effort to hammer the business press—not just the trade press which *was* covering the industry. I've got a copy of a booklet here called the DP Public Relations Review dated October '76 and there are a number of articles in it which are very software industry specific. So trade publications were talking a little bit about software here and there, but the big problem was that we had not cracked the business press. That was the big goal—to crack the business press—*Business Week* and *Fortune* and *Forbes* and so on. We designed a game plan in '77 where we would set up regular and continuous appointments with the press. We would come up with topics that we thought were newsworthy and offer them up to the press. When we got a bite, we would bring in the CEOs that were relevant to that subject. In so doing, we hoped that we would increase awareness and understanding and, eventually, get coverage from these publications.

The first success story was when we finally cracked *Business Week*, which wrote what they called a platform article. We had learned that it was almost impossible to get coverage from *Business Week* until they had done a platform article, which is kind of a baseline article: broad-based, significant, maybe even a cover story. And once you got one of those, it was much easier to go back and get them to then take pieces of the story and cover them in more depth with more reporters involved and so forth. It was approximately early 1980 when we finally did get that.

Sturtevant: September 1, 1980, *Business Week*.

Crandall: It was a cover story and there was a picture of a computer box with the top opened up and the title of it was "The Empty Computer," meaning the computer was empty without software inside. That opened the gateway for many more articles and then it spread throughout the rest of the business press. I won't jump in right away with what I think the impact was. I know that our goal was to generate acknowledgement in the buying marketplace that software had a value, that you paid money for it, instead of it being something that was bundled and seemed like it was free.

The second goal that we had was to try to open up the equity markets to the concept of software firms being public. There were a number of timesharing firms that were public, Comshare being one. Comshare went public in 1968 so it had been public for a long time. ADP went public in '61 or something like that. So there were services firms that were public, but software firms going public was the next goal and that was another goal of this campaign.

So that meeting that John Imlay and I had was a key meeting. John really picked up that game plan. I had it as a goal and a strategy of the 1978 administration, which was the year I was President, but he was definitely the most aggressive with it over time.

We also decided that we needed to get ADAPSO itself, as an organization, more ramped up about itself and more of an enthusiastic, fun-loving organization. It was a very serious, mission-oriented organization, and continued to be, but we wanted to kind of mix it up. I know many in this room will remember that we decided to pull off a stunt at the meeting in the spring of '78, which was in Phoenix. We hired the head of the International Brotherhood of Magicians of Phoenix to do an illusion, which involved a nailed-together crate that had in it secret ingredients that he brought from his mountain top to solve one of the industry's major woes. Which at the time clearly was IBM. [*Laughter*]

Jerry, I think you arranged for a caricaturist to draw a picture of me as Superman with a big A on my chest for ADAPSOMan that I used as a slide in my incoming speech as ADAPSO President. Because all we were doing in those days was fighting problems. Well, John had arranged for a real Superman costume emblazoned with an A on the chest. You know, real blue tights with the red pants and so on. He had me dress up in it in secret in the back of this big room. We must have had about a thousand people at that meeting. So the magician does some magic tricks to warm the crowd up and brings out this big trunk. He had a way of opening the trunk and tipping it over so you could see it was empty.

So then he said, "Oh my god, it's empty, they shipped it to me empty, they made a mistake. I'm going to have to use all my magical powers to transport what we need from my mountain top retreat. But here is the problem we're dealing with." And he had three huge Styrofoam letters: I, B, M. He threw them into this apparently empty crate. Closed it up, nailed it, spun it around and did all this hocus-pocus stuff. I was, in fact, in there, really cramped up, in this outfit. After he did his hocus-pocus and reopened the box, I grabbed the letters and jumped out. I literally leaped out, which I had to do to get over the sides, with the red cape flying behind me and I started ripping the three letters, I, B, M, apart. And Bernie Goldstein jumped up and said, "Oh my god, he's breaking up IBM." [*Laughter*]

At which point, about six IBMers left the room. I couldn't tell if they were ticked off or what. But that started a number of higher profile, more entertainment-oriented activities that went along with the image campaign. That went on for years. So that's a bit of introduction and some memories. I'm sure some more memories will get jogged as we go along. What we want to talk about are any further recollections of what we did in the image campaign, what our goals were, and what the effect was on the industry and on individual companies.

Maples: Let me just add that IBM was very anti-press and anti-publicity. IBM was very, very closed and managed all the information flow to their customers. They didn't want to give information to anybody else. It was a very closed, controlling environment so that any little company had a hard time trying to get any kind of press. There was hardly any press prior to this time and any conflicts were pushed underground.

Maguire: That underscores the problem that we had.

Maples: Absolutely.

Maguire: That was the biggest part of the problem. I made a lot of trips to New York for those breakfast meetings with *Fortune* editors and *Forbes* and *Business Week*. And speaking from my perspective as a software product marketer, it was extremely difficult trying to sell into an IBM account, extraordinarily difficult, because there weren't many IBM customers that had a lot of software from the independent software industry. That was the image that I personally was trying to push, that we were really an industry. That *Business Week* article, I think, talked about the independent software industry.

Crandall: Oh, yeah, the article covered the independent software industry very extensively.

Maguire: That was the first time anyone other than those of us on the inside talked about the independent software companies as an industry per se, and that was part of the problem of cracking the IBM users. Because of IBM controlling the information, they didn't see us as a viable industry. At Software AG, we were selling database systems, the engine of their future information systems, and they saw us as a very high risk.

Albert: This is a footnote, but when I took over the software industry and the services industry for IBM, I became involved with ADAPSO and I met John Imlay who was running MSA at the time.   At one point in our discussions, I said, "What do you call yourselves?"   And he said, "Well, Sam, you're a hardware company. We would call ourselves an independent software vendor."   So the term "ISV" was really created by John and since that time I've been on a mission to erase it from the industry, because, when you think about it, there is no such thing as an independent software vendor. I've been trying for many years to get IBM to call it "SV," software vendor, and I almost succeeded.   I talked to a very high-level IBM marketing executive about four or five years ago and I told him, "This doesn't make sense. If you don't ever want to be included in the list of software vendors, keep calling them ISVs on your charts, because then they are ISVs, and then there's IBM which is an SV."   I said, "You're all SVs."   So I had him convinced but the next time I saw his pitch he was still using ISVs. After he finished his pitch, I said, "Why are you still using ISVs?"   He said, "Sam, I wanted to erase it but my communications guy told me nobody would know what I was talking about.   They don't know about SVs, they know about ISVs."   So I wrote a couple of articles in *Enterprise Systems Journal* titled "Telephones, ISV's and Other Antiques," and I still can't get rid of it. So it's just a footnote that John Imlay and I extemporaneously created the term "ISV."

Regarding what you said about IBM controlling the press, they never realized that the press isn't controllable. That worked to their disadvantage over time. Now I think they are a little better at PR but not that much better.

Maples: But, you know, the early data centers all used accounting machines that weren't programmed. You only had the hardware which you programmed uniquely. But it wasn't called programming, it was wiring the boards and so you didn't deal with programming as such.   It was all just hardware. So the idea that there could be an independent software industry didn't make sense.

Maguire: Most of the people I dealt with once the *Business Week* article came out knew that independent meant non-IBM.

Albert: Yes, that's right. That was correct.

Maguire: After that issue, they knew that we were okay. And after that *Business Week* article I started parading users to *Computerworld* that had interesting stories about using our software, and *Computerworld* was much more receptive than they had been five years earlier.

Bride: At *Computerworld*, we talked about independent everything. It was anything that was not-IBM. Independent peripherals, like independent disc drives. You know, how you could put a Mohawk drive onto an IBM system and it would work and would be cheaper. So "independent" became a commonly-used word for non-IBM. I hadn't really reflected on that until this discussion.

I didn't start going to ADAPSO conferences until right after that *Business Week* article appeared which is when *Software News* started up. It always struck me how few of the business press ever came to those conferences and, in fact, how few of my colleagues in the trade press came. Sometimes there would be three or four press people. I know it wasn't for lack of trying on ADAPSO's part. It always puzzled me, because the *Business Week* article could have started it. You would have thought that *Fortune* would have followed, *Forbes* would have followed. As companies began to go public, which was beginning to happen by then…

Dreyer: Less than a year away. It started really in '81.

Bride: You would think that the press would flock to ADAPSO, but it didn't happen.

Sturtevant: I'll make a couple of observations. First of all, in our heyday, on average we would get ten or twelve reporters from various publications to the conferences. I think one of the reasons that it was always difficult to get more was because a lot of the decision-making in the boardroom was closed to the press. That made things a little less attractive, as far as news availability. But at the same time, there were tremendous stories to be had at the meetings and we did a decent job getting the press there. One of the things that I'm pleased about is that, by my count, in the eight years that I was there, we generated over twenty-five hundred articles on behalf of the industry and the association that we could lay claim to.

One anecdotal story that's kind of interesting. In 1979, I'd been on staff for six weeks. I got a call from a guy by the name of Al Berkeley who was then with Alex Brown & Sons. He said, "I understand that you guys are the association that represents the software industry." I said, "Yeah." He said, "I need to get smart on this. This is the next big thing." I said, "Okay." He came to my office and we spent about four hours going through old INPUT reports on the size and shape of the industry and various background materials. That was the beginning of Al's getting tremendously involved in the industry and the association. Ultimately he became the president of NASDAQ. But it also was critical in terms of Alex Brown bringing a number of our companies to IPOs in the '81, '82 time frame.

Maguire: Not only reporters, but right after this article in '80, underwriters started showing up at our conferences. Al Berkeley, however, was in my office in Reston, VA, getting to know Software AG in 1979 before the *Business Week* article.

Crandall: I'll chip in. I know Al very well. We've talked about those days and he will tell you that his whole motivation was not so much for the betterment of the industry. He was trying to figure out how to make a name for himself in the investment banking world. At the time, Alex Brown had made a corporate strategy decision to try specialization but didn't know how to do it. Al knew he had no specialty but he figured if he got to say the same words five times over then he was a specialist in those words. That was the basis of his calling you up, Dave, and saying, "I've got to get smart with the software and services industry." He became the guru and the software specialist within Alex Brown. That got to be very successful for them and they did the early software IPOs. It's very important that you raised that because that is another very key element in the success of the image effort and Al was a major contributor to that.

Albert: He visited me at IBM, as a matter a fact, during that particular period of time. He was a really very professional person who became so knowledgeable about the software industry that I invited him to IBM to address some of the people who were dealing with the software community.

Sturtevant: A couple of other things related to that. The association was producing an industry newsletter called *Update* that was distributed to about two thousand financial analysts, primarily on Wall Street. It listed all the current publicly traded companies in the industry with their quarterly results, and it had articles that referred to what was happening in some of these new industry sectors like software.

We also started having financial analyst conferences. The idea, frankly, was stolen from AEA which did financial analyst conferences in Monterey for the electronic companies. We said, "Let's put ours right in Wall Street's backyard at the Waldorf-Astoria Hotel in New York City and have our companies that are trying to position for IPOs do presentations." The first one of those we held was, I believe, in 1980 and we had probably thirty or forty analysts in the room. Which was pretty good because we didn't have a lot of background with them. Peter Cunningham from INPUT and Julie Johnston were working on producing an annual industry survey that showed statistics on the industry: how big the industry was independent of IBM's numbers. We had three industry segments that we talked about in those days: professional services, software products and processing services, including timesharing.

By 1981, we had over a hundred industry analysts present at the meeting and a lot of CEOs came and pitched their companies. Al Berkeley became the chairman of the program and our biggest cheerleader, and eventually he took it over as a program run by Alex Brown because they could, frankly, fund it a hell of a lot better than we could. So we copied the idea from AEA and Al stole it from us, but we got our objective accomplished. The analyst community was paying attention to the industry and our companies were able to do IPOs.

Maguire: And, boy, did Alex Brown draw the analysts. I remember making a presentation and they had 750 analysts there. I had a 35' x 35' display behind me for the slide projector in a big auditorium. I mean, the interest just exploded.

Grier: Can you differentiate between the kind of work that you did to present the software industry to the investment analysts and work that you did to increase sales, particularly the work you did to gain access to IBM customers? Was there a difference in the way you approached these problems?

Sturtevant: Well, from a PR standpoint, the best thing that the association could do was get coverage and articles on behalf of its members. And, frankly, just get Rick Crandall's name or John Maguire's name or John Imlay's name on the Rolodex of all of these business publications so that when something broke the reporters would know who to call. These guys went into the *Wall Street Journal* time after time after time and it didn't result in coverage for a long time, but we established credibility. And, in time, when stories did start to come up where it would make sense to pick up the phone and call someone, their business cards were on the Rolodex.

Maguire: Yeah, there was some overlap but, mostly, it was sequential. We first had to get the sales in order to get the numbers to go public.

Crandall: The image campaign had both as equal objectives: to get a higher profile in the investment community, as well as a higher profile in the customer community for the purpose of getting more sales. The fact of the matter is that when a company goes public it doesn't only get the money from the IPO, it gets a higher profile in the broader market. It's just a fact. So there is really a blurring between those two objectives.

Dreyer: It was also a marketing tool for the association to bring in new members, new blood into the organization. You can show companies what you are doing and convince them to get on board. Dave reminded me of the situation with Alex Brown. That was a coup, actually, even though we lost direct control of the event. All of a sudden, the analysts were taking a very strong look at our industry and a lot of successful things occurred as a result of it.

Crandall: I have a question for the room on a subject that Sam Albert was responsible for. In 1982, Sam organized a conference for the first time at IBM which I'm sure they referred to by some long and complicated name.

Albert: It was called the Application Developer Conference.

Crandall: But we referred to it as the great IBM software love-in. There were CEOs from 75 software companies, as I recall, and we noted that there were some CEOs that were very specifically not invited.

Albert: Those were CEOs from systems software companies as opposed to application software companies. I remember that. In fact, I went to Burt Grad to try to understand who should be invited.

Crandall: So the message that IBM gave at that conference, really for the first time, was that they wanted to work with us. Prior to that conference it was just about impossible to partner with IBM. We were not acknowledged to exist or, if we were, we were irrelevant or too tiny or not going to be around for very long, or whatever. At this conference, IBM executives paraded up on stage, and some sounded like they were reading from a script somewhere and didn't really have any idea what they were saying.

The message was that IBM was opening the doors now and didn't have all the niches plugged and wanted to partner with us.

My question is whether that meeting and some subsequent ones actually had an impact on the overall industry. The reactions to that specific meeting at the time were varied. If you talked to the people walking out of the room, some of them took it seriously and said this is an opportunity. Others said, "There's no way. This is some kind of an IBM hype thing to kind of patch up some of the grievances."

Maguire: I was in that camp.

Crandall: It was right at a time when my company, Comshare, was redefining itself from being a timesharing company to being a software company. We had software products but we were not known as a software company. So we decided that we had nothing to lose and we might as well grab onto this. First of all, to see if it was real. I was always one who liked doing that, trying something to see if it was for real. Secondly, if we could accomplish something with IBM, it would help us adopt an image of being a software company.

In fact, we succeeded. In January of '84, we announced a partnership with IBM that generated more press than the sum of the entire press that Comshare had had since 1966. It was absolutely incredible how the press picked up on this announcement of our relationship with IBM to supply decision support software. So that was another huge PR-related step forward for us as an independent software vendor. We became immediately credible to the marketplace. But I know there were a lot of vendors, yourself included, John, that felt there was nothing to this. Looking back, did it prove to have value at all in contributing to PR for the independent software industry?

Albert: There was a constant concern within IBM as to whether the software industry was friend or foe. This is what IBM constantly debated and there were people within IBM whose attitude was: nullify ADAPSO, get them out of the way, thwart whatever their agenda is. I was a minority voice on the other side that said, "No, wait a minute, these guys could be helpful. They really complement IBM, they don't compete against IBM." That was a constant struggle. So I think the Application Developer Conference in 1982 was a watershed event in terms of IBM's positive thrust toward the ADAPSO organization and towards software firms in general.

Maples: One thing that we haven't talked at all about was when IBM unbundled its core services.

Albert: 1969.

Maples: No, it was '70. To some extent, that's what created the ability to have an industry in software. Prior to that, hardware companies thought software was a freebie that drove hardware. And I think that is what started the need for publicity and public companies and so forth.

Albert: You know, ever since ADAPSO was formed, IBM had a bastion of defense to make sure that it wouldn't go anywhere.

Crandall: Well, one of IBM's representatives to ADAPSO, Amby Carr, was the most maddening individual that I ever dealt with because he was Mr. Barrier. You just could not get past him no matter what.

Albert: Exactly.

Crandall: And that's what IBM felt like to many people inside ADAPSO. The whole organization was just this impenetrable barrier.

Albert: Well, he was in an area that covered marketing practices and corporate concerns and things like that, so that was his role, his responsibility. I was this innocent person who went from consultants, CPAs, and lawyers, to software and services, and mine was a marketing role. So I constantly had fights with Amby and others. I never had to get approval from them but they really didn't like my thrust.

Crandall: I'd like to transition this conversation a little bit to see what recollections we have about the effect of all these efforts. Good effect, no effect, effect on business, or effect on selling productivity, or whatever. What was the outcome?

Maguire: I had a few thousand copies made of that *Business Week* article. [*Laughter*]. And I used them all. [*Laughter*] Big impact.

But I want to go back to another point that you made. When you signed that agreement with IBM, you were in a different situation than we were.

Crandall: That is correct.

Maguire: When we got down to IBM versus Software AG, it was a slug fest. We were going after the engine and they were, too. Out in the streets, in the marketplace, we were fighting them everyday, and they were fighting as hard as they could, too.

Albert: How did you resolve that?

Maguire: By losing to them. Because the enemy was not only IBM, it was the people within the customer's organization that saw their future tied to IBM's IMS. They were the experts. It was a hard system to learn, okay? They were the experts inside the customer's organization and I can tell you many, many stories of where the game was fixed. I'll give you two. Large insurance company in San Francisco. We won the technical evaluation. Database studies were very common in that day and age, and we got the highest score. It goes up to the executive that the IBM account rep takes to lunch all the time. What he did was have them change the weightings on two criteria. All of a sudden, out of nowhere, the size of the company became heavily weighted, the number of database experts within one hundred miles became paramount. I had one person in Oakland, they had a hundred down in San Jose. I lost the business. The other one was in Boston, an insurance company. I could never prove it, but I was told that for a benchmark, the internal people, maybe with some suggestions from the IBM people, pre-sorted all of the updates against the database in the middle of the night. So the updates flew through IMS like reading the data straight off a tape. And then when they ran Adabas, those updates were in the random sequence they would typically be in and it ran much slower.

Albert: But Software AG was a very successful company.

Maguire: This is 1981, '82, '83. We'd just gone public so we weren't there yet.

Albert: It was IMS versus your product?

Maguire: Yes, always. And I was always very professional when I lost the sale and said, "Well, if it doesn't work out give me a call later." I personally closed a hundred of those accounts several years later—where they tried IBM's product, spent a lot of money, and then came to Software AG.

Albert: This is with a relational database?

Maguire: It was sort of relational. Oracle was purely relational. But Adabas was designed to do the bread and butter of all kinds of production, from query to sequential processing. But I'll never forget that benchmark in Boston. They won the benchmark. Later on their sister company in England became a customer, and they eventually converted from IMS to Adabas in Boston. But that was common, once a week for me.

Albert: I do remember the duels over those two products. But, you're right, Rick had a different kind of a company.

Crandall: I understand. I just was stirring things up to get some substantive comments.

Sturtevant: There was another thing we did that helped to get a lot of additional coverage for the industry. The September 1, 1980 *Business Week* story was big but, obviously, they didn't have, as they do now, an IT department with specific reporters assigned to cover IT on a regular basis. So we employed a strategy to show these guys that there was enough financial clout and horsepower here that they had to cover this regularly.

Albert: As a beat.

Sturtevant: Right. And the way we managed to do that was through the back door, but it worked very well. In 1981, we did a special advertising supplement on the industry and we got a number of our members to buy ad space, full pages in most instances. What we did, much to their surprise, was to sell twenty full ad pages. Well, that was the biggest special ad section that they had the whole year. So they said, "By God, there are real advertising dollars here. If we start writing more about these guys and set up a department, gee whiz, they will come."

We did this for two years. The third year I went back and they said, "No, we'll take care of it this year." Because, obviously, there was a cut coming out of the ad dollars in terms of the cost to do it. And I was told off the record that their editorial people were embarrassed because we played the editorial content so straight. It wasn't like an advertising section which is touting just one company. Because it was covering multiple companies, we had to be very careful that everything was on the up-and-up. So the editors said that it was better copy than they were providing on the industry and we were embarrassing them.

Albert: So ADAPSO wrote the advertorials?

Sturtevant: We wrote the first couple advertorials and sold the ads, and then, lo and behold, *Business Week* formed a department to actually cover what we do.

Maguire: I get *Business Week* every week and it's still there.

Crandall: Mike, I'm wondering about this from a Microsoft or a PC perspective because, at the tail end of this period, there was tremendous activity already on the PC front. I imagine there wasn't any concern about how to get press because it was such an electric new area, but was there any impact or carryover from any of this?

Maples: Well, I think the PC guys figured out PR and getting press much better than the mainframe guys ever did. I've commented a number of times that Microsoft's shadow has always been much bigger than its body. It did that through pure PR. Microsoft is willing to take credit for anything that happens anywhere. Where IBM would always try to keep their name out of the press, Microsoft was always trying to get their name into the press. The most stark contrast between IBM and Microsoft was the whole issue of PR. At Microsoft, six to eight weeks before you announced a product, you'd go on a long-lead press tour. Then you'd go on a short-lead press tour and you'd have all the executives ready for press conferences. You did everything to get press. At IBM, you'd avoid telling them anything till the day of the announcement and then you'd give them a press release.

And so I think that the microcomputer companies developed the ground swell. The customer set was consumers, it wasn't the IT department, and the only way to ever reach them was through some indirect means. You could never reach them through *Computerworld* or a direct sales force. So, I think the micro guys figured out early that PR was much more important to the dissemination of their product information than it was to companies selling to IT departments.

Sturtevant: But, Mike, in some respects, you're dealing in part with a different time and place. For example, when I started in 1979 in PR with ADAPSO, I assembled a press list of the various reporters that were in the trade publications related to the industry. There were seventeen publications. That was it.

Maples: I agree that the time was more ripe in the mid-80s. If you look at the number of PC magazines started, I bet it dwarfed the number of other technology magazines. I bet that in 1984 there were more PC magazines on the rack than all of the other computer trade publications combined. I think it was just a recognition that the PC companies didn't go to the IT department with a direct sales force.

Dreyer: I'm looking at this from a different perspective, which is one of membership. We had Milt Wessel standing before Judge Edelstein in the IBM case to get the gag rule lifted. That was notoriety, that was exciting, that was publicity. And we had headlines in *Computerworld* that said: Feisty ADAPSO attacks the banks, and the accounting industry, and the telecommunications industry. All of those things we were able to promote to the industry, which recognized that ADAPSO was doing something for them besides having conferences. We got very tangible results from these things. We may have not won the cases, but our strategy was to hold at bay all of these deep-pocket companies who were trying to get into the industry. So we accomplished a lot of things and we reached our peak of a thousand companies because we were doing activist things and protecting the industry.

Sturtevant: That aspect of it certainly made PR on behalf of the association and the industry easier. This gets a little beyond the timeframe you're talking about, Rick, but not by a lot. I couldn't help but watch the Enron thing with some amazing replay in my head of the Big Eight wars we fought. We had tremendous press at the time because we were challenging whether the auditing firms could in fact be independent and also be consultants. It all came back. It took twenty years but it's finally come back.

Crandall: I think from a historical perspective, it's probably useful to divide the benefits and the results into several categories. Some had to do with how software companies produce business. Others had to do with how software companies go public. A third had to do with how does the trade association gather membership and gather power so that it's really the advocate organization that the industry needs, and needs increasingly as it grows. I think we've really got three buckets. There may be some blur between the financial and the business-building side. The other really had to do with increasing ADAPSO's profile so that it could represent its members more powerfully.

I'm going to try a summary here and then see if there are additional thoughts to be added to it. If we take an overview of our industry, we had a problem which was that we were not recognized as a separate industry. That had to do with the way in which the industry was born, almost literally like a rib out of IBM. We used promotion of an image as a strategy to achieve an awakening in the marketplace. The objective was to get access to the public equity markets and also to get an easier, more productive ability to sell our products and our wares. And that was successful. We only have a few software vendors in the room today but if you talk to many more, all will say that we did accomplish both purposes as evidenced by the data.

Almost simultaneously, or just a few years afterwards, we had a tremendous new element of software come on the scene which is the PC software. I think it's right to say that the PC industry didn't so much learn from ADAPSO as it learned from its own needs, having started as consumer product companies. In fact, by hiring people from traditional consumer products companies, the PC software vendors were much more expert at marketing than the prior software industry ever was. But with regard to long-term impact, the combination of the success of that early program at ADAPSO and then the even more skilled approach that the PC software companies took made working on image a permanent strategy of this industry. Although it started with very little in the way of marketing abilities, it wound up as an industry that has highly-valued marketing abilities. And that's become a permanent part of the fabric.

Maguire: Good summary.

Crandall: Julie, do you have any comments?

Johnston: I think that Dave and Jerry have covered it well but I'll point out that, at the beginning, we had to define the industry. I remember Rick doing a lot of work on that. When we were writing articles, we had to find words to communicate to people who didn't understand software at all: what these companies did, what these products were, what was application software versus systems software. It actually was mundane and boring work but we had to do it.

Crandall: Thank you for reminding me. We had a Research and Statistics Committee at ADAPSO that I chaired for several years. The job there was to figure out how to define the industry and figure out its segments, and figure out a way of representing what those were, and describing what those were. While we provided some of the fodder for the image effort, it had another audience, which was the industry analysts at the time: IDC and INPUT and Quantum Science. We wanted to influence them to get on the same bandwagon with regard to how the industry was defined because it was such a confusing mess that they were talking about. We felt we'd never get anywhere with the press until we got common definitions, so that was actually another effort that I forgot about.

Sturtevant: With that foundation, we could walk in with a report by an independent research firm like INPUT and lay it down in front of a reporter and say, "Look, $9.5 billion this year in processing services and $2.4 billion in independent software products." And so forth. And there was credibility because we could then compare and contrast those numbers with other industries. Without that foundational work that Julie was doing…

Dreyer: Very important work…

Sturtevant: It was critical because if you walk in and you can't answer the question: How big is this market?, your conversation's over.

I definitely remember in early discussions with financial analysts that there was real concern as far as doing IPOs or major investments with software or professional services companies because there was nothing tangible for them to grab onto. I remember one analyst saying to me, "How can these companies go public? Their assets go down in the elevator every night."

Crandall: Actually that battle was fought on many fronts including with the accounting firms and with the FCC and Feds and so forth as to what is this asset. Today, the value of intellectual property is well-recognized.

We're getting close to three o'clock so thank you all. I think we had a pretty complete discussion.

Contracts Reference Directory Workshop

Moderators: Burt Grad and Phil Frana

Rapporteur: John Gracza

Participants: Dick Thatcher
                       Mary Jane Saunders
                       Jay Goldberg

Grad: This is the session on the Contracts Reference Directories that were produced at ADAPSO starting in the late '70s and continuing, I guess, for another five to seven years. One thing we'll talk about is the period of time covered. Each of you please identify yourself by name, what your affiliation was during the '70s and '80s, and what your affiliation is now.

Saunders: My name is Mary Jane Saunders. From January of 1983 till about March of '89, I worked for ADAPSO and I helped put together two of the contracts that are in the directory—the software product acquisition agreement and the software product maintenance agreement.

Grad: Those were in the second of the two volumes.

Saunders: They were the first microcomputer software contracts.

Goldberg: Jay Goldberg. I was the founder and CEO of a company called Software Design Associates which I started in 1968 and ran through 1985. I was chairman of ADAPSO in 1987. I broke the professional services group away from the software products group into its own section and headed up the development of the contract for the professional services industry.

Grad: What are you doing today?

Goldberg: I'm the managing partner of a venture fund called Hudson Ventures. We invest in software companies.

Gracza: I'm John Gracza. I was on the staff at ADAPSO from, I believe, 1987 to 1992 or '93. I began as Director of Statistics and Research and then became very active with the software group.

Thatcher: I'm Dick Thatcher. I joined ADAPSO with the formation of the software section in 1970 in Denver, Colorado, and remained in

ADAPSO through, I guess, the late '80s. I was on the Software Division Board for many years and on the ADAPSO Board for a number of years. I got involved in the contracts project because Burt grabbed me and put me on the project.

Grad: What was your company affiliation?

Thatcher: Atlantic Management Systems, originally called Atlantic Software.

Grad: What happened to Atlantic Management Systems?

Thatcher: I sold it to AGS, Larry Schoenberg's company, one of many companies he bought including one of Jay's companies. Today I am in the investment banking business with Investec PMG Capital.

Grad: And you continued to stay active in ADAPSO when you were working with AGS?

Thatcher: Yes.

Frana: I'm Philip Frana. I'm an historian at the Charles Babbage Institute. I run the National Science Foundation Software History Project there.

Grad: A very major project funded by a significant grant that they got from the National Science Foundation. I'm the moderator, Phil is the co-moderator and John is our rapporteur.

What we're going to try to do is develop a chronology: when the project got started, and how it developed. And then, I'd like to spend time on how these contracts were used, what value they had, what difficulties arose. There were a number of contracts done in different time periods. We're not going to go into depth on many of them, obviously, but if there were certain things that you think were particularly significant, let's bring them out and talk about a particular contract.

We've asked Phil—looking at it from a historian's perspective—what kinds of things would he think might be of interest. So he'll ask some questions or ask us to elaborate.

The scope is anything to do with the directories or the use of these contracts over the entire time period. I don't remember when we first started to talk about producing a contracts directory. Does anybody remember?

Thatcher: I'm going to guess '73 or '74.

Grad: That early?

Thatcher: I know why the project got started but I can't tell you exactly when. In the early days clients just signed our standard license agreements without questioning them. But then they started to get their lawyers involved and so it was not uncommon for me to find myself, besides selling software and taking care of clients, negotiating with their attorneys. And that became an expensive and time-consuming process, besides the fact that it delayed the signing of contracts. We were dying. That was the most urgent motivation: to get deals done on a timely basis. And, Burt, you and I had an early discussion about the possibility of facilitating this process to reduce its cost and expedite getting it done. At the time somebody—it was probably you, Burt—raised the analogy of the architects. How the AIA, the American Institute of Architects, had standard contracts that were used as a framework for their engagements and so the idea germinated from there.

Grad: Help me here. In the back of my mind there's a recollection that we started a committee that Larry Welke was active in but it didn't result in anything for a period of time. We didn't have a lawyer on the committee initially, to my knowledge. Esther Roditti got involved at a later point in time.

[*Ed. Note: Esther Roditti's name was Esther Schachter at the time under discussion.*]

Goldberg: That was the late '70s

Grad: It was late '70s before I remember anything specific happening.

Goldberg: That's when Esther got active in trying to put together the first of the directories.

Grad: That's my recollection as well.

Thatcher: But it took a couple years to get to that point.

Grad: Yeah, because we tried to get it going for a period of time. I know Larry worked at it and it just didn't germinate. But there was a need. Who got Esther involved? Do any of you remember?

Thatcher: I thought you did.

Grad: I may have. I don't remember.

Thatcher: We decided that we needed a combination of industry expertise and legal expertise. And so special groups representing different sectors of the industry were formed and Esther was a part of each group. There was a team of IT services players—occasionally we met in Esther's apartment in New York, as you recall—and a software products group. Then there was a VAR group. Esther would draft the contracts and circulate them to those people.

Grad: Milt Wessel, who was ADAPSO's General Counsel at the time, was not involved in this process to my knowledge.

Thatcher: That is correct.

Goldberg: In fact, it was the opposite.

Grad: He was nervous about the project.

Saunders: He didn't like the idea.

Goldberg: There was a great deal of caution on the part of the ADAPSO attorneys that we not do anything that would be perceived in any way as collusion or as violating antitrust laws. They cautioned us on that in all these efforts. Every time we would try to do something the association was concerned that it would appear as though the industry was getting together to force its terms on the market.

Grad: That's a very good point. The term we used to refer to these documents—which Esther probably came up with—was: "a form contract with alternative clauses."

Goldberg: That was the basis for the alternative clause format. Nobody wanted to have one contract that all of us as vendors were going to present to customers.

Grad: Companies might have ended up with the same contract but it was a matter of making choices among the alternative versions of the clauses. I'm recalling that Esther must have collected twenty-five or thirty contracts from different software companies. The first contract that was done, the Program License Agreement for an End User, was for a software product. An end user, of course, in this case is a company, not an individual.

We got twenty-five or thirty contracts as samples. I remember that we had a problem because the companies didn't want to give us their contracts. Their contracts were private and they didn't want others stealing them. They were willing to let Esther look at them and use them to create a new document but not copy them. We got IBM's contract. We must have had thirty of them. Do you remember some of the companies that contributed their contracts?

Goldberg: I don't know, but you would have to assume it was the usual suspects, which would be the people on the SIA board. So you would assume ADR, Informatics, TSI...

Thatcher: Pansophic. And we submitted ours, of course.

Grad: I wonder if Esther has any record of which companies contributed. That was a really tough thing. I remember we negotiated with each company. How could they be sure the other people wouldn't see their contract? You know, you have this concept of ADAPSO, this conflict between sharing and competing, and here is a wonderful example where it was to our general interest to share information, particularly for the smaller companies.

Frana: Do you remember who refused?

Saunders: Everyone.

Grad: There were some that never gave.

Thatcher: People were reluctant but I think that once the process got started and got institutionalized to a certain extent there was a lot more openness about it.

Grad: I think later on, after the first three or four got done, it was easier.

Saunders: I disagree. It continued to be a problem to get people to give us contracts. We spent a tremendous amount of time begging people and promising that we wouldn't use them wholesale, that when the contract agreement came out they would not be able to recognize their contract as a whole. And the problem with following through on that promise was that there were some contracts that were excellent. The IBM contracts, in particular, tended to be very favorable to the software company, which is what we were trying to accomplish. So we had to actually build in clauses that were less effective in order to follow through on the promise.

Grad: The point I think we're picking up here is that there were a number of different reasons why this seemed to be a good project during that time period. What was happening at the end of the '70s that made this project particularly valuable? Can any of you remember?

Goldberg: Well, I remember one of the discussions. There was a pretty significant focus on providing benefits to members so there was a lot of discussion about what SIA could do that would have value to its members. The members were paying a lot of money in legal fees and so there was a sense that we could reduce legal fees for software companies, particularly the young ones, by providing something they could take to an attorney and say, "I've got these alternative contract clauses. What would you recommend?" And there would be reduction in the legal fees. So one of the motivations was clearly economic.

Grad: I'd forgotten that completely.

Thatcher: It's true.

Grad: Yes, I remember now that we were talking about insurance policies and all kinds of things that would have financial value and benefit the smaller companies.

Goldberg: Because they had no money. These were companies that were struggling because the industry was just in formation. There were some big companies that were doing well but the little companies were all struggling and couldn't afford first class legal fees.

Grad: I'm assuming that we must have started this project in the '77-'78 time period.

Goldberg: I got interested in ADAPSO in '76. That was when I became a member and this had not started then.

Grad: That's a little later time period than we discussed earlier so something triggered getting it started. The buyers were getting more sophisticated, more powerful, and we were starting to see some very unfriendly contracts that didn't give us any protection.

Saunders: This was one of the things that Milt Wessel was most concerned about. We were drafting these documents with the idea that you would use them with lawyers, but we were doing such a comprehensive job by providing the alternative clauses that Milt was concerned—correctly, I think—that people would just take these forms and put together their own contracts without consulting with lawyers. And they would end up in a worse position than otherwise because they wouldn't know what they had actually proposed and agreed to.

Grad: The way the alternative clauses were done, which was Esther's idea, I think, is that she gave the reasoning as to why you would use or not use each clause. Or if you were faced with such a clause by one of your users, you would understand what the implications were.

Goldberg: Why that was so important was because most of the people in the software industry, particularly in the small companies, didn't really understand the significance of a lot of the clauses. They just didn't understand it. And so one of the purposes that this served was to educate software entrepreneurs about why tax treatment was important or why intellectual property was important because in those days there was just a naiveté about the business.

Thatcher: I'll tell you how you can figure out when it got started. Our first committee meetings were held at the conferences. Dave Sturtevant reminded me of that and handed me a flyer from a 1979 ADAPSO conference where I was chairing a meeting of the Contracts Committee. At one point the Contracts Committee meetings were featured events at the conferences. If you go back through the ADAPSO press releases about the conferences you'll find the first one where they announced the committee.

Grad: Unfortunately, that kind of material wasn't saved in the ITAA files. I have in my records some minutes of meetings from '75 through '77. I'm going to look back through those and see I can find anything. I think we're talking about the '77-'78 time period for starting this project. This first volume shows June 25, 1979 as the publishing date and I assume that that's the original date, that this isn't a later version. Do you remember, Mary Jane?

Saunders: I started with ADAPSO in January of '83 and this is what I remember being told at the time. This Directory was something designed to provide a benefit to members. We had remarkably few tangible benefits we could hand members and when people signed up for membership they always wanted to know what they were going to get. It was a major selling tool during the early to mid-'80s.

We decided which contracts would be done in response to the way the industry or, at least, the membership of the association, was evolving. I was most directly involved in what were then called microcomputer software contracts. There was a marked difference in the contracts we were putting together for that group compared to what we had done previously for the professional services and software products companies. I suspect that Ron Palenski knows the most about the early days of the Contracts Reference Directory because he and Mike Nugent preceded me on the ADAPSO staff by a couple of years.

Grad: I know that Ron eventually took over drafting the contracts in the directory. At some point, we decided not to continue to pay outside counsel and Ron picked up that responsibility.

Saunders: It was for financial reasons.

Goldberg: I think it was a lot later, though.

Grad: It was about '83, '84. I remember having a discussion with Esther in which I told her that Ron was really capable of doing it. She was a very, very good drafter—still is, I'm sure—but there was a point in time that we wanted to shift it over to Ron for financial reasons. She was not very happy with that, if I remember.

Saunders: Milt also wanted that. Milt was very good at teaching us how to be lawyers. And one of the things he wanted was to take over this process and move it in house so that the lawyers who were working on staff at ADAPSO could learn more about how the industry operated.

Goldberg: Kind of a countercultural move for an attorney.

Saunders: It was, but he was very countercultural. I think from the early to the mid-'80s on, all the contracts were drafted by the lawyers in house.

And we *all* did it because Milt insisted that we all do it so that we would learn this process.

Grad: One of the things that maybe Jay and Dick might talk to is whether this was something that was reasonable for an association to do. I guess we all thought so at the time, but did the lawyers for the software companies get upset about having this kind of a document produced by the association? Does anybody have any idea? Did your lawyers object, Dick?

Thatcher: Well, we didn't have any permanent counsel. We used outside counsel as little as necessary because it was expensive. When we started the company, we had very good counsel who knew something about intellectual property, unlike many of the companies. But it was *very* expensive. So we took whatever would work and was cheap.

Grad: Be specific. The first contract was a program license agreement. You were licensing products. Did you use this Contracts Reference Directory or did you continue to use your own contracts?

Thatcher: Oh, we used that. Not only did we use it, when we sent the contract out, we actually let the prospect know that this had the imprimatur of ADAPSO. And I felt, frankly, that that helped reduce the amount of pushback that I would get from the client or his attorneys because he wasn't just dealing with a little software company, he was now dealing with something that had the imprimatur of a national organization.

Grad: You were selling to fairly large companies and you were a very small company still in that time period.

Thatcher: Correct.

Grad: How about you, Jay?

Goldberg: We did the same thing because we had a products group and we had a professional services group and both groups used the contracts. But I think you might want to put it in the context of the buyers' perspective in that era. Because the buyers of software had no knowledge and their attorneys had no knowledge, so it wasn't simply educating the vendor as to what these clauses were about, it was also educating the customer. They were used to signing contracts from IBM, but in those days IBM didn't have separate software license agreements.

Grad: That's not a correct statement. They did have a separate software license agreement.

Goldberg: But customers just signed it. They would never go to their counsel to argue about IP or to argue about tax, they just signed the contract. So when you would try to sell software to a large company, their legal department had really no understanding of the issues.

Grad: You didn't show the Contracts Reference Directory to your customer, did you?

Goldberg: No, but what we would say was that this grew out of an industry association. We did the same thing that Dick did. If they were interested, we would refer them to ADAPSO's counsel to discuss the wording of the clauses. But they never actually did. More often than not, they would just accept the clauses.

Grad: Interestingly enough, I think that if they had read some of the pros and cons on these things, it would have made them a much too well-educated buyer.

Goldberg: Right.

Thatcher: What went out on our letterhead was our contract but we let them know what it was based on.

Goldberg: But on any of these issues like acceptance periods, license, who owns the software, etc., the in-house counsel in these big companies was completely naïve. They understood how to buy hardware but none of them really understood how to buy software. So this really served a dual purpose although we didn't intend it that way. I think it actually educated the buyers about what the issues were.

Grad: I've heard the point of view that the contracts that are used today by software companies or services companies are incredibly one-sided. That they are biased toward the vendor. Do you think this Directory may have contributed to that in some way?

Goldberg: Absolutely.

Grad: You think it did?

Goldberg: Absolutely, because I think it gave companies a feeling that what they were doing had some grounding and had an association behind it. I had a small software company and when I was going to sell software to New York Telephone which had a whole raft of attorneys, I could actually say that the reason that clause is in there is because this big trade association debated the issues, consulted with lawyers, and this was the result.

Grad: I left IBM in '78 so I must have left about when ADAPSO started working on this. The first IBM software contracts had to be in '69-'70 when they started delivering software for the first time at a price. I know I worked on a software contract at IBM. But that isn't what triggered ADAPSO's doing this. Competing with IBM was not a factor. This had to do with dealing with our customers.

Thatcher: I'll go back to a point I made originally. For us, the motivation was to get the deal done. And, Jay, you were right about the other side not understanding things and, as a result, just dragging the contract negotiations out. In those days, we were trying to get traction. Of course, 1970-71 was a horrible time but, even in the mid-'70s, we were trying to get traction and it was not unusual that we were really screaming for somebody to sign a deal so we could bill on it—we always billed 50% up-front—and get the cash so we could make the payroll. So when I ended up dealing with a lawyer who was dragging things out for thirty or forty-five days, it was real serious.

Grad: Did you have that same experience in the services area, Jay? Was there a delay in getting contracts signed caused by the lawyers or was that not a problem?

Goldberg: It was the same issue. Although the issues were a little more straightforward and easy to understand than they were on the products side, it was an era when big companies hired consulting firms and they didn't have master agreements. Today it's all boilerplate. In those days we would present them with our agreement, they would send it to their legal department, and it would take a long time to get their approval. The difference was we very often began the work before we had the signed contract which was harder to do in the software products business. We would operate more on faith. If we had a purchase order, we'd go in and start doing the development.

Grad: You could bill against the purchase order.

Goldberg: That's right.

267

Frana: Were the contracts often violated?

Goldberg: All the time, regularly.

Grad: Are you talking about services or software?

Goldberg: Services and, I suspect, in products as well. But certainly in services. Violated by the customer, absolutely.

Grad: Do you remember that in the products area, Dick?

Thatcher: The big concern that we had initially was, of course, unauthorized copying of the software. But for us, it turned out, that rarely proved to be a problem. Once or twice we discovered that it had happened. Once was with the Washington Post. I ended up calling Katherine Graham's office and getting referred to one of her top officers. We had found out that the head of IT had taken a copy of our product and was using it in another location. I think it was a subsidiary. We confronted him about it and asked him to pay for a second license. We told him he could use it but he had to send us another ten grand. He denied it but we had very sound proof. I had a phone conversation with one of the top officers and told him we had solid evidence that the guy had violated the contract. It was settled very quickly and we got a second license. But that was very rare. It really wasn't much of an issue for us. Remember, this was not PC software where theft is a significant issue. This was all mainframe and mid-range stuff.

Grad: At that time, using the software on multiple computers under a single license was a greater concern than piracy.

Thatcher: The other big issue for us was payment terms because, for us, cash flow was always important. But we could track violations on that very easily.

Grad: Jay, on the professional services side, what kind of violations occurred?

Goldberg: Well, the one that was most commonly violated was the non-hiring clause. Every professional services company had a clause in its contract that said that the client couldn't hire an employee of ours for a period of time after the contract ended. When there was a dispute, it was always about hiring. The one other problem area had to do with fixed-price contracts.

Grad: Let's deal with both of those because they were both interesting. On the hiring issues, the professional services companies were—I hate to use the pejorative term "body shop"—putting people on site either under time-and-materials or fixed-price contracts.

Goldberg: The issues were different.

Grad: Was the first professional services contract a time-and-materials agreement or a fixed-price agreement?

Goldberg: I believe the first one was a time-and-materials agreement because that was the easiest one to do.

Grad: You would put your people on customer premises performing specific work usually alongside some of their own people, right?

Goldberg: Yeah, fixed-price contracts were typically our own people, and with time-and-materials contracts, it was typically blended.

Grad: And, invariably, if they thought they saw somebody good, this was a cheap recruiting opportunity.

Goldberg: Absolutely.

Grad: What did you do about it?

Goldberg: Only once did I actually elevate it to upper management—at Equitable Life Insurance—and it wound up costing my company dearly.

Grad: Is that right? How? In what way?

Goldberg: Well, they hired one of our people. We objected. In most cases when that happened, I would object and show the customer the contract. They would say, "Yeah, you're right. Can we pay you a fee?" We always wanted to preserve a customer relationship so we would say, "Absolutely." And we would charge them a fee. But the guy at Equitable Life said, "Go screw yourself." I escalated it and wound up with a very senior executive who said, "How did this ever get to my level?" He wrote me a check and we did no more work at Equitable Life.

Grad: Wow. That's a pretty painful lesson, isn't it?

Goldberg: Yeah. In those days, if you decided to take on a customer you did it with great caution.

Grad: So the contract terms were fine but the issue was how do you enforce them in an effective manner.

Goldberg: Most customers lived with them or negotiated through them. Every now and then you got a recalcitrant customer, but I think they were the exception in those days. I think today it's very different. Today the customers define *all* the terms.

Grad: Let's switch now to the fixed-price contract.

Thatcher: Well, before you do that, this is exactly the foundation of the 1706 battle.

Grad: What is the 1706 battle?

Saunders: The independent contractor issue.

Goldberg: I'm not sure they are connected.

Saunders: Oh, I think they were. ADAPSO wasn't the first association to pursue it, but ADAPSO got deeply involved in it when the professional services company saw the advantage.

Grad: What is 1706?

Saunders: It was Section 1706 of the Tax Reform Act of 1986 which imposed rules on the tax treatment of independent contractors, making it difficult for people who had been employees to become independent contractors. There was a movement afoot among many programmers to set up themselves up as independent contractors who worked through body shops. They sought significant tax advantages such as being able to deduct the cost of their basement office and that sort of thing. I can't remember which industry group it was that went to Congress and got this little provision into the tax reform act. And then all hell broke loose.

Grad: I remember a gentleman named Jay Goldberg becoming the bête noire of a bunch of people because of 1706. Can we put that on a side note here and come back to it?

Goldberg: Yeah. I'm not sure they are connected.

Thatcher: You don't think there's a link? You don't think the right to hire someone is a link?

Goldberg: No, because that right to hire would have been whether you were an independent contractor or full time employee.

Thatcher: Okay.

Goldberg: I think it was a completely separate issue. It was an important issue in the evolution of the industry but not related to the contracts issue.

Thatcher: I'll never forget Tony Stepanski who ran AGS Professional Services who felt very strongly that the client didn't have a right to hire his employees, just like you did.

Goldberg: No, he felt much more strongly than I did because he would actually sue. He actually went after employees.

Thatcher: But clients countered with, "Well then, I'm going to deal with firms who use independent contractors who I can treat as I wish."

Goldberg: But even the firms who specialized in using independent contractors had the same clauses. That's why I don't think there's a connection.

Thatcher: Did they? That's interesting. Okay. I didn't fully appreciate that.

Saunders: One thing that I observed over the course of the time that I was involved in this at ADAPSO, and then at the Software Publishers Association, is that these contracts were very pro-vendor and they initially didn't have any warranties. And for a long time they continued to be presented without any warranties.

Several voices: No. No, no.

Saunders: Yeah, they were. They were as-is contracts. But, in practice, you guys were providing warranty service. You didn't want to put it in the contracts, but in order to maintain the customer relationships you were providing warranties.

Grad: Are you talking professional services? Are you talking products?

Saunders: All of them.

Goldberg: I don't think so. Let me go back to my recollection of what the situation was at that time. We were all companies that had no assets. And our customers were the largest companies in America. The idea that any one of those companies could literally, with one lawsuit, put any one of us out of business was a terrifying prospect. So we developed as much protection as we could so that if our software screwed up, we'd give the customer back his money, but we wouldn't be responsible for anything beyond that.

Thatcher: Consequential damages.

Goldberg: Consequential damages was the big issue because these software companies went from payroll to payroll. Even the biggest of the companies, because they were growing so fast, were just literally keeping up with payroll. We were terrified that a large company would put in our payroll system or our accounting system, something would get screwed up, people would be paid incorrectly, and the customer would come back to us for the damages that they had incurred, not what they had paid for the software.

Saunders: But you were able to get that accepted and into the final contract by having these be industry-sanctioned agreements.

Goldberg: Absolutely. That is exactly how that happened. But I believe today that it's the same, isn't it?

Saunders: No, it's not. Now you get ninety days.

Goldberg: Ninety days of what?

Saunders: Ninety days of warranty coverage.

Goldberg: That's just a pricing issue. When maintenance starts is simply a pricing issue.

Saunders: No, I'm not talking about maintenance, I'm talking about the basic warranties that are provided under any professional service agreement or product license agreements these days.

Grad: I've been involved as an expert witness in some lawsuits and all the contracts I've looked at—Computer Associates or GEAC agreements, for example—say no consequential damages, period.

Saunders: Consequential damages is a different issue. That's a limitation on liability.

Grad: Almost all of them have an arbitration clause, limiting the right to sue.

Saunders: Right.

Goldberg: The warranty just had to do with when the customer started paying maintenance. You could warrant the product for a year and then maintenance would kick in. Or you could warrant the product for ninety days and then maintenance would kick in.

Grad: She's using a different term, Jay.

Saunders: Right.

Grad: Let's see if I can help interpret. The warranty concept is that I commit that something will perform your task correctly. What software companies commit to is that it will perform what we say it will do correctly. That is not the same thing.

Saunders: As to consequential damages, of course, they always had, and continue to have, limitations on liability.

Grad: The contracts I've seen, which relate to mainframe software, not PC software, guarantee that it'll do what I say it will do. If you point out to me that it's not doing what I say it will do, then I will correct it to the best of my ability to make it do what I say it will do. I go no further.

Goldberg: Our companies all say that today.

Saunders: All say that today, but the contracts under discussion didn't say that.

Goldberg: They all said the software would perform in accordance with the documentation.

Thatcher: That kind of wording is not in that 1979 license agreement? I thought it was.

Saunders: No.

Goldberg: I bet it is. In accordance with the documentation. That's the way it used to be phrased.

Grad: Article 13 of the Product License Agreement with End User talks about warranty of performance and provides different alternatives. We're not going to go through the wording in detail but warranty was one of the major issues and we were saying to the companies in this agreement...

Goldberg: We give you this documentation and the brochure and we guarantee the product will do what we say. We would also say that if you modify the product in any way that the warranty no longer applied.

Grad: In the Contracts Reference Directory, we told the software company if you choose this wording, here is what you're subject to, here's what you're protected against. We didn't tell them whether or not to include the warranty clause. They made the choice. They may have turned around and said to their customers that this is what the industry said they should do, or this is what other people do. We were trying to be very careful because it was a very sensitive issue. Milt really was concerned about it.

Goldberg: Fixed-price contracts for professional services were much more difficult because the customers didn't understand the development process. It's still a problem today in fixed-price contracts but, in those days, it was much more of a problem because the buyers were so naïve and uneducated. So the analogue we always used was building a house. We would have a design document agreed to by the customer. We would sign a fixed-price contract to develop to those specifications. And then the customer would change the requirements. So the language in the contract for changing the specifications, and doing additional work, was always crucial. That's where all of the disputes occurred. I'm not sure that problem's been fixed. I think it's probably still a problem today. The only difference is today the customers are much more aware of the ramifications of changing the specifications and so there's a more business-like approach to it than there was in those days.

Grad: I know that, in general, the view in the '70s was that if you took on a fixed-price contract, there was no way the customer could ever specify it well enough. Even if they *had* specified it well enough, they were going to change their minds and there was no way you were going to be able to renegotiate your price once you had a fixed-price contract in place. I think that the companies that belonged to ADAPSO during the '70s did very few fixed-price contracts. It was death. The customer was powerful. If you wanted to keep the customer, they could get away with changing anything that they wanted. The only customer that I can remember that we would do fixed-price contracts with was the government. The federal government did have a process for changing the requirements.

Thatcher: Change management.

Grad: There you had a change management process. But other companies didn't.

Thatcher: The Big Eight really were the early players in fixed-price contracts but they were also the early players in effective change management.

Grad: Was Andersen a leader in change management methodology?

Thatcher: Yeah. Part of the reason that they developed Method One was to have a methodological framework so that people could agree on milestones as they went along and deliverables throughout the implementation of a system. Then it became a marketing approach where the Big Eight would—this is anecdotal, but I think it's pretty valid—bid a job knowing full well that, with an effective change management system, the job was going to end up being three, four or five times the size of the original bid.

Grad: The companies that were providing services to the Federal Government—CSC and the others—would low-ball, underbid, to get the contract, because they were banking upon a number of changes being made over the two or three years of the contract. The Federal Government had an engineering change process and the companies felt that the customer wasn't going to switch vendors in the middle of a project. If you maintained good relations with the purchasing agents, you would get authorization for changes and the contracts would end up two, three, four times as large.

Thatcher: I think that was basically borrowed from the engineering business.

Grad: Absolutely. I think it was because of the government experience in dealing with hardware change in the aircraft industry and so forth.

In the time that we have left, I'd like focus on the first two contracts a little bit and then maybe the ones you worked on, Mary Jane. How did the process work? Dick, do you recall the process of getting this first contract, the Program License Agreement, in place? Do you remember the sequence of events? If you remember any of people involved, it would be helpful.

Thatcher: It started before Esther got involved. We tried to pool some contracts and do it on our own. And it became clear very quickly that that was unrealistic because of fears that Milt had, and the fact that none of us were lawyers, and that none of us had the time to pull all this stuff together. And I think you're the one, Burt, who promoted getting professional help to drive the process. That's when you brought Esther into the equation, and it then became a team effort led by Esther, supported by company executives in each particular area, whether it was software products or professional services or VARs or what-have-you. There were a series of meetings and she established a process for creating the contracts. The first step of the process was to send your contracts to Esther. Then she would do a cut-and-paste to create a draft which got circulated through the committee several times for comments, and then it was finalized.

Grad: My recollection is that we tried to do this within SIA. We had a Contracts Committee and people wouldn't give us their contracts because they had no confidence that the contracts wouldn't get passed around. We solved that problem by bringing in a third party. My memory is that it was probably Oscar Schachter, who was very active in SIA, who suggested Esther.

SIA was both software products and professional services at that point. The two groups hadn't split apart yet. I think we probably started on the Professional Services Agreement about the same time, Jay.

Goldberg: We would meet at Esther's and Oscar's apartment. We'd meet in their kitchen or living room and there were usually five or six people there.

Grad: Do you remember some of the people who worked on the Professional Services Agreement?

Goldberg: Oscar was one of them.

Grad: He was with Advanced Computer Techniques, Charlie Lecht's company, at the time, I think.

Do you remember any of the other people who were involved Jay?

Goldberg: No, I don't.

Grad: Dick, do you remember some of the people involved in the software product contract? Any recollection? Did we have an IBM representative working on that one?

Thatcher: We did. Was it Ed Kane?

Grad: No, it was somebody from their legal side. It was a lawyer, not a businessman.

Goldberg: I sure don't remember an IBM attorney at any of these meetings.

Grad: You don't?

Saunders: Yeah, there were. There were IBM attorneys.

Grad: Certainly later on there were.

Thatcher: I don't recall an IBM attorney being involved but I do recall IBM input.

Grad: Let me read the titles of some of the articles in the Program License Agreement first and then I'm going to do the same for the Professional Services Agreement and see what you remember as being the most significant or most difficult.

- Parties and Definition
- License Grant

The concept of a license was central to everything, right?

Goldberg: People were beginning to understand that they couldn't sell software. In the early days, people would actually sign a contract of sale for the software.

Grad: So this was very significant.

Goldberg: Yes, but I think that by that time period everybody understood that you had to license software, not sell it, to retain ownership rights to it.

Grad: By the end of the '70s that was clear.

- A whole article on Program Support Services: what did maintenance cover, when did it kick in

The typical practice then was one year "free" maintenance as part of the initial license agreement. Later on, maintenance couldn't be included in the license agreement, it had to be a separate transaction from an accounting standpoint.

- Training, maintenance, program support, call-in service, whatever else you want to do
- Data conversion
- Consultation
- Enhancements

We never did figure out a way to define enhancements other than to say, we'll give you what we choose to give you. That's effectively how it has always been done—no one is entitled to anything in the way of enhancements. One of the problems is putting a value on the commitments you've made. If you've committed to doing enhancements, what have you committed to?

Thatcher: Well, it really depended on how you structured your deal. For example, if you read John Cullinane's article in the *Annals*, he started charging an annual support fee. You paid an initial fee and then paid an annual support fee and that went on forever and you got everything. So it wasn't an issue.

[*Ed. Note: Volume 24, Number 1, of the* IEEE Annals of the History of Computing *was distributed to all attendees at the meeting.*]

Grad: Couldn't they release a new feature or a separately-priced capability that wasn't included?

Thatcher: No, it was all thrown in.

Grad: Well, Syncsort did something very similar to that.

Thatcher: As long as you kept paying...

Grad: You got whatever.

Thatcher: When you stopped paying, you couldn't use the software any more. I don't know if he had a recovery process or not.

Grad: He was able to get away with that then. That's interesting, because most companies would not sign that kind of agreement now.

Goldberg: It was an annual license.

Thatcher: Didn't Computer Associates use that model? I think they did.

Goldberg: There was a guarantee to the customer that you would keep the product current if IBM came out with a new generation computer or system software modifications. So that was essentially what you guaranteed.

Grad: That's right.

Goldberg: If the hardware or the systems software changed, you would keep it running.

Grad: And that was an issue because the customers would say, "We've paid all this money for the software, we want to be able to keep using it. You can't put me out of business by jacking up the annual rates." Of course, when a company was acquired by Computer Associates, among others, the rates just took off.

Frana: How did you handle the customers that didn't want to upgrade?

Goldberg: That became a real issue because you would wind up with multiple versions of the product to be maintained. So eventually there became a mandatory upgrade where you would tell your customers that you would maintain software going two or three versions back, or for a period of time. And if they didn't upgrade, then you could no longer support them. That became a really big issue.

Grad: And, of course, the license agreement specified that it's yours to use, but you have no right to resell it. Even transfer rights were blocked in many cases.

Saunders: Moving it from computer to computer was sometimes blocked.

Thatcher: To reinforce what Jay said, we had a policy that if you stopped paying for maintenance but then you called for support, you had to go back and make up all the payments that you missed before we would answer your question.

Grad: Yeah, you never got a free ride. In some cases there was a penalty charge because, otherwise, the customer would just wait until he needed to make a support call and then just make up the missed payments. That was a no-loss proposition for the customer.

Frana: Did you institutionalize the change? Did the customer always know when a new version was coming out?

Thatcher: Many companies did. They developed a regular schedule of new releases and upgrades. On top of that, with the influence or evolution of user groups, the change process actually got institutionalized in conjunction with a user group which would submit requests for upgrades. The company would decide which of those requests it wanted to incorporate in the next release. There would be an agreement either formally or informally with the executive committee of the user group, and that was what was in the next release.

Grad: Almost every product company ended up with these user groups. We didn't have much activity in ADAPSO related to user groups, did we? They may have been modeled after the original IBM SHARE and GUIDE.

Thatcher: A very important function.

Goldberg: Yeah, but I have a feeling that it is one of those areas where everybody felt proprietary about what they were doing because everybody had their own style.

Grad: Did you ever have a user group for one of your products?

Goldberg: Oh, yeah, we had many of them.

Grad: I know you did, Dick.

Thatcher: Well, it was great for promotion. They initially started as parties for our customers. And then they became sales sessions as well as parties. Then, in many cases, the users took them over. They became organizations that were truly independent of the software company.

Grad: But the contracts didn't really address the user groups. That was an evolved process. The other articles here include:

- Property Rights
- Proprietary and Trade Secret Information
- Liability and Default

No way we're going to go into this in detail, but the range of coverage was very broad.

Goldberg: Property rights was an important issue. A lot of the software products were built in conjunction with customers. For example, we would start out with a core product and then some company would tell us they'd like to have a particular feature. If it was a feature peculiar to that company, we handled it one way. But we handled it differently if we thought we could sell that feature to a hundred other companies. We would negotiate ownership of the modifications differently in that case and provide maintenance of the modifications.

Grad: Did you write separate contracts for those?

Goldberg: Yes. The issue of ownership was crucial because if you did something for a customer, you wanted to make sure at the end of the day you owned the rights to it.

Grad: In your professional services companies, who owned the work you did for the customer?

Goldberg: We would always try to own it and the customer would always push back.

Grad: Did you win in many cases?

Goldberg: Usually not, because they were smart enough to know that it was work for hire. But occasionally we would. If we saw an opportunity to develop it further, we'd negotiate to own it. A lot of software products were built out of professional services contracts.

Grad: I remember Dick Thatcher setting up an agreement for four or five sponsors to pay for developing a new product.

Goldberg: Right, that's exactly how it was done because we didn't have the money to build it.

Grad: The sponsors paid for developing it and they got a license to use it when it was done.

Goldberg: I would bet that if you went back and looked at the history of the successful products in the business, you would find more than half, perhaps the vast majority, were customer-funded developments. You'd find a customer, build something for them, and then you'd say, "Hey, that worked pretty well. can I sell that to other people?" Then you would negotiate ownership. That wasn't in the contracts we're looking at now because it deals with licensing a product once it's become institutionalized.

Thatcher: I recall discussions about drafting a sponsorship agreement in one of the meetings because it became a very complex process, with issues of ownership rights and royalties. One of the players who was very active in that space was ISA, Insurance Services of America, which had, I think, fifteen or twenty large insurance companies as customers.

Grad: Also Anacomp and Hogan Systems in banking. Big, big money involved. They never finished a product but... [*Laughter*] ...they got hundreds of millions of dollars out of sponsorships.

The articles in the Professional Services Agreement were:

- Parties and Services; what was the scope and site?
- Modification and Cancellation
- Term
- Payment
- Staffing; who owns the people, whose employees, that kind of thing.

Did the issue come up about when people worked for a customer for more than a certain period of time on the customer's site, they became a de facto employee of the customer according to the IRS?

Goldberg: That was later. It was an IBM-driven issue. IBM was the first one to really understand that and they put a six-month limit on their employees working at a customer's site.

Grad: Was this the late '80s maybe?

Goldberg: Yes.

Thatcher: It's still, by the way, an important issue today. Staffing companies are rotating people all the time.

Grad: Your people were on the customer's site but they were your employees. You were paying their social security, etc.

Goldberg: Yes, but there were companies that used so-called 1099 employees which was the 1706 issue.

Grad: Is that at the same point in time or is that later?

Goldberg: Same point in time. It was a big issue in ADAPSO. I had a problem because I came down on the wrong side of that.

Grad: Yes, you did.

Goldberg: I really thought that Section 1706 was something that ADAPSO should figure out how to deal with. Jack Courtney, who was ADAPSO Chair in 1988, was vociferous on the issue and, in fact, got ADAPSO to oppose companies that used independent contractors instead of full-time employees. I thought he was wrong because it would prevent companies that used independent contractors from ever joining ADAPSO, which it did.

Thatcher: Right. It resulted in the formation of the National Association of Computer Consultant Businesses.

Goldberg: That's exactly right.   Which today is an incredibly large organization. From a membership standpoint, I always had the view that the association should work to represent a wide range of constituents and not take a position that would exclude parts of the industry. There were others that felt that the association existed for its current membership and should promote its interests. That's where our views crossed.

Grad: Jack Courtney was the president of Computer Task Group at that time.

Thatcher: There never would have been an NACCB were it not for the 1706 issue. All of those people would have become part of ADAPSO.

Grad: One article in the Professional Services Agreement was Warranty of Performance.

Goldberg: Yeah, we essentially said to our customers—to your point, Mary Jane—that we're not responsible for anything.

Saunders: Right.

Goldberg: You pay us and we're responsible for nothing.

Saunders: Right. That was my point. It was not really a limitation of liability.   It was telling the customer that they really were not getting anything. It was being provided as-is, and that the software company owned it, not the customer. They got the right to use it for a limited period of time.

Grad: This agreement—let me make sure I'm right here—says Professional Services Agreement.   Is this only the time-and-materials agreement, or does this include fixed-price work?

Goldberg: We had multiple versions. We had a time-and-materials agreement, and we had a fixed-price agreement.

Thatcher: What's the date on the Professional Services Agreement?

Grad: October of '79.

Thatcher: Really? So it followed right after the Product License Agreement.

Grad: I think these two were going on in parallel. I think Jay and the people he was working with were doing one, and Dick, you and I and others were working on the other one. And then, I think, there may have been a delay. Yeah, December of '80 is the next one, which is a Computer System Agreement with End User.

Goldberg: That was the old service bureau agreement.

Grad: Well, I don't think so, because the next agreement is called Batch Processing Services Agreement.

Thatcher: I think the one called Computer System Agreement was for VARs.

Grad: I think the VAR agreement was the third one done. I don't know if we were calling them VARs at that point in time or not.

Goldberg: We called them OEMs.

Grad: The Batch Processing Services Agreement was done by Esther and is dated October of '80. The Computer Services Agreement is dated December of '80. The next one in this book is the Remote Processing Services Agreement. It was done by Ron as the Assistant General Counsel in 1982.

Let's see, they are not in the book by time sequence. I'd forgotten that. The next one is also by Esther who is identified as Special ADAPSO Counsel-Contracts. This is called a Non-exclusive Marketing Representative Agreement. That's using a third party to sell your products.

Thatcher: What was the date on that?

Grad: The date is July '81. Here's another one that she did that is copyrighted in '82, without a month—An Exclusive Distribution Agreement. How about the book you have, Mary Jane? Let's look at that.

Saunders: The first one is the Software Product Acquisition Agreement done by Esther in February, 1983.

Goldberg: That's when you are buying a product from another developer to remarket or reuse.

Saunders: I started with ADAPSO in '83 and the Software Product Maintenance Agreement was one of the first projects I did.

Thatcher: Was that for PC's or for mainframes?

Saunders: It was for mainframes. Work on PC contracts didn't start until '85. This next one is an Exclusive Distribution Agreement (International) which Ron did in November, 1983.

Grad: Because by then the international market was big business for the software product companies.

Saunders: This next contract is incorrectly attributed. The name on it is Bob Daunt but this is something I actually wrote in 1985. It's a Warranty Drafting Aid. If you look at this and the Software Publishing Agreement, which was in '86, this was at the point where the PC guys were trying to decide whether to join ADAPSO or form their own organization. So there was a lot of emphasis on creating product that would be of value to them. One of the critical issues for those guys was how to deal with warranties.

Goldberg: The shrink-wrap issue.

Saunders: Right. This Warranty Drafting Aid is actually not a whole contract. It is just the part of the contract that involves warranties because that is what the shrink-wrap license was.

Goldberg: This may seem trivial today but, in those days, when you sold software to a big company, they got a piece of paper that they had a chance to review, and then they could accept the terms of the contract or reject them. The PC software guys handed you a box and in the box was a warranty or disclaimer. The question was: If a customer wasn't going to sign it, what was the contractual relationship? Because, for the first time, there wasn't a negotiation, there wasn't a signature.

Grad: They put it under plastic so you could read the thing before you opened the box.

Goldberg: Today, customers understand that it's a license agreement. But in those days there was really a question as to whether it was binding.

Frana: But it has changed back a little bit, hasn't it? Because now you accept/decline if you purchase the software.

Saunders: Yeah, because it's smarter that way. But because the agreement had to be on the back of the box, it really forced us to pick and choose those things that were important. What was important was that this was a license to use, not a sale. Also to put in the reservation of rights for the Federal Government so that they didn't end up owning it. And then the warranty provisions. That was it.

Goldberg: There was no accept/decline because nothing was online. Today, you download, you scroll and you click yes. But in those days what you got was in a box. You installed it on your computer. You weren't connected to anything.

Grad: "Accept" meant you ripped open the plastic. The minute you opened the plastic cover, you accepted it.

There's a Non-exclusive Software Distribution Agreement for Microcomputer Software here and, again, it's aimed directly at the PC industry.

Saunders: It is the original software contract, sort of modified, with a new label on it, so that we could say, "We put this together for you PC guys."

Grad: We had at that point brought the PC software people into ADAPSO and were trying to set them up as a separate section. Esther Dyson, the editor of *Release 1.0*, and Paula Brooks, president of Unitech Software, were the two key people trying to organize that.

Goldberg: And then the big issue arose with the piracy lawsuit.

Saunders: Right. We were going to file the first piracy lawsuit but the ADAPSO Board wouldn't pursue it and Ken Wasch did.

Grad: This is when SPA, the Software Publishers Association, run by Ken Wasch, picked up that issue and did an incredibly good job with it. SPA became the association that most of the PC software companies joined.

Goldberg: They came to us first.

Saunders: They did come to ADAPSO first.

Goldberg: The ADAPSO board had a heated discussion because of what they wanted us to do...

Grad: Who's "they"?

Goldberg: Microsoft and a handful of other PC software vendors. They said, "We want to bring a series of lawsuits against the major corporations in America for illegally copying our software and we're looking for a trade association to work with us on it. We insist on your funding support and the use of your name." And there was a very heated discussion at the ADAPSO board.

Grad: Were you Chair at the time or was this before you were Chair?

Goldberg: It was either right before or when I was chairman. So I was either Vice-Chairman or Chairman.

Saunders: You were chairman in '86?

Goldberg: '87.

Saunders: Yeah, that's about the time. We were going to sue American Brands.

Goldberg: And that was another argument I lost. I felt that it was important for us to step up and represent all constituents, but a lot of the guys from the timesharing and network services companies were terrified that the big companies that were going to get sued would turn against them.

Saunders: I left ADAPSO in March of '89 and became General Counsel with SPA.

Grad: You were considered a traitor and a turncoat. You do understand that? [*Laughter*]

Saunders: I knew that. But I did it because I wanted to be involved in the piracy litigation. I then ran their litigation program. In addition, what the SPA membership wanted was exactly the same thing that the ADAPSO membership wanted. So there was an entirely separate Contracts Reference Directory that I developed at SPA.

Grad: You stole it?

Saunders: I stole the idea.

Grad: Did you steal the contracts? [*Laughter*]

Saunders: No!

Thatcher: Make sure this conversation is being recorded.

Goldberg: It was entirely reverse engineered. I want the record to note that she's not blushing. [*Laughter*]

Saunders: No! I didn't steal the Directory! Believe me!

Ron called me up and said, "It's copyrighted." I said, "I know it's copyrighted." He said, "You can't take it." I said, "I know, I don't want it." He said, "It's good." I said, "I'm going to do a better job." And what we did that was different was that we provided it on diskette.

Grad: Well, that's clearly different. The words were the same but, hey, it's electronic. It's different. [*Laughter*]

Saunders: But that was important.

Grad: Anyway, this Software Publishing Agreement was clearly done to appeal to Microsoft. Mike Maples, a top executive at Microsoft, was a very active member of SIA. The decision to create a separate ADAPSO section for PC or microcomputer software companies was a very hard decision because we felt that the two groups had more issues in common for *business* software than issues that were different. Not necessarily so for consumer software.

Goldberg: Yeah, but the groups were different culturally.

Grad: The ADAPSO microcomputer section never succeeded. SPA grew, and then they went on to include game software and educational software.

Goldberg: In retrospect, they really were different and there was very little recognition at the time about the differences.

Grad: We were business software people, selling to big companies. Theirs was a whole new culture dealing with selling millions of copies instead of a few. I think that it made a difference.

The next one here is the Non-exclusive Distribution Agreement for Microcomputer Software.

Thatcher: Can we stop on that point? Notice that, for historical purposes, two major trade associations—NACCB, the National Association of Computer Consultant Businesses, and SPA, the Software Publishers Association—both started, in effect, out of ADAPSO, each driven by a single, very compelling issue. Then they evolved into more comprehensive trade associations.

Grad: Interesting, because I think what Ken Wasch offered was his agreement that they would litigate. Well, they would negotiate or litigate, but they would go to the companies and do something about it.

Saunders: He agreed to litigate. But we also started negotiating as a result of me not being twelve people.

Goldberg: It was all about litigation.

Grad: Let me just finish these last two agreements. Mary Jane, you did the Non-exclusive Distribution Agreement for Microcomputer Software in 1986, again following that same theme. And then there's a Site Licensing Agreement in 1986 which was done by Joe Ruble?

Saunders: Yes, Joe was the junior attorney and I was very, very tied up in the 1706 issue by that point.

Grad: The last one in this book is dated 1986. You can see the shift in emphasis covering all the sections. The point you make, Dick, is an interesting one. This reflects the evolution and changes that did and didn't take place within ADAPSO. It covers just a seven-year period. But that was a period of incredible change, and the contracts provided benefit for software products, professional services, and service bureaus.

Goldberg: Benefit and standardization. I think standardization is one of the main things that came out of it.

Grad: But that was tricky. We had to be very, very careful.

Goldberg: It felt that way to me. We were always very conscious of the issue. But I don't mean standardization from an antitrust perspective. It was a real thorough discussion of what the issues were, and what the positions were with everybody disseminating the results to customers.

Grad: A thinking-through process and an educational process.

Goldberg: Yeah, that's what I mean by standardization. Because even at the end of this, we did not have the same contracts. I'm sure at the end of this process, if you had looked at Dick's contracts and at my contracts you wouldn't know that they had come from the same source. But they contained a lot of the same meat.

Grad: I've had a chance to look at some contracts by Computer Associates over the course of about twenty years. I've had a chance to look at the GEAC contracts, which are the old McCormack & Dodge and MSA contracts, and to see how they had changed over time. Lawsuits have often hinged upon what is industry practice, and this Directory is part of the evidence that has been used in a couple of these trials. I've used these contracts as representing industry practice.

Thatcher: I think the other thing that ties in with Jay's earlier comment that you're really educating the client is that, in the late '70s and early '80s, we were also educating the lawyers. There were a lot of lawyers who were seeing intellectual property as an emerging practice and didn't really know a lot about what was going on in that space, and they came and sat in on some of our meetings.

Frana: That's very important. Historians sometimes try to put two things together that don't seem to go together and they struggle with it. These are very logical, very clear, very eloquent solutions to the problems. But was it the weighty issues that were driving this activity? Or was it the fact that you guys have logical, clear, elegant programs? It seems like gifted programmers as artists would innately understand the whereas, the wherefores, the kinds of things that get put into these contracts. Not true?

Grad: That was part of the educational process, to get the business people to see the risk of inadequate contracts.

Goldberg: In fact, that really *was* the problem.   A lot of programmers had set up companies and were selling software and couldn't see the importance of contracts.

Grad: This was a real education to them.

Frana: That surprises me.

Goldberg: It's hard to understand the naiveté of both the buyers and the sellers.   This was a new business and the issues were not straightforward and clear.   And programmers were really the least-equipped to deal with business issues, maybe.   I used to be a programmer.   Were you a programmer, Dick?

Thatcher: For a little while, until I realized what my strengths were.

Goldberg: I was a programmer for six or seven years in the early stages of my career.   First of all, none of us had business school training or backgrounds.   It's not like today.   We all had either a liberal arts education or a technology education.   There was no place that you could learn this stuff.   There wasn't any place that you could go.   So a programmer and a salesman would start a software company, usually because they did a project at a big company and developed something that they thought had value. Then they would take it and try to resell it a hundred times.   And it was all done on a shoestring, starting out in somebody's house with a credit card used to cover expenses or whatever.   There was no road map, I guess, is the right way to put it.   So when you would talk about these issues, not only did people not understand them on the buying side, but even on the selling side. You had to educate the software entrepreneur about why it was important.

Thatcher: Go back and look at the agenda for the conferences.   How do I sell a software package? How do I hire people? All the basics of business. They received their education in ADAPSO.

Grad: Luanne Johnson makes the comment that she got her MBA at ADAPSO meetings.   That's how she learned to run a software company.

Thatcher: And this was the legal side of the business.

Goldberg: The analogue to me is the Internet. If you look at this whole bubble with Internet entrepreneurs—guys who were 23 years old, 25 years old, 27 years old and didn't know anything. They just got a tiger by the tail and rode with it. That's the way it was with us, only over an extended period of time. Time was compressed in the Internet boom but, if you look at all the stuff that occurred, we were going through the same things in the '60s and '70s. Only it took fifteen years instead of a year and a half.

Frana: I guess when I read through these I saw modular programming.

Grad: Absolutely. We did that. There is hardly anything technologically you'll come across in the '90s or late '80s that we weren't doing in the '60s and '70s.

Goldberg: You're reading about web services now, right? Web services is modular programming.

Saunders: But it was done in that style to avoid pitfalls that Milt Wessel saw from a legal perspective. One observation I can make as a still practicing lawyer is that these Directories have had tremendous impact on the legal profession because they spawned a number of other books with model contracts. One of the reasons ADAPSO stopped drafting them is because people in the private sector started coming out with similar books and we began promoting those instead. There was a book on drafting forms and agreements by Richard Raysman and Peter Brown that was quite good. What you see as a result is that there is now an entire category of books on drafting license agreements and other computer-related contracts.

Grad: Let me close the session. There is one other comment I'll make. Esther Roditti has written an article about the history of contracts in the industry and about the intellectual property issues. She's promised that we'll be able to get a copy of that. Thank you very much.

Industry Roundtables Workshop

Moderators: John Rollins and Jeff Yost

Rapporteur: Linda Schnell

Participants:

Betty Blankenship	Gary Durbin
Buck Blankenship	Nathan Ensmenger
Joe Blumberg	Larry Schoenberg
Barbara Brizdle	Larry Welke
Bart Carlson	Jack Yeaton
Bruce Coleman	

Rollins: Welcome to the session on Roundtables. Let's go around the table and please state your name, your company or companies that were affiliated with ADAPSO, and roughly when that was, so that we have a time frame for talking about roundtables.

Coleman: Bruce Coleman. In the '70s, Boole & Babbage; in the '80s, Informatics.

Durbin: Gary Durbin. Mid-'70s through '80s, Tesseract Corporation.

Schoenberg: Larry Schoenberg with AGS Computers. I believe I'm the only person who was a member of multiple roundtables at the same time. They were the first and second roundtables that existed. I have some notes prepared by Gil Mintz, one of the partners in Broadview Associates, who was the moderator of the first roundtable.

Ensmenger: I'm Nathan Ensmenger. I'm an historian at the University of Pennsylvania.

Yost: Jeff Yost. I'm the Associate Director of the Charles Babbage Institute and I'm an historian of business and technology focused on computing and software.

Carlson: Bart Carlson. My first association with ADAPSO was with a company I had called National Systems Laboratories, Inc. That was the late '70s to the early '80s. Then I was associated with another company called Group 1 Software until about '86. And then I started Napersoft which is still a member of ITAA.

Welke: Larry Welke. At the time, I was with ICP. I was also involved in one of the first roundtables.

Yeaton: Jack Yeaton. I founded Merit Systems in '76, and was a member of ADAPSO from about '78 to '91 or '92.

Rollins: And I'm John Rollins. Just one company, AZTECH Corporation. Founded it in 1968, sold it in 2000. I was the CEO from 1970 until 2000. I've been involved with four different roundtables, one of which still meets twice a year. Actually, I'm in charge of planning the upcoming fall meeting of that roundtable.

Larry, I have a copy of the same notes from Gil Mintz and there's one section of it I thought I'd read because he has some deep historical knowledge that I think surpasses that of most of us. He refers to it as the Presidents' Roundtable though not all the roundtables were for company presidents. We'll talk later about other kinds of roundtables that were formed.

"Originally, it was the "Presidents' Roundtable"; only CEOs were eligible—it was later expanded to include other senior officers.

"The original concept, I think, came from the auto industry, where there were "Dealers Ten" groups—10 Cadillac dealers, etc.; the idea being that non-competing homogeneous businesses can share techniques and gestalt...

That sounds like Gil.

"...gestalt to the mutual benefit of all.

"When I was CFO of ADP ('63 -'73), we held semi-annual roundtable meetings; the Presidents of our payroll operations in multiple cities would share techniques and statistics—the result was excellent. As clever and payroll-savvy as ADP was, we always learned from our regional Presidents at these meetings. It was also kind of inspirational—'how come Boston generates a better gross profit than I do in Philadelphia.'"

So that's a little background from Gil on how this came out of the auto industry and then from ADP and was imported into ADAPSO.

Schoenberg: I honestly don't remember that one way or another. I will tell you that we ought to give credit to the person who really started it, a man named Brinson Weeks who was with Computer Management Corp. There probably aren't a lot of people here who ever knew Brinson but I first heard about the roundtable from him. He was starting one with a group of people who felt they had interests in common but were not significant competitors with each other. They were mostly processing services companies—about twelve of them, I think. At the time of ADAPSO's 25th Anniversary, I gave the original notes, which included the size of each of the companies and the comments made by the people introducing themselves at the first meeting, to the association. I guess those notes are all gone now.

Rollins: What year would that have been?

Schoenberg: Buck, what year was that meeting, do you know? Buck was in the group.

Blankenship: We've been agonizing over that ever since the morning meeting when John raised that question. I'm not sure. I would say mid-70s.

Rollins: Buck, please introduce yourself for the tape.

Blankenship: I'm Buck Blankenship. At that time, I was with Data Processing of the South in Charlotte, North Carolina.

Rollins: So what would you guess the year would be? Give it a guess.

Welke: I have it pegged in my mind as '78.

Schoenberg: The second roundtable was for people from software companies and it started a year or two after the other one.

At any rate, Brinson had the original idea. Milt Wessel, who was ADAPSO's General Counsel, raised the issue of the possibility of antitrust violations in these meetings and felt that there should be a disinterested party in the room. We didn't want a lawyer there, and so, Gil Mintz became the moderator. I don't know whether Gil is implying that he helped create the roundtables. I don't honestly know whether he did or didn't. I do know that Gil was a moderator. A few years ago, I looked through my notes from that first meeting. My company was the largest one and we did $4 million a year.

Rollins: Well, I was in a roundtable that first met in 1980. I resurrected a list of the members of that roundtable. None of the others are here for this reunion. That roundtable met over a period of years—I think 3 or 4 years—until it evaporated and turned into another roundtable which I joined in the mid-'80s.

Each roundtable, by my recollection, was characterized by some commonality of business type. The first one I was in was processing services companies because AZTECH was in that business. We were a big data center at that time. And the other members of that roundtable were doing similar things. The next roundtable I was in was one that was moving from processing services into turnkey systems.

Then I went onto a third one and then, finally, the fourth one, which Bart Carlson is also on, along with ten other people strictly from software companies. So as the industry evolved, I moved to different roundtables as my business changed.

Yost: Was there someone who ran the meetings? Was there a moderator?

Carlson: We switch our moderator every single meeting. Whoever is hosting the meeting is the moderator for that meeting and picks the location, makes all the arrangements, handles the financing and bills everybody for their share of meals, etc.

I started with the one I'm currently on about ten years ago, in the early '90s. At the first meeting, I was asked to take minutes. I was trying to impress this group, so I took a lot of notes and a few days later, I wrote them all up and distributed them. And the fellow who hosted that particular meeting called me up and said, "Bart, whatever you do, kill that. Get rid of those notes. We don't want those kind of notes floating around."

Well, we never took that kind of notes again in the subsequent ten years. That was my first learning experience with the roundtable, about what we wrote down and what we didn't write down.

Blankenship: Let me pick up on Bart's comment and Larry's earlier comment about Milt's concern about whether this activity was an antitrust violation. I was astonished at our first meeting at Hilton Head Island that one of the things we did was to compare our financial statements. Remember that, Larry?

Schoenberg: Absolutely. That's how I remember what the revenues were.

Blankenship: Larry was making far more profit than anybody else there. I was kind of suspicious of him. [*Laughter*]

Rollins: One thing that I'd like to try to do is to identify every roundtable that ever existed by type of firm or by date or something so that we have some historical record. Buck, I've got your list of the very first roundtable, the one that Brinson Weeks was involved in setting up in the late '70s. I've got lists of the members of the four different roundtables that I was on and I'm wondering if there were other roundtables that we can identify.

Brizdle: At one of the conferences, I had a conversation with Walter Brown about roundtables in general and we thought it would be nice to get together a group of people who were in the business of *supporting* the software businesses. So we talked to Burt Grad about it and he loved the idea and set up a roundtable of people whose business was selling consulting services to the software companies. That included Joe Blumberg, who is here in the room, and Walter Brown of the Walter Brown Group, Esther Roditti, an attorney, Larry Welke, Pat Landry of Specifics, Inc....

Welke: Esther Dyson, publisher of Release 1.0.

Brizdle: Esther Dyson was a very early member. And Lee Keet.

Blumberg: Lee didn't come in until later.

Brizdle: But I can't remember the year we started.

Blumberg: Larry Welke facilitated our first meeting.

Brizdle: Larry, do you remember when it was?

Welke: Early '80s sometime.

Blumberg: It had to be '85 or '86.

Brizdle: And then Burt, with his inimitable skills in organizing, kept us together for years. He was really our administrative point person. Oh, and then Elizabeth Virgo joined later.

Rollins: Good. I've got a list of all those names you mentioned. That's very useful.

Welke: Let me make a comment in response to what you said earlier, John. You said that the roundtables you were on were discipline-oriented; just one industry or one segment. The one that I was on with Larry Schoenberg and Bruce Coleman was as diverse as you could get.

Rollins: That was Roundtable No. 1?

Schoenberg: No, that was No. 2.

Brizdle: Was it actually called Roundtable No. 2?

Schoenberg: Yes, it was called Roundtable No. 2 at the time. The question is whether we can come up with the names of the original members. It would be difficult. From professional services companies, there were Dave Campbell, Jay Goldberg, myself, Bob Jones of Computer Dynamics, Stuart Monchik of Monchik Weber...

Coleman: Dan Fylstra of VisiCorp for awhile. No, on second thought, he wasn't part of that original roundtable.

Schoenberg: Allen Hufft from UCC.

Brizdle: What year was this?

Schoenberg: Well, that's what we don't know. But it was about a year or two after the first was formed. It could have been as late as '80. Bob Cook of VM Software was another member.

Blumberg: The roundtable you're talking about was going when Rick Crandall first brought me to ADAPSO in '78. Because of that roundtable, I made the suggestion that we create a Human Resources Roundtable for software and services companies. That wound up becoming the Computer Services Personnel Association. That kicked off in '79 and I know that there were a couple of roundtables going on then.

Schoenberg: Peter Cunningham of INPUT was in Roundtable No. 2, and so was Rick Crandall.

Welke: And then John Maguire came on.

Schoenberg: I think Maguire may have been an original member because either the first or the second meeting was in Atlantic City and Maguire organized it. I got the previous day's newspaper delivered to my hotel room. I knew then how sleepy a town it was. [*Laughter*]

Rollins: Larry, what happened to that first roundtable that you and Buck were on?

Schoenberg: As people left the industry and some of the companies merged, it sort of dissipated.

Blankenship: Doug Altenbern of Endata came later.

Schoenberg: So did Marty Kogon of National Dynamics and Art Kramer of Praxa Data Centers.

Blankenship: Maybe two years after we started.

Schoenberg: In the Accounting Workshop this morning, we were talking about antitrust and I suggested that perhaps the reason why the roundtables survived longer than other ADAPSO programs was because they were doing something that was only marginally acceptable. That may be exactly why they were able to succeed. [*Laughter*]

I said it this morning and I'll repeat it now: I never once in forty years ever had a conversation with a competitor about pricing. But if you think that having a conversation about costing...

Rollins: And margin.

Schoenberg: ...does not give you a hell of a lot of insight into pricing... It's only people in the software products industry who don't think that, because they don't think that there's a connection between cost and price. [*Laughter*]

Yost: Was there any effort to keep direct competitors from being in the same roundtable?

Schoenberg: No.

Coleman: Oh, yes, there was.

Rollins: Wait a minute, there's a difference of opinion here. I thought everybody was going to say that there were no direct competitors on the same roundtable because that was my experience. So let's talk about it.

Coleman: I think the rules were that if someone who competed directly with a member wanted to join a roundtable, the member had to agree to it and be comfortable with having a competitor in the room. Is that how it played out?

Schoenberg: Ultimately. I don't know if that was an early rule.

Carlson: That was definitely a rule we had and to this day anybody can nix a candidate coming in for competitive reasons. Even if it's a minor competitive reason. There have been several people who wanted to apply and we didn't let them in.

We also decided to broaden the focus beyond software products but that didn't work for us. We added some professional services people sometime in the early '90s, but within two or three years we decided that was not our forte.

Rollins: Any further comments on letting competitors in? I want to talk about that some more.

Brizdle: We, too, had that issue because there were two people who were members of the Consultants' Roundtable who were both selling research services in competitive situations to the industry: Pat Landry and Warren Culpepper of Culpepper Associates. I don't really remember how that was resolved but I remember that it was a *very* difficult situation. Joe, can you help me?

Blumberg: It was resolved in a...

Brizdle: Huff.

Blumberg: Oh, in a real huff, yes. Pat actually walked out of a meeting and said that if Warren was allowed in the group, she would not participate.

Rollins: So what did you do?

Brizdle: Warren resigned.

Blumberg: They were originally in two different businesses. Warren was in the sales compensation business which meant they didn't compete, but then he wound up going into the customer satisfaction business, and he had to resign from the roundtable because he was then competing with Pat.

Schoenberg: I was accused at one time of using the roundtable to make acquisitions, which is untrue, because I never had a conversation about acquiring a company at a roundtable meeting. But the facts are that I bought three companies that were in a roundtable I was in. You talk about a conflict, what do you do when a guy who works for you is in the roundtable?

Rollins: What *did* you do?

Schoenberg: They left the roundtable. One of them, Jay Goldberg, came back after he had left the company a number of years later.

The other thing is that everybody's business evolved. When we started, there was a group of us in what you would today define as identical businesses but we weren't competitive because we were in different locations.

Rollins: You were in different geographic markets, so it was OK.

Schoenberg: And since that time, we've had much more complex issues than those created by competitors. When there's an issue that can't be discussed openly in front of a member, that person simply agrees they will not show up during that discussion. We've had innumerable cases with people who were on the boards of other people's companies where their issue was a problem with the company, and one guy or the other had to leave the room.

Rollins: That's a good segue. I'd like to talk next about what features of a roundtable make it successful. Obviously, one is that you have to be able to talk openly, which means that you can't be competitors as in the example we just talked about with Warren Culpepper and Pat Landry. What other features of a roundtable would make it successful?

Coleman: One of the adjectives we always used is that a person must be "zingable." And that means the ability to have open and prickly discussions.

Unidentified voice: We call it being blunt. *Really* blunt. Candid.

Welke: The other thing we had as an unwritten rule was that, if you get a message from any member, no matter how many other messages you had on your desk, the roundtable member's message came first. We all adhered to that and gave preference to the roundtable members. So it really did get to be a very, very personal relationship that we established.

Blankenship: John, adding on to Larry's comment in the morning session on ADAPSO Conferences, somebody made the point that trust played a very great role.

Rollins: It was key.

Blankenship: And I think that was magnified in the roundtables. I know the group we were part of had a high degree of trust in each other and we spoke with great openness. It was heartwarming. It was a very good experience.

Rollins: Trust and integrity.

Brizdle: But trust was developed. That came from the nature of the conversation.

Schoenberg: It was assumed.

Rollins: And then confirmed.

Coleman: Periodically, we would reinforce—particularly when there was a new member—that what is said in this room goes nowhere. And you honored that. For about five years, I kept track of tips that I could have acted on and didn't. And if I had, I would have lost my shirt on them. [*Laughter*] The good news is that I couldn't do it because of the confidentiality. But whether it was personal or business, you just didn't talk about it outside of the meeting.

Rollins: In the roundtable I'm in now, we have several public companies and when they get into areas which are not disclosed publicly, we all have to make note of that fact because we simply cannot act on the information they are providing to us.

Carlson: One of the other things that happened with this particular group, too, is that we started to bring our spouses with us to our getaways in the winter time to the Caribbean or Hawaii or Mexico or wherever we were. We also had a fall meeting, and after five or six years, the spouses had become such good friends that they wanted to be part of the fall meeting, too. So it expanded to become a social event beyond the business function. Some of the roundtable members, like John, have sold their companies and they're retired, but they're still part of the roundtable because of the social aspect.

Rollins: We have four or five of our dozen members who have sold their businesses and are doing other things. They're involved in new startups, they're consulting, or whatever. Just to finish, though, on what makes a successful roundtable, are there other things that are necessary ingredients?

Schoenberg: It's not just what makes it successful but what keeps it going and I think that last comment that the introduction of spouses made it practical to continue was an important one because without that you couldn't really do it. But another important factor was a decision made by at least several roundtables that if you didn't show up a couple of times in a row you were out.

Rollins: Right.

Schoenberg: It didn't matter whether you would really be thrown out or not. It sent a very clear message that it was highly insulting not to come and that you could not carry on a conversation where you had lost the train of thought. After all, seeing someone twice a year is not a lot. So if you miss one time, you are really out of the flow. I think creating a perception that you would be dropped from the roundtable if you missed a couple of times was an important element in maintaining the continuity of the roundtable, whether or not it was enforced.

Rollins: What about preparing for roundtable meetings? Did you often have emails going around or, in the old days, snail mail, where you'd ask for input from the different roundtable members on topics to be discussed? Gil Mintz, in the notes he wrote up, refers to a grid that would be filled out ahead of time asking certain standard questions about roundtable members' businesses so comparisons could be done during the roundtable meetings. Was preparation important?

Blumberg: We had a pretty set agenda. There were certain things that took place in the morning of the session but if we had something that we wanted to get input on from the rest of the group, we put ourselves on the agenda to present something in more detail, and got a specific slot in the afternoon to deal with it. Most of the time, it was a strategic issue or a problem that you were dealing with that you wanted extra input on.

Blankenship: Joe, we did the same thing. It was an organized thing in the sense that we treated the roundtable as an unofficial board of directors. Someone would present a business problem that he had to this group and seek advice from the other members. I presented a case at one meeting and the conclusion of my "board members" was that I really needed a high-powered marketing guy. My company was OK but we were in a sort of a limbo. So I approached one of our roundtable members, Lou Pfeiffer of A. O. Smith Corporation, and he joined my company as our marketing guy. That was one way you'd lose roundtable members. You hire them.

Rollins: I've made that exact comparison so many times when people have asked me about the roundtable meetings. I describe it as being an informal board of directors just as you did, Buck. It's more than a board of directors, though, because these are all CEOs who have walked in the same shoes. In many cases they've made some of the same decisions, whether good or bad, that you're trying to make and so you can go to them with your problems. I've never had a case where there weren't people at the roundtable who had experience with the particular issue or decision that I was trying to make. Whereas, if I took it to my AZTECH board of directors, they wouldn't have anywhere near the amount of experience with that particular issue. So it's a supercharged board of directors.

Carlson: We have different formats for our winter and fall meetings. Our format for our February meeting is Wednesday through Sunday. We come in on Wednesday and get together with a cocktail reception with dinner after that. We meet in the mornings and we play golf in the afternoon and we'll all be together in the evening.

Our fall meeting is a little more condensed. We come in on Thursday night, and meet just Friday morning and play golf Friday afternoon. Or we'll meet all Friday and half of Saturday and play golf the rest of the day and then leave on Sunday.

We also have a general format that we've used for over ten years. We go through all twelve company updates, where everybody gives a presentation on what's happened in the last six months. And then we submit issues that members want to get on the agenda for that last day. That last day is where we deal with specific things, out of the ordinary course of business. Those are submitted ahead of time and distributed to the group a week or so before the meeting. You can add one at the last minute but, obviously, nobody's going to have thought about it without advance notice.

Rollins: What we're hearing is that the roundtables served a real function and some have continued to this day without support or endorsement from ITAA. They just live on and on because they're doing something useful for all the members. I'd like to explore how many roundtables are still in existence.

Welke: In our meetings there was usually a certain amount of time that was allotted to the discussion of what the hell was going on in ITAA. Or ADAPSO. And what do we want to do about it. Sometimes we wanted to do something about it and other times we said, screw it, it's not worth the effort. If they want to shoot themselves in the foot, let them go ahead and do it.

Carlson: I want to add another thing that's happened with our group. Members of the roundtable are now members of the real boards of directors of the companies in multiple cases. Two of the roundtable members are on the boards of companies that I happen to own. Several others are on the boards of other members' companies. It just kind of blossomed as a by-product of that trust.

Rollins: To Larry's point about discussing ITAA issues, that would come up periodically in roundtables I was in but we would usually say, "Geez, this is not our problem, we want to talk about roundtable issues." And so we wouldn't spend much time on it. Even though we would worry about it, we would rationally move on to what we felt, correctly, were more important issues for us.

Carlson: Isn't that a factor of the times, though? Maybe the ones that you were on in the '80s spent more time on it than the ones you were part of in the '90s.

Rollins: Well, we talked about it in the '90s at a couple of meetings, too, but we quickly dispensed with it and said, "Let's not spend any more time on that."

Schoenberg: One of the reasons why that changed over time is the stage of life that people were in. Our roundtables tended to move from basic core business issues to broad-based business issues to personal issues, to family issues, to retirement issues, to investment issues. I have to believe that these are the patterns that occur in every group.

Rollins: Exactly.

Schoenberg: But there's one other thing that I think made the group that Larry's talking about a little bit more focused on ADAPSO issues because there was an unusually high percentage of people in the roundtable who had been Chairman of ADAPSO. This makes a big difference. Since so many had been the Chairman of ADAPSO, it's not shocking that they were a little bit more involved and concerned about what was going on.

Rollins: Good point.

Schoenberg: I'm intrigued by the fact that the roundtables had similar formats. That wasn't an obvious decision but we had the same thing: one long meeting which was social, one short meeting which was business. But I wonder if we're not reflecting some broader social/cultural issues here. The need for these kind of groups which seems to be *so* prevalent and they're always justified the same way—that this is the only place we have peers to relate to. Yet, in fact, they seem to go so far beyond that. Everybody seems to have some need for this kind of social interaction.

I'm also intrigued by the fact that most of the people were not socially involved with each other except in the roundtables. They're involved enough to be able to respond and yet removed enough that they don't have a direct personal involvement. It's easy talking about someone's problem or someone's personal life when you're not a part of it. It doesn't matter because you don't see the other people who are involved. So I think there are some very broad issues and I would be interested in knowing what happens in other industries. We can't be alone. That's why I'm intrigued by Gil's comment. He presented it as an issue for all business. I wonder if it was.

Ensmenger: This is interesting to historians because we recognize that if we want to understand all of your companies, we have to understand how people are networking, how they're hiring people, how they're making decisions and learning. These kinds of practices, I believe, go on in all industries. But those interactions disappear from the historical records. So this will be probably the only documented evidence of the existence of these groups. And the question is can we begin to preserve this even more? Are there notes from sessions? If you're writing your memoirs, make sure to include these.

Brizdle: No, no, no, you wouldn't want to. You might note who was there and what the topics were.

Ensmenger: Which is the problem that historians have. A lot of the records that survive—annual reports, marketing brochures, milestones, product releases—don't talk about the three versions that didn't get released because they failed. And, for most historians, those are much more important and yet they're not kept.

Coleman: By the trust bond that we have and what's talked about, the difficulty is you just can't do that.

Brizdle: Have you been able to identify all of the individual groups?

Rollins: I think as best we can. What do you think?

Durbin: There was a CFO roundtable.

Schoenberg: There were many others.

Carlson: A lot of them were started and died along the way. I don't think there are many others still going.

Rollins: Let's try and figure out which ones are still in existence. Larry, you're on one.

Schoenberg: I'm on two.

Brizdle: OK, so there are those two, plus the consultants' roundtable, and the one that Bart and John are on.

Rollins: That are still in existence?

Brizdle: Yes, well, I don't know if the consultants' one is still in existence. We're having a meeting tonight, does that count?

Rollins: Sure, absolutely.

Yost: I was thinking about what Nathan said on recollections and I think that it might be possible to write a little about the types of issues that came up that might give historians a better sense of the range of issues, without identifying specific companies or problems Another question I have is: Was there a great difference in the size of companies and as there a sense of the roundtables as a means to help smaller companies build capabilities or managerial knowledge through a type of mentorship?

Carlson: The makeup of ours is that it started out primarily entrepreneurial and, over time, professional managers joined. There is, in my observation, a difference between these two types, in background and how one approaches problems, if nothing else. Not to say that there aren't tons and tons of things in common but there are some differences. The age range is fairly close, within ten years from the lowest to the highest, with one exception. That one person, in his late 40s, is maybe fifteen years out of the age range. Everybody else is in their mid-50s to early 60s. So there's a homogeneity in age.

Rollins: That's the age today. This roundtable has been going on for 10 years, so the range was 10 years younger when it got started.

Carlson: And in recent years there's quite a range in revenues. There wasn't that big a difference when we started but it has changed dramatically, as much as a hundred times difference in size.

Rollins: Jeff, to answer your question, I believe there needs to be a fair amount of commonality and companies of roughly the same scale or at least similar sophistication of management style. And you have to have some similar interests—golf is a common thread among many of the roundtables as you've probably noted—or an interest in going somewhere with spouses to a nice resort—someplace warm in the winter time, like the Caribbean, Mexico, or Puerto Rico. That sort of thing. That's what makes a roundtable succeed over many years.

Yeaton: And stay together.

Brizdle: I think it could be quite the opposite. Because, as these companies have evolved, some of them are far more successful than others, for one reason or another, and therefore some members would be interested in taking their spouses to an exotic place while others might not have the wherewithal to do that or are focused on their business. So it would seem to me that it could be divisive within a roundtable.

Carlson: I guess there's a certain level of success in our roundtable so that a trip is not an issue. The differences come out not on spending a few thousand dollars for a trip but on spending a few million or tens of millions on investments. Those kind of differences are certainly there but the wherewithal to take a trip, at least in our case, is not an issue for anybody.

Schoenberg: One intriguing thing that no one has mentioned is what happened to women? Why haven't they been more involved in roundtables? One of our roundtables has had three women in it, I think.

Coleman: Yes, three.

Carlson: We've had one in the history of our roundtable.

Schoenberg: Well, I remember the first time that the software roundtable invited a woman, she turned us down because she said she didn't think she could learn much from us. I remember it well because it was Mr. Welke who did the inviting. We could never decide what she was telling us because Larry was the interpreter of it.

Welke: I don't know if she didn't like the group or she didn't like me.

Schoenberg: What about this issue of differences in size? Because we had this issue.

Welke: But when we started, there wasn't a single member that exceeded $2 million in sales. If somebody even approached $2 million, you thought they were pretty damn big. At the end some were ten times, a hundred times, that size and there were some companies that had not grown at all. They just were stuck for some reason.

Brizdle: I remember being part of one that was not successful and I wonder why it is that some of them were not successful. My sense is that it was a very disparate group that had come together without a core group, so nothing kept it together. I wonder whether some of the roundtables that did work had a core group of people committed to the roundtable, as opposed to that one which was five strangers thrown together and didn't last at all. At least some of those people, including Mike Blair of Cyborg, are in the roundtable you're in, John.

Rollins: The core group of my current roundtable first met in August of 1990. So it's been going for 13 years as of the moment. To support what you said, Barbara, the third of my four roundtables, had only one meeting. And it was very disparate group. Lot of different backgrounds: processing services, software, and consulting. We had one meeting in Miami and talked at the conclusion of that meeting about having our next meeting in Mexico. But it never happened. There wasn't a core leadership group, which is what you are talking about.

Brizdle: Either a core leadership group or...

Coleman: A leader.

Brizdle: Someone who was willing to make the phone calls to make it happen.

Blankenship: There may be another force at work here in whether these roundtables survived or even formed effectively. Looking at the list of the members of the first roundtable, all of these people were good friends before the idea of a roundtable even surfaced. We all knew each other and had seen each other at ADAPSO for years. Judging from some comments I've heard from those roundtables that are yet surviving, they represent people who are just good friends apart from their professional relationship. So my suspicion is that that is a factor of some importance in their forming and their surviving.

Rollins: I'd like to respond to our historians across the table by asking if people have specific recollections to submit, in generic terms, of issues that may have been resolved at roundtable meetings. I've got one that stands out in my memory when AZTECH was going through a transition. We went through so many evolutions from punched cards on main frames to timesharing to turnkey systems to DOS to Windows to the Internet. The industry was changing so rapidly, it was such a dynamic environment that there were no models for where you were going.

So you'd go to the roundtable meeting and try to ferret out some ideas on a revenue model or a business model. When I was moving from processing services into selling software, I was very uncomfortable because I'd built the processing services business around recurring revenues where you could bill every customer every month for all the stuff you did for him. AZTECH was very solid and stable and grew at a nice 20-30% annual rate. And in software, it looked like it was all this choppy water. I took this issue to the roundtable and came out with a support program that we christened AZTECH-Care. We included lots of support, free software backup, free newsletters, free membership in the users group, telephone hotline access, fax line access, online modem support, etc. We started charging 1.5% a month, which meant that 18% of what they had paid for the software, we'd get back each year in support revenues. Because it was so feature-rich, it succeeded beyond my expectations. It was ideas that came out of a roundtable session that enabled me to do that. My revenue base solidified and, with that 18% per year add-on revenue from all the software sales, I was able to keep building the base until eventually it got to the point where over 80% of all the revenue was from AZTECH-Care. In fact, later on we came out with AZTECH-Care Plus and added more services and raised the price to 24% per year. And that was purely a roundtable idea.

Brizdle: What year?

Rollins: I don't remember what year that roundtable meeting was but it must have been in the early '80s. Any other ideas for our historians who are looking for specifics about something you may have learned at a roundtable?

Schoenberg: Well, I can think of a lot of things but the problem is I don't have permission to repeat the stories. But I can tell you one that I will always remember in which the person didn't take the advice. We had someone in the roundtable who got involved in a lawsuit and both parties' positions were very understandable. It dealt with royalty payments for software and the man who was making the presentation said, "We're thinking of settling this case if they will agree to pay us $5 million." And Jay Goldberg, who is a member of the group, said, "How about paying them the $5 million instead?"

It was such a shocking idea, but you cannot imagine how right it was. In fact, both companies went out of business because they ended up in a legal action that produced no money for anybody and put two companies out of business. So in this case, the advice was not followed, but it's the kind of extraordinary advice you could get from this group that you wouldn't get from your regular board of directors. Who would ever think of advising somebody to pay the money rather than take the money? I don't know how serious Jay was, literally, but his point was right. This is not a winner. Get out.

And I think as often as not, the really best advice has been: don't go into that business, don't touch it, keep away from that approach. One of the issues I remember constantly discussing was the issue of a COO, a No. 2 guy. Should you hire a COO? I seem to recall that Bruce was part of that discussion.

Coleman: Yes, it came up because I was one once and I'd never do that again. I said, "You know, the COO is only a Band-Aid that won't work. The bleeding is at the top and you're putting the Band-Aid around the neck." [*Laughter*]

Carlson: I think that some of the best advice I've gotten out of the roundtable has been what not to do. I did that, it didn't work; if you do it, you're probably going to throw away money. Also ways to resolve the big business issues like how to handle compensation and what works best with sales commissions. But it was also a bunch of little things like: What are the tools that you use to run the business? What are you using to keep track of support calls?

Rollins: What are your metrics?

Carlson: What are you using to do this or that? We'd poll the group and we'd have three people using that and two people using the other. So it's probably safe to use one of those two, as opposed to trying something that hasn't been tried before. So there was a lot of that kind of stuff that just came as a by-product besides the big issues. And very, very valuable.

I believe the value is cumulative and it's a function of time, because as people get to know you, as well as your business, better, then the advice becomes better. They've seen your track record and know what you've done with the advice you were given before.

Rollins: Very good. Other examples of benefits from the roundtable meetings?

Blumberg: One of the things I can relate that was important to our roundtable was the fact that as consultants to the industry we weren't very good at marketing ourselves.

Brizdle: We did it in the halls of ADAPSO conferences.

Blumberg: Yes, so the roundtable spent time on some of those issues and there was a lot of advice and a lot of counsel given on how to do things. I think it's probably safe to say that there were frequent occasions when that advice was not followed. The group tended to be somewhat hostile when that happened and it got to the point where you were embarrassed to report back that you had not followed the advice and counsel of the group. So that prompted some of us to do things in quite a different way. We were committed to having taken some steps in the right direction if we were going to show up at the next meeting.

Rollins: A little peer pressure. It works.

Schoenberg: How many people obtained professional help through their roundtable? For example, it could have been an investment banker, it could have been a lawyer, it could have been whatever. There must have been a lot of that.

Brizdle: Outside expertise, you mean?

Schoenberg: Yes, outside expertise. It would be the most natural thing in the world. I don't remember it happening.

Rollins: You mean having a professional attend the roundtable?

Schoenberg: No. Someone says, "I have this problem, who do I hire?"

Carlson: We've done a lot of that: Here are the two people in the world you ought to talk to about that problem, here are their names, here are their addresses.

Rollins: Investment bankers, head hunters

Brizdle: I thought you were talking about something else. I thought you were talking about asking somebody with specific knowledge to come and make a presentation.

Schoenberg: Well, that's a good question, too.

Yeaton: Larry, didn't we have two sessions on topics that weren't industry-oriented? Didn't we have two sessions where we had someone come in for part of one of the three workdays?

Schoenberg: You're right.

Yeaton: Estate planning was one of them.

Carlson: I know we've talked about it over the years and I think we've had someone in once or twice. I can't even remember who it was and we certainly didn't do it as much as we could have.

Rollins: It's not part of the model that survived.

Yeaton: We had one guy talk about estate planning, which shows how our group is aging, but what made it really interesting was that at the next meeting people got to share what components they had already put in place of the things that were mentioned. That was very helpful. Because then you find out what they had learned and they may be able to give you some advice.

Schoenberg: I have another question. I think one of the most difficult problems that I ever dealt with in the roundtable was not at the roundtable itself. It was the process for adding people. And the process for people leaving. I'd like to hear what people did about this sort of thing because everybody must have had it. It was not a good feeling.

Yeaton: Well, in the case of the last two or three times we added people, there were recommendations made and sent out ahead of the meeting. So if you had concerns, you had a chance to discuss it then.

Schoenberg: But what about the other way, Jack?

Yeaton: When they're leaving?

Schoenberg: Yeah. I'm certainly aware of people who were encouraged to leave and it's not a good feeling. Also, when you want to bring someone in, people always say they'd like to meet them first. Well, what do you do? You invite them and then *don't* invite them again? It's very difficult.

Rollins: We've dealt with this over a period of years in our roundtable and I can tell you how we finally decided to handle it. I think it works pretty well. If you want to bring someone new in to replace someone who has left for some reason, we distribute the information ahead of time like Jack's roundtable does. So everybody has a chance to read it and make sure there's not a competitive situation because we want to avoid that for the reasons we discussed earlier. But we also invite the new person, once there's consensus that we should, to one meeting so that they can "try us out." Now, who's trying who out? It's a two-way tryout, really.

Schoenberg: Have you ever turned anyone down after doing that? If not, you don't have a process.

Carlson: We have. And we've also had the case where we had people on the roundtable and we had to go have a little private discussion that they were not invited back. It's no different from terminating any kind of relationship. Two of us had that conversation with a couple of different people who were not invited back. There was nothing in writing--nothing whatever--it was just a private little meeting. It was not fun, by any means.

Schoenberg: And what were the reasons for not wanting the person to stay?

Carlson: There were two situations that I'm familiar with. One was that the person had an incompatible business model and there was just a total disconnect within the meeting. In the other case, the person was a jerk. To be honest.

Rollins: And they were counseled out and successfully so. We have two new members that we have just invited to attend our fall meeting, so we're going to be trying it again. They are younger CEOs of software companies, one from North Carolina and one from this area. They're invited to our fall meeting so they can try us out. We'll see how it goes.

Blumberg: The process that we used was that information about a new candidate for the roundtable was circulated to the group. Then we were asked to try to get an opportunity to meet with that person at a conference or elsewhere, and get some idea informally as to whether they would or wouldn't fit in. And then a decision would be made at the next meeting as to whether or not we would invite them to attend one of our meetings. In a couple of cases, after they were invited to attend a meeting, they stayed and we found that they fit in with the group. Then in other cases, the person just wasn't invited back. In one case, the issue was one of honesty. We just weren't sure that the information we were getting was the straight information. And that just didn't fit with the group. In another case, it was a personality that didn't mesh.

Schoenberg: I have another kind of question that intrigues me about the roundtables that I've been involved in. That one that Bruce is in is a particularly ornery group. He used the word "zingable". What intrigues me is that those of you who have been around ADAPSO a long time would be amazed to hear some of the people in that group described as zingable.

So my question is this: Did you find that people adapt to the ethos of the group? My answer is, "Yes, they do." It's amazing. People I thought would never talk about themselves opened up. We have one guy in our group who is the last guy you would expect to talk about himself and he told us about his sex life after a prostate operation. I mean, this is a pretty extreme change of personality. [*Laughter*] I think somehow the context made it comfortable.

Yost: Was there ever a situation where, because of mergers or acquisitions, a company in the group became a competitor and one person had to go for that reason?

Welke: They didn't necessarily have to go if they became a competitor.

Schoenberg: I acquired several companies that were in the roundtable and they all left. Although as I said before, one of them rejoined the roundtable several years later after he left the company.

Rollins: Nathan, do you have any questions you'd like to toss out?

Ensmenger: I realize that we're approaching the end of our time so I'll hold for now. I should say that this is exactly the kind of thing that we wanted to get out of these workshops from our perspective.

Rollins: Great!

Blumberg: One thing that should be something chronicled somewhere is what happened with the Human Resources Roundtable. It was seven companies that were all in the IT services world and the reason we got together was to share compensation information. Milt Wessel was paranoid about what we were going to do and how it was going to be done. The people who were there from GE were paranoid that there was a tape going someplace and that these conversations were being recorded. But we did meet and agreed to share compensation information confidentially.

Then we agreed to have a third-party firm collect this information and feed it back to us. And after we had done this for about two years, ADAPSO understood that this wasn't a bad thing, this was actually a good thing, and they adopted it as their own compensation survey and took over the responsibility for running it. The roundtable that the seven of us started became the Computer Services Personnel Association in 1979 and eventually had a membership upwards of 100 companies. I think it's still operating today.

Rollins: Were there any other roundtables besides the CFO and Presidents' roundtables?

Blumberg: There was a marketing roundtable.

Brizdle: There was an aborted effort to start a marketing roundtable but it didn't fly.

Rollins: No meetings?

Brizdle: We had one or two meetings at ADAPSO conferences but the members were all independents so it was very, very difficult to get the funding to travel. I don't believe we met more than two or three times.

Rollins: We're out of time. Anybody want to make a final comment for the tape? Something you want to say that you haven't had an opportunity to say?

Terrific. Thank you all very much for participating.

[Chorus of thank yous and applause]

GLOSSARY OF TERMS AND ACRONYMS

ACT Advanced Computer Techniques

ADAPSO Association of Data Processing Services Organizations, founded in 1961. The name was changed to the Information Technology Association of America (ITAA) in 1991.

ADP Automatic Data Processing

ADR Applied Data Research

AEA American Electronics Association

AICPA American Institute of Certified Public Accountants

AISC Association of Independent Software Companies. Merged with ADAPSO in 1972.

API Application Program Interface

CBEMA Computer and Business Equipment Manufacturers' Association. The name was changed to the Information Technology Industry Council in 1994.

CCIA Computer & Communications Industry Association

CCITT Comite Consultatif Internationale de Telegraphie et Telephonie. Replaced in 1993 by ITU-T, the Telecommunications Standardization Sector of the International Telecommunications Union.

CDC Control Data Corporation

CICS Customer Information Control System, an IBM teleprocessing monitor

Computer Inquiries, First, Second, Third A series of investigations conducted by the FCC in the late 1970s and early 1980s to consider the impact of telecommunications regulations on competitive conditions between basic service providers and enhanced service providers.

CONTU   Commission on New Technological Uses of Copyrighted Works

CRITA   Council of Regional Information Technology Associations

CSC   Computer Sciences Corporation

CTG   Computer Task Group

DB2   A relational database from IBM that was originally developed for its mainframes.

division/section   A sub-group within ADAPSO which represented a specific industry sector such as software products or processing services. These groups were called "sections" when they were first formed in the 1960s but the name was changed to "divisions" in the late 1980s when they began to manage their own budgets and have staff dedicated to their programs.

DSL   Digital Subscriber Line

EAM   Electronic Accounting Machine

EDS   Electronic Data Systems

FASB   Financial Accounting Standards Board

FCC   Federal Communications Commission

FUD   Fear, uncertainty and doubt. A marketing strategy used by a dominant or privileged organization that restrains competition by not revealing future plans.

GUIDE   An IBM user group

ICP   International Computer Programs

IIA Information Industry Association

INPUT A market research company focused on the computer software and services industry.

I/O Input/Output

IP Intellectual property

ISAM Indexed Sequential Access Method

NACCB National Association of Computer Consultant Businesses

NCR National Cash Register

NBIS Network-Based Information Services, one of the ADAPSO subgroups called sections or divisions.

OCO Object Code Only

OEM Original Equipment Manufacturer

PTT A post, telephone and telegraph administrative agency of a national government.

RF Radio Frequency

RPSS Remote Processing Services Section, one of the subgroups within ADAPSO.

SAA System Application Architecture

SBC Service Bureau Corporation

section/division A sub-group within ADAPSO which represented a specific industry sector such as software products or processing services. These groups were called "sections" when they were first formed in the 1960s but the name was changed to "divisions" in the late 1980s when they began to manage their own budgets and have staff dedicated to their programs.

SHARE An IBM user group

SIA Software Industry Association, the name initially adopted by the software section within ADAPSO.

SNA Systems Network Architecture

SPA Software Publishers Association. Merged with the Information Industry Association (IIA) in 1999 to become the Software and Information Industry Association (SIIA).

Type I, Type II, Type III, Type IV programs Categories assigned by IBM to programs that were distributed to customers on request. Type I were systems programs produced and maintained by the product divisions. Type II were applications programs produced and maintained by the marketing divisions. Type III were various utility and application programs contributed by IBM systems engineers which were not maintained or supported by IBM. Type IV were various utility and application programs contributed by IBM customers which were not maintained or supported by IBM.

UCC University Computing Company

User group An organization of users of a particular hardware or software product.

VAR Value Added Remarketer

VM Virtual Machine, an IBM operating system which can run multiple operating systems within the computer at one time.

VPN Virtual Private Network, a wide area communications network provided by a common carrier that provides which seems like dedicated lines when used, but backbone trunks are shared among all customers as in a public network.

VSE Disk Operating System/Virtual Storage Extended

WIPO World Intellectual Property Organization

Index

About the Author

Luanne Johnson is the President of the Charles Babbage Foundation and the former President of the Software History Center. She has served as the President of the Information Technology Association of America (formerly ADAPSO) and as Executive Director of the ADAPSO Foundation. In 1971, she founded a software company, Argonaut Information Systems, Inc., and ran it successfully for 15 years during part of the turbulent period described in detail in this transcript.